Troubling Multiculturalism

It can be easy to imagine that Child and Youth Care practitioners are inherently or naturally attuned to issues of diversity and colonization as they pertain to multicultural practice. While there are excellent culturally attuned practices that are happening in the field of Child and Youth Care, when it comes to collecting stories of cultural diversity and, more specifically, the problematic unfolding of some of these stories, there remains hesitancy in the field. This hesitancy, in part, is due to assuming we are practicing in postcolonial times, where all the messiness, the doubting, and the pain have been 'dealt' with.

The authors of this volume suggest otherwise and their chapters represent an important contribution to the field. They are a diverse group of practitioners but they share a common concern that the term multicultural practice grooms hegemonic interventions that do not critically examine issues of power, difference, colonialism, Whiteness, or species, to name a few. Although the title of this book is *Troubling Multiculturalism*, the language within stretches this term, troubles it, and at times, reinvents it.

This book was originally published as a special issue of *Child and Youth Services*.

Hans Skott-Myhre is an Associate Professor in the Child and Youth Studies Department at Brock University, Canada, and is the author of *Youth Subculture as Creative Force: Creating New Spaces for Radical Youth Work*.

J.N. Little is an Instructor in the School of Child and Youth Care at the University of Victoria, Canada.

Troubling Multiculturalism

Edited by
Hans Skott-Myhre and J.N. Little

LONDON AND NEW YORK

First published 2014 by Routledge

2 Park Square, Milton Park, Abingdon, Oxfordshire OX14 4RN
711 Third Avenue, New York, NY 10017

Routledge is an imprint of the Taylor & Francis Group, an informa business

First issued in paperback 2018

Copyright © 2014 Taylor & Francis

All rights reserved. No part of this book may be reprinted or reproduced or utilised in any form or by any electronic, mechanical, or other means, now known or hereafter invented, including photocopying and recording, or in any information storage or retrieval system, without permission in writing from the publishers.

Notice:
Product or corporate names may be trademarks or registered trademarks, and are used only for identification and explanation without intent to infringe.

British Library Cataloguing in Publication Data
A catalogue record for this book is available from the British Library

ISBN 13: 978-1-138-02356-7 (hbk)
ISBN 13: 978-1-138-37924-4 (pbk)

Typeset in Garamond
by Taylor & Francis Books

Publisher's Note
The publisher accepts responsibility for any inconsistencies that may have arisen during the conversion of this book from journal articles to book chapters, namely the possible inclusion of journal terminology.

Disclaimer
Every effort has been made to contact copyright holders for their permission to reprint material in this book. The publishers would be grateful to hear from any copyright holder who is not here acknowledged and will undertake to rectify any errors or omissions in future editions of this book.

Contents

Citation Information	vii
1. Introduction: Troubling Multiculturalism *J.N. Little and Hans Skott-Myhre*	1
2. "We Need to Talk About It!": Doing CYC as Politicized Praxis *Elicia Loiselle, Sandrina de Finney, Nishad Khanna, and Rebecca Corcoran*	4
3. Child and Youth Care To-Come *Scott Kouri*	32
4. Stories of Another Kind: Engaging in Generative Conversations in Pedagogical Spaces *Marie Hoskins*	63
5. Journeying With Youth: Re-Centering Indigeneity in Child and Youth Care *Dawn Zinga*	84
6. Unsettling Representational Practices: Inhabiting Relational Becomings in Early Childhood Education *Fikile Nxumalo*	107
7. Postcolonial Entanglements: Unruling Stories *Veronica Pacini-Ketchabaw*	129
8. Reconceptualizing Multicultural Discourse as Shifting Geographies *J.N. Little and M. Walker*	143
9. Fleeing Identity: Toward a Revolutionary Politics of Relationship *Hans Skott-Myhre*	155
10. Conclusion: Sketching the Outlines: CYC Multiculturalism(?) *Hans Skott-Myhre and J.N. Little*	171
Index	181

Citation Information

The chapters in this book were originally published in *Child and Youth Services*, volume 33, issue 3–4 (December 2012). When citing this material, please use the original page numbering for each article, as follows:

Chapter 1
Introduction: Troubling Multiculturalism
J.N. Little and Hans Skott-Myhre
Child and Youth Services, volume 33, issue 3–4 (December 2012)
pp. 175–177

Chapter 2
"We Need to Talk About It!": Doing CYC as Politicized Praxis
Elicia Loiselle, Sandrina de Finney, Nishad Khanna, and
Rebecca Corcoran
Child and Youth Services, volume 33, issue 3–4 (December 2012)
pp. 178–205

Chapter 3
Child and Youth Care To-Come
Scott Kouri
Child and Youth Services, volume 33, issue 3–4 (December 2012)
pp. 206–236

Chapter 4
Stories of Another Kind: Engaging in Generative Conversations in Pedagogical Spaces
Marie Hoskins
Child and Youth Services, volume 33, issue 3–4 (December 2012)
pp. 237–257

Chapter 5
Journeying With Youth: Re-Centering Indigeneity in Child and Youth Care
Dawn Zinga
Child and Youth Services, volume 33, issue 3–4 (December 2012)
pp. 258–280

CITATION INFORMATION

Chapter 6
Unsettling Representational Practices: Inhabiting Relational Becomings in Early Childhood Education
Fikile Nxumalo
Child and Youth Services, volume 33, issue 3–4 (December 2012)
pp. 281–302

Chapter 7
Postcolonial Entanglements: Unruling Stories
Veronica Pacini-Ketchabaw
Child and Youth Services, volume 33, issue 3–4 (December 2012)
pp. 303–316

Chapter 8
Reconceptualizing Multicultural Discourse as Shifting Geographies
J.N. Little and M. Walker
Child and Youth Services, volume 33, issue 3–4 (December 2012)
pp. 317–328

Chapter 9
Fleeing Identity: Toward a Revolutionary Politics of Relationship
Hans Skott-Myhre
Child and Youth Services, volume 33, issue 3–4 (December 2012)
pp. 329–344

Chapter 10
Conclusion: Sketching the Outlines: CYC Multiculturalism(?)
Hans Skott-Myhre and J.N. Little
Child and Youth Services, volume 33, issue 3–4 (December 2012)
pp. 345–353

Please direct any queries you may have about the citations to clsuk.permissions@cengage.com

Introduction
Troubling Multiculturalism

J.N. LITTLE
*School of Child and Youth Care, University of Victoria,
Victoria, British Columbia, Canada*

HANS SKOTT-MYHRE
*Department of Child and Youth Studies, Brock University,
St. Catharines, Ontario, Canada*

Child and Youth Care is an international community that is bound together by our dedication to children, youth, families, and the communities in which they live. Due to our geographical distances, varied cultural contexts, political realities, and a plethora of social issues to be addressed, it is easy (even tempting) to imagine ourselves as inherently or naturally attuned to issues of diversity and colonization as they pertain to multicultural practice. And yet, when an e-mail request was received on CYC-net in 2011 asking for a comprehensive resource for multicultural practice in CYC, the response was not overwhelming. This is not to say there are not excellent practices that are happening in the day-to-day praxis[1] in which we engage; rather it suggests that when it comes to collecting these stories of cultural diversity and, more specifically, the problematic unfolding of some of these stories, there remains hesitancy in the field. This hesitancy, in part, is due to assuming we are practicing in postcolonial times, where all the messiness, the doubting, and the pain have been "dealt" with. The authors of this volume suggest otherwise and their words are an important contribution to the field. They are a diverse group of practitioners but they share a common concern that the term *multicultural practice* grooms hegemonic interventions that do not critically take up issues of power, difference, colonialism, Whiteness, or species, to name a few. Although the title of this issue is "Troubling Multiculturalism," the language within this issue stretches this term, troubles it, and at times, re-invents it.

Elicia Loiselle, Sandrina de Finney, Nishad Khanna, and Rebecca Corcoran open the issue by reflecting on their experiences as queer, First Nations, racialized practitioners, academics, and activists, to offer the reader an opportunity to draw on their rich narratives to subvert rigid, exclusionary notions of CYC. They present a robust challenge for practitioners to consider the arbitrary binaries set up in practice that are barriers to effective and respectful critical work. Readers will resonate with their complex practice vignettes offered.

Scott Kouri continues this challenge by questioning notions of stability in identity and brings forth questions regarding the tension of problematizing CYC identities and practices from the very context of CYC. He asks us to consider understandings of hospitality are taken up as a way to think CYC contexts, communities, and relationships as an openness to the unexpected coming of the unanticipated other: a CYC to-come.

Marie Hoskins takes up the difficulty of holding a White identity while grappling with the historical and present implications of colonization and racialization. She presents the tensions of wanting generative conversations but recognizing her privilege in them. Her prior work "tiptoed" around what she considers the fundamental component—relationship—and reflects on the emotional work required of us in dismantling dominant discourses regarding cultural differences. Dawn Zinga follows up Hoskins's nuanced reading of Whiteness by questioning the "nods" given to diversity in many programs, without significant structural change. Specifically, she speaks to centering "indigeniety" in CYC against a liberal discourse and the challenges, tensions, and successes in doing so.

Fikile Nxumalo takes up early childhood spaces as a risk for social justice and equity through "static representations of difference and diversity" (p. 281), and suggests more fluid assemblages would offer the greatest hope for all children and those who care for them. Veronica Pacini-Ketchabaw, also exploring the world of early childhood, tangles our ideas about separation and difference through her exploration of the cultural child. She draws on the methodological critique of figuration, which in her words can be described as "reclamations that have 'real' meanings, a kind of personification and, simultaneously, *a making of knowledge*" (p. 313). The making of new knowledge(s) as it relates to understanding culture is, in our opinion, of highest priority for the field(s) of CYC. J.N. Little and M. Walker ask us to consider how some of these aforementioned questions are brought forth in post-secondary classrooms, and explore how multicultural discourse reifies White-centered conceptualizations of diversity.

Hans Skott-Mhyre's contribution asks an important question, *who are your people?* This question, in turn, asks readers to consider not only their familial location and ancestors, but to ask who their people are in the field. How do we connect with others outside of dominant and fixed practices? How do we, in his words, "signify the possibility of belonging" (p. 330) with understanding how we describe ourselves as always incomplete?

All authors speak to the need for frank and reflective dialogue and a deep questioning of hegemonic multicultural practice. Our/their stories are ones born of relational encounters against the backdrop of practice, pedagogy, and policy. It is our sense that the authors would agree these can never be separated. But, they can be re-imagined in ways that invite dialogue, sustain healthy critique, and ultimately make the lives of children, youth, families, and communities better. We anticipate these forward-thinking authors will inspire others to critically reflect on their practice, challenge static notions of multiculturalism, and engage in curious conversations. A special thank you is warranted to our amazing peer reviewers, who expanded the conversations, asked the curious questions, and are acknowledged as fearless warriors in their own dedication to social justice in the field of CYC and its allies. Thank you!

NOTE

1. The authors wish to stress that by CYC praxis they are acknowledging all dimensions that include, but are not limited to, frontline practice, teaching, advocacy and activism, and policy development.

"We Need to Talk About It!": Doing CYC as Politicized Praxis

ELICIA LOISELLE, SANDRINA DE FINNEY, NISHAD KHANNA, and REBECCA CORCORAN

School of Child and Youth Care, University of Victoria, Victoria, British Columbia, Canada

Like many others seeking to make room for alternative voices in the narrow canon of CYC theory and practice, our work is steeped in theoretical and activist perspectives on colonialism, neoliberalism, normativity, social power, and social change. This critical, multidisciplinary lens is too often cast outside the realm of authentic CYC. In this article, we share our simultaneous struggles with and passion for our work and the CYC field and consider what can be gained from a critical ethic of practice, research, and activism. Our transtheoretical framework, drawn from Indigenous, postcolonial, queer, feminist, and poststructural perspectives, helps us unpack how coming together critically, hopefully, productively enables us to trouble exclusionary notions of CYC. We present vignettes from our practice and research that explicitly challenge the assumption that critical practice is somehow less effective and less responsive to the realities of the diverse children, youth, families, and communities with whom we work.

So they're all—teachers and stuff—like, "Oh, talking about racism is too hard, it confuses the kids so we should not do that to them," like we're too dumb to understand what happens to us every day? I think it's more like an opposite situation, like, I mean, they don't want to talk or they're scared about racism because they're the group of power. They don't give us...credit that we understand and, yeah, we need to talk about it! (Priya, 16, social justice activist)

In this article, we engage with ideological diversity in the field of child and youth care in an effort to honor and make sense of the experiences of young people like Priya, who are stressing that "we need to talk about" issues of social inequity that "happen to [them] everyday." Drawing on our different experiences as queer, straight, Indigenous, racialized, White, and able practitioners, academics, and activists, we problematize a dominant and now predictable response to critical analysis in our field; a response that undermines the value and necessity of critical frameworks by insisting that they detract from practice and even limit our efforts to connect effectively with children, youth, and families. Like many others who seek to make room for alternative voices in the narrow canon of Child and Youth Care (CYC) practice and theory, our practice is steeped in theoretical and activist perspectives on colonialism, normativity, social power, and social change. This critical, multidisciplinary lens is too often cast as outside the realm of authentic CYC, even though all of us (and many other critical practitioners) are trained and practice in the field. Through a series of narrative vignettes drawn from our practice and research, we challenge a dominant idea that we need to "protect" young people from critical language and conversations out of a misguided developmental approach that assumes children and youth do not or cannot understand the systemic injustices they experience every day. We take the position that it actually harms young people to assume they are neither aware of these issues nor already engaged in multiple forms of resistance, action, and transformation.

"REAL" CYC

Our contention that critical theories have been constructed as irrelevant and even hazardous to "real" CYC practice is evidenced in discussions and debates about the field, such as a recent discussion on the use of academic research and jargon in child and youth care on the International Child and Youth Care Network listserv (http://www.cyc-net.org). This discussion is addressed in the special issue of the *International Journal of Child, Youth and Family Studies*, edited by White and Pacini-Ketchabaw (2012) and in a response by de Finney, Little, Skott-Myhre, and Gharabaghi (2012). This listserv debate was incited by the question, posted by a practitioner, "why are people speaking about the field in ways I don't understand?" This generated a "spirited, and at times fractious, discussion" (de Finney et al., 2012). Critical concepts and language that were unfamiliar to many practitioners were framed as academic "jargon" and dismissed by several dominant voices in the field as disconnected from real, frontline CYC practice. Posts from the listserv debate read: "The biggest issue... for me and those like me, is the relevance of the language [of critical theory] to the realities of the work and the field" and "[How is this language of critical theory] helping those who... are busy trying to help the children find the food, the shelter, the safety they need now?" In response to questions like this, it is our hope that this article makes explicit the ways in which critical concepts like neocolonialism and neoliberalism are not only relevant for the lives of children, youth, and families, but are the very forces that shape the realities of poverty, homelessness, and multiple forms of violence they experience. Further, our vignettes show the vital importance and the multiple possibilities of engaging these critical concepts in collaborative practice with children, youth and families.

While the critical practice moments we share later in this article are not all specifically CYC examples, they occur across and offer critiques of diverse sites of practice where CYC practitioners also work (education, child welfare, residential care, and child-, youth-, and family-serving agencies, etc.). Further, it is our intent to show how we might engage with critiques of and possibilities beyond dominant foundational concepts of CYC practice (such as relational and developmental practice and individualized care). Our framing of transformative CYC praxis as always imperfect and evolving demonstrates our hopeful struggles as CYC-trained people and our own entanglements with the foundational concepts of our field and our work as CYC practitioners, researchers and activists. As such, it is our hope to offer salient contributions about critical praxis to current discussions shaping the field of CYC.

A TRANSTHEORETICAL APPROACH TO CYC PRACTICE

As a discipline, child and youth care is already transtheoretical in its orientation, and our approach builds on this strength. The multidisciplinary praxis approaches we present here are shaped by an ethical commitment to doing CYC practice as politicized, critical, and radical social change work alongside children, youth, families, and communities. We will show how, in our practice and research, we draw on feminist and political analyses of neoliberalism and capitalism; Indigenous, postcolonial, and anti-racist feminisms; poststructural and posthumanist perspectives; queer theory; material analysis; and desire-based frameworks. We have explained these theories and concepts in more detail elsewhere.[1] We are aware that by simply listing them here, we risk alienating practitioners who are unfamiliar with these orientations. However, we ask readers to bear with us in a spirit of open-mindedness and possibility, because here our desire is to move beyond definitions to *show how* we use these ideas and concepts in everyday praxis moments to engage critically and meaningfully with children, young people, and communities.[2]

THE COLONIAL CONTEXTS OF CYC PRACTICE

Before we move into our practice stories, it is important to provide a brief overview of the colonial contexts in which all CYC practice in the Americas (and other colonized countries across the world) is embedded and in which we situate our vignettes. Canada, as a "settler society with a history of genocide and colonization" (Razack, 2002, p. 89), has maintained its colonial authority over First Peoples through policies that have included forced sterilizations and scientific experimentations; deliberate infection with lethal diseases such as smallpox; forcible removal of entire communities from their homelands to allow European immigrants to access desired territories; preventing Indigenous people from voting, studying, travelling, meeting in groups, practicing their culture, and participating in business; and incarcerating thousands of Indigenous children in residential schools where they were subjected to physical, spiritual, sexual, emotional, and cultural abuses (Battiste & Semeganis, 2002; Lawrence, 2004; Smith, 2005). Given this constant assault on every aspect of their societies in the name of building Canada, it is a testament to the strength and spirit of First Nations that they maintain their political, social, land-based, cultural, spiritual, and linguistic traditions.

Colonial policies are deeply embedded in current conditions and ideologies that shape the lives of Indigenous people (Schutte, 2007; Sinclair, 2007). Even today, Aboriginal people in Canada are governed by the 1876 *Indian Act*, which "rests on the principle that the Aborigines are to be kept in a condition of tutelage and treated as wards or children of the state" (Indian and Northern Affairs Canada, 2008, p. 172). These colonial processes sustain a system of chronic poverty, social exclusion, and political and cultural disenfranchisement for Indigenous people, with particularly dire effects on women and girls—as we explore later on. These effects are particularly salient for CYC practice. In Canada, for example, Indigenous children constitute approximately 9% of the child population but roughly half of all children in residential care (Child Welfare League of Canada, 2003; Bell, 2012; Trocmé, Knoke, & Blackstock, 2004) and in the justice system (Artz, 2012; Fechter-Leggett & O'Brien, 2010). Yet, social services for First Nations are underfunded by 20%–25% as compared to those for non-Aboriginal Canadian children (Trocmé et al., 2004).

We use the term neocolonialism to theorize this active coloniality and to focus attention on North American society as dominated by normative social values and practices that have systematically, over many generations, positioned Indigenous cultural and social norms as inferior (Lawrence, 2004). That is, dominant, White, middle class, patriarchal values of individualism, rational choice, and self-realization are embedded in capitalist, neoliberal structures that function through what Lugones (2007) calls the "coloniality of power" (p. 186). Under this social paradigm, responsibility for failure to achieve educational and economic success is attributed to minoritized[3] youth, families, and communities, rather than understood as a product of the systemic racism, classism, homophobia, and so on, that dispossess Indigenous, racialized, poor, and queer people of educational and employment opportunities (Harris, 2004; Fine & Ruglis, 2009). Thus, "under a neo-liberal social order, structural inequities are embedded in socio-cultural, economic, and political structures....that are enacted in [minoritized people's] everyday lives" (de Finney, Loiselle, & Dean, 2011, p. 90).

Using decolonizing frameworks (Alexander & Mohanty, 1997; Simpson, 2011; Smith, 2012; Tuck, 2009, 2010), we take up analyses of patriarchal binary gender systems (sexism), compulsory heterosexuality (heterosexism), class divisions, and racialization/racism as mutually constituted products of settler colonialism and imperialism as they are continuously reconstituted under late modernity through "global, Eurocentered, capitalist domination/exploitation" (Lugones, 2007, p. 196). That is, we aim to unpack and resist (in this article and through our practice) the ways that neocolonialism and neoliberalism shape the overlapping structural inequities faced by the young people, families, and communities with whom we work.

THE VIGNETTES: MOMENTS OF ENTANGLEMENT

To illustrate our struggle to make sense of what young people are telling us about the complex geopolitical and sociomaterial conditions of their lives, we aim to unpack, disturb, and transform normative/neoliberal/neocolonial framings of bodies, social relations, place, justice, practice, and theory. Our goal is to explore how taking up alternatives to these dominant frameworks in/as CYC practice, while difficult, produces needed openings for engaging with the complexity of people's lives. In sharing our simultaneous struggles with and passion for our work and the CYC field, we hope to show the imperfect nature of critical practice even as we challenge the assumption that it is somehow less effective and less responsive to the realities of the diverse children, youth, families, and communities with whom we work.

We have found Eve Tuck's (2009, 2010) explicitly anti-colonial, desire-based research/praxis framework helpful in understanding how critical practice can better account for both the ongoing impacts of structural inequities and the hope and possibilities of collective engagement and action. Tuck (2009, 2010), an Aleut community and youth practitioner/researcher, draws on Indigenous epistemologies to theorize desire as *smart*, explaining that it accumulates wisdom over generations. She notes that a desire-based framework "recognizes and actively seeks out complexity in lives and communities. It dismisses one-dimensional analyses of people, communities, and tribes as flattened, derelict, and ruined" (Tuck, 2010, p. 639). She goes on to quote Gordon, who explains that this framework acknowledges that "we all possess a complex and oftentimes contradictory humanity and subjectivity that is never adequately glimpsed by viewing others as either victims or superhuman agents" (Gordon, 1996, p. 4, as cited in Tuck, 2010, p. 639).

We turn now to our vignettes to demonstrate that young people not only understand the systemic injustices they experience, but are also actively engaged in resisting them *and* generating multiple "becomings" (Deleuze & Guattari, 1987)—imperfect, hopeful, and needed alternative possibilities outside of dominant neocolonial frameworks.

Becoming Resurgence: Founders, Helpers, and Other Myths—Sandrina de Finney

The young people I work with typically live in contexts of social exclusion shaped by gendered, racialized, and sexualized violence and discrimination, active colonization operating at multiple levels, and racial and class stratification. Many of them are all too familiar with legally enforced forms of "care"—foster and group care, institutionalized care, the (in)justice system, and so on. Many also participate in initiatives, programs, countercultures, movements, and communities—such as the community-based, participatory, action-oriented practice and research projects I describe here—that offer alternative accounts and engagements with the norm. In this vignette, I present moments of creative exchange and possibility with young people I have had the honor of working with across several different contexts of my work as a researcher, educator, practitioner, community activist, trainer, and volunteer. I hope to articulate how I simultaneously commit to and struggle with enacting an always partial and always evolving critical, politicized ethic of child and youth care. At the heart of this committed struggle is the urgent need to unravel and disengage the multiple, intersecting threads of minoritization that underscore the contexts of CYC practice. In this work I draw on Indigenous and postcolonial feminist theories and practices and, more specifically, ideas of presencing and resurgence (Lee, 2011; Simpson, 2011) and smart desire (Tuck, 2009, 2010).

"Founders"

I begin with a story about working with a group of Indigenous girls during an intensive summer research internship that was part of a much larger social-change project conducted in partnership with several organizations, facilitators, researchers, and youth/girls groups.[4] In this vignette, the girls engaged in Photovoice,[5] a participatory method that uses photography and critical analysis to disrupt dominant narratives and re-center Othered bodies and perspectives. Over several days, the girls used cameras and journals to explore spaces where they felt they belonged and did not belong in Victoria, BC—a colonial city named after Queen Victoria that is built on the unceded lands of the Lekwungen Nation. Afterwards we sat together—all of us First Nations—sharing food, pictures, and stories to generate an analysis of "what's going on here." During these collective art/relational/action sessions, multiple entanglements came together: the power of silence and denial, the palpable discomfort of identity politics, immeasurable sadness and grief, the sharing of hopeful, sacred stories, an ethic of collaboration, and the spirited contestation of colonial narratives. In one example, 11-year-old Sienna took a picture of a prominent monument in downtown Victoria that celebrates British Columbia's "founding fathers." She explained:

> This picture is called "founders." I took this picture because they say they "found us" and I find it a bit weird that they say they "found us." We were here before they ever came and we had our own territories and we knew what was going on.

Sienna's picture (Figure 1) and analysis aptly articulate how, across Canada, diverse and ongoing Indigenous communities are constructed as inconsequential to a nation imagined as a benevolent British (and in some settings, French) colony. In this convenient colonial reimagining, Indigenous ecologies, knowledges, and societies are erased through ubiquitous markers of imperial hegemony celebrated in statues, monuments, and town, street, and building names, among others. Razack (2002) links colonial appropriation to a mindset that "not only enabled White settlers to secure the land but to come to know themselves as entitled to it" (p. 129). As Sienna suggests, this process serves to reinforce the problematic construction of Indigenous people as static relics of the past, as peripheral to contemporary Canadian society, and as inferior to the dominant population (Dei, 2000). The girls' contestations of this problematic erasure and systematic minimization was a salient theme in our conversations; they explained that such knowledge manifests in their lives as deeply gendered and sexualized racial slurs and stereotypes. In one discussion,

FIGURE 1 Founders, photographed by Sienna. (Color figure available online.)

Rianna, a 15-year-old First Nation youth leader, spoke animatedly as she contested the narrow roles available to Indigenous girls:

> Let's see... there's the drunk, the ho, like all Native girls are on the street. There's the dirty Indian, broke. There's the whole Indian woman in a blanket thing, with the braids, like 200 years ago. The whole Pocahontas thing. That's what we have to choose from.

Rianna's friend, 16-year-old Seeka, a First Nation girl who lives on reserve, jumped in: "No wonder... Native girls disappear and stuff and it never makes it to the news."

Downe (2005) argues that "the abuses experienced by Aboriginal girls over the past 130 years are not isolated occurrences; they are connected through a pervasive colonial ideology that sees these young women as exploitable and often dispensable" (p. 3). Because the colonial mindset of entitlement is deeply embedded in the dominant Whiteness of Canada's institutions and structures, Indigenous girls and women continue to be pathologized and criminalized for being victims of gendered and sexualized violence. They are seen as less grievable; their exploitation is less deserving of public empathy, of government resources, and of comprehensive social, economic, and political interventions. As Rianna and Seeka explain, this damaging narrative casts Indigenous girls as "voiceless," broken objects of colonial imagination, obscuring their complex experiences, knowledges, and strengths—their "smart desires."

"Helpers"

The examples I share highlight the need for courageous, expansive conversations and risk taking in our field. These are honest, complicated moments of everyday practice and research; they occur because young people have a lot to say about intersecting processes of minoritization, whether or not they have the "right" language to describe their active knowing and living of the complicated layers of social power. The children and youth I work with want their "helping" relationships to involve information and critical language about why things are the way they are, and strategies for transformation and radical reimaginings. They want to represent themselves against and outside of limited and limiting psychological explanations of "low self-esteem," "treatment resistance," or "disordered attachment" that pathologize and victimize them. One especially problematic construct of practice that they critique time and time again is the superficial, essentialized approach to "diversity" and "multiculturalism" that is typically employed in youth programs. As an example, Hannah, a 16-year-old who described herself as "a strong warrior woman," talked about attending a group in her community where "there was so much racism, it was brutal, like brutal. And the counsellors didn't wanna talk about it, they always avoided it." When I asked, "What do you think they are scared of?" she replied, "Of losing their power.... They want us to cut out totem poles but they won't talk about racism."

The kind of trivializing denial that Hannah describes constitutes a deeply troubling ethical breach in dominant conceptualizations of diversity and multiculturalism. Such conceptualizations assume that young people are not already aware of and engaged with issues that have shaped generations of their families, and that effective "care" and "helping" should involve apolitical, uncritical, color-blind "relational practices" that are disconnected from what is going on in their lives and communities under the blanket of global neoliberalism. Why, I wonder, in the context of a helping relationship, do we teach young people to understand complex, loaded psychological labels like "attention deficit hyperactivity disorder" and "post-traumatic stress disorder" but say (as I have been told many times) that using words like colonialism and racism "puts ideas in their heads" or is "too complicated" or "too theoretical for them to understand"? What are we saying about young people when we assume that psychopathologizing them meets their needs, but that naming the political, social, and economic forces that impact their lives—and ours—does not?

I once facilitated a cultural camp for First Nation children and youth in care. We had invited Elders and cultural teachers who spoke at length about the history of residential schools, the Sixties and Millennium Scoops, and the urgent need for foster care planning that sustains social justice and cultural and community connections across generations. Fifteen-year old Jayden's reflections really summed up the need for us to engage with young people in difficult political conversations about Canada's colonial history:

> Nobody else ever took the time to even explain to me, "Hey, guess what? There was residential schools and stuff, that's what happened to your mom." Like, the Canadian government and churches forced her to give up her culture and she was so abused. And yeah, it finally made sense, it's not just "your family had problems" but it's more, it's a whole Canada-wide problem that they forced us all Natives to give up our culture and everything that made us strong. So it's not, wasn't our fault and they never explain it to us that way. It's just like, "Oh, your mom is messed up so we're taking you away."

Jayden was all too aware of what Corcoran (2012) describes as "the hegemonic control of the state over access to basic cultural information" that "is representative of a very deliberate and intimately damaging policy of colonial assimilation and forced marginalization that continues to impact thousands of Indigenous families" (p. 71). Jayden reminded us that normative practices are not entirely static and irrefutable: they are also malleable, contestable, even if only partially. He spoke about what it meant to him that a worker was willing to seek out connections to his community and background:

> The first time I met her she told me what Nation I am. It was in my file the whole fuckin' time... It took her one day to tell me more about my

> family, where I'm from and all, than I never heard from being in care for six years. She actually drove to my community for a coming home ceremony. She was the only non-Native person there. She stood by me.

I hear Jayden's words as a powerful call to becoming *more*, both subversive and interconnected. How do I honor it without dissolving into guilt, burnout, or theoretical paralysis?

To begin, I draw on Leanne Betasamosake Simpson's (2011) notion of presencing. To engage in presencing means to implicate ourselves fully in the tangled process of decolonizing child and youth care work, since "colonialism does not only occupy our lands, it also occupies our minds, bodies and narratives, and re-occupying these spaces is a form of resurgence" (Lee, 2011, para. 4). What might a framework of resurgence and presencing teach us about coming together differently, critically, hopefully, productively, to subvert exclusionary notions of what constitutes "care" and "helping" under an ongoing colonial order? The lesson I take away from the experiences of the young people shared here is the power of strategies and practices that sustain hopeful disruptions to our current engagements with ecologies of being, in the face of deeply entrenched structural inequities. Jayden, for instance, participated in a youth consultation process that helped us shape a new Indigenous-focused foster care/adoption governance policy for a local agency. The girls I worked with enacted a radical collaborative ethic of action and praxis through critical education videos and workshops that they/we have presented to numerous youth and community groups, schools, and organizations. Presencing is explicitly decolonizing and contingent upon different conceptualizations of place, ecology, being, and relationship than dominant Eurowestern modern and postmodern concepts; it teaches us how "becoming radical together" is both made possible and made complicated in everyday moments of collaborative engagement. In these moments, in our efforts to name and make visible silenced experiences, to embody spirited other becomings, we get entangled together, made accountable in the space of imperfect praxis and other possibilities.

Becoming Complex: A Spirited Inquiry Into the Culture of Care—Rebecca Corcoran

My work as a child, youth, and family counselor with young people in the care of British Columbia's Ministry of Children and Family Development (MCFD) compels me to explore conceptualizations of foster care as they are understood and experienced by young people in the system. I have found that much of the work and research with young people in this area fails to make connections to sociocultural barriers, and that complex conversations of life, love, loss, creativity, resistance, and new possibilities are overshadowed by more rigid, prescriptive, and clinical conversations focused on pathology, problematic behavior, and broken attachment. Eve Tuck (2009) writes: "It is our work as educational researchers and practitioners, and especially as community members, to envision alternative theories of change, especially those that rely on desire and complexity rather than damage" (p. 422). In my collaborative research and practice with young people in foster care, I attempt to embody Tuck's encouraging vision of movement toward desire and complexity and away from a focus on deficit in hope that this creates space and opportunity for difference, and engagement in critical discussion/analysis.

As we assert in the introduction, the context of BC's foster care system cannot be separated from a history of violence and assimilation rooted in colonialism (de Finney, Dean, et al., 2011). Richardson and Nelson (2007) explore how ongoing practices, including the use of specific techniques, and assessment tools, construct Indigenous families as counter to the "norm" and seek to assess deficiency and dysfunction. Similar to Tuck, they argue instead for the importance of attending to dignity, and responses to challenges, and for the necessity to acknowledge power imbalance and social context. Moving with this intention, I draw on a transtheoretical framework informed by concepts central to the works of Foucault (1982), Deleuze and Guattari (1987), Tuck (2009), and Skott-Myhre (2008), in order to depart from harmful practices and reductive forms of research and to create space for complexity.

The following vignette is an assemblage of art, quotes, and analysis chosen from my master's thesis (Corcoran, 2012) to exemplify the complexity that emerged from my rhizomatic, arts-infused exploration of the lived experiences of foster care alumni. Rhizomatic inquiry invites exploration of movement, connections and expansion in and between the lines of power, resistance, desire, and possibility and thus offers opportunity for departure from linear/reductive methods. The practice of art in research can lend to this expansion and seeks difference and multiplicity rather than an answer. I approached this work with the multiple, shifting hats of being/becoming researcher, practitioner, activist, advocate, and artist. I am English born, and a settler here in Canada; my ancestral history is English and Irish. I have not been in government care, as appears to be the case for the majority of researchers in this area of study, illuminating the importance of more collaborative approaches to practice and research. I therefore, situate myself tentatively in relation to this research space and am deeply indebted to the collaborators who came forward to participate in this research; they spoke openly about their memories of complex everyday moments "in care," their hopes for change, and their desire to be involved in that change.

"FOSTER CHILD"

In a one-on-one interview, collaborator Mandy described ideas of becoming a "foster child." Powerful imagery of becoming invisible and not being seen or heard—of becoming a ghost—arose in both her art work (Figure 2) and the following conversations:

> You're a ghost. You are put into these homes but you never belong there. And holidays come, and their family has come in, and you're just there. You are not heard, not seen... you're just there. You know when people want you to disappear you are really easily made to disappear, and when you're growing up and trying to become a productive person in society, you are a ghost!

The dividing label "foster child" legitimizes limits to familial and cultural/historical information and to foster children's control over their own lives. As Mandy explains, adults have access to this information, highlighting how policy, institutions, and professionals construct their expert roles with children in care. This division is ingrained across multiple categorical shifts from "child" to "youth" to "adult." Mandy reflects that children are assured, "It's not your fault,"

> but then when you grow up, different things that social workers say and foster parents say make you feel like it is your fault. Like the judgments that they put on you—"Well, I guess I am bad then"—you're not told those things like you're a pre-teen or a teenager. You are bad. You're just bad and that's why you're here.

Mandy's words bring to life the developmental progression from "innocent child" to "manipulative teen." A child is seen as in need of protection; a youth should be self-sufficient, self-determined, a citizen-in-becoming. Here, the "under-performing youth in care" is contrasted against the norm of the

FIGURE 2 Collage by Mandy. (Color figure available online.)

liberal humanist subject—a middle class, able, straight, White youth who is "rational" and can "succeed." A young person who cannot measure up to this standard is damaged, broken, and delinquent. Skott-Myhre (2008) speaks to how the creative force of youth "becomes subject to the definitions of psychological development and emotional health within the taxonomic descriptions of adolescence, with its focus on deviance and pathology, risk and resilience" (p. 13). Connecting to a need to embrace complexity—messiness—is movement toward new ways of viewing behavior, movement away from pathologizing, individualizing, and further isolating ways of viewing young people.

BECOMING COMPLEX/SPIRITED

In my exploration of new ways to think about resistance, desire, and wisdom, I looked to Tuck's (2010) notion of desire as becoming intentional, agentic, and smart to allow for complex readings of context to relate how young people and foster care alumni produce new possibilities in the midst of damaging situations. As my collaborators and I created art, discussions of Indigenous knowledge and belonging connected in many ways to layered, complicated experiences of spirituality. It is difficult to put parameters on any definition of spirituality, and perhaps it is contradictory and even unnecessary to do so. Still, spirituality and spiritual knowing shaped not only the collaborators' experiences, but also our process of inquiry and our methodology. Irwin and de Cosson (2004) describe creating art as "a deeply spiritual act giving voice to the inner longings of the spirit with an attitude of receptivity and openness" (p. 57). Art can also rupture linear academic approaches to research, reaching beyond the limitations of structured interviews into new spaces. As an example, collaborator Emily created a collage with the words "Action is the answer/Awareness is enlightenment/Innovation is the future/Dare to dream" (Figure 3). I see in her art piece an invitation to awareness, innovation, and action—and an urgent call to move into new spaces that acknowledge vitality, dignity, respect, and power, as well as the importance of collaboration.

Each of the collaborators in this project spoke to becoming loud, learning rights, and becoming political. Participation in collaborative research can itself be read as an act of resistance or response to challenging experiences in the culture of care; it also allows insights into what works, and opens possibilities. Including young people and foster care alumni in research and policy is pivotal to reshaping the field because it connects to the need to acknowledge and honor multiple ways of knowing, including Indigenous knowledges and lived experience. My hope is that, as researchers, practitioners, and collaborators, we continue to explore alternative and critical approaches as counterpoints to dominant, hegemonic psychological research/practice that perpetuates the erasure of young people's complex experiences.

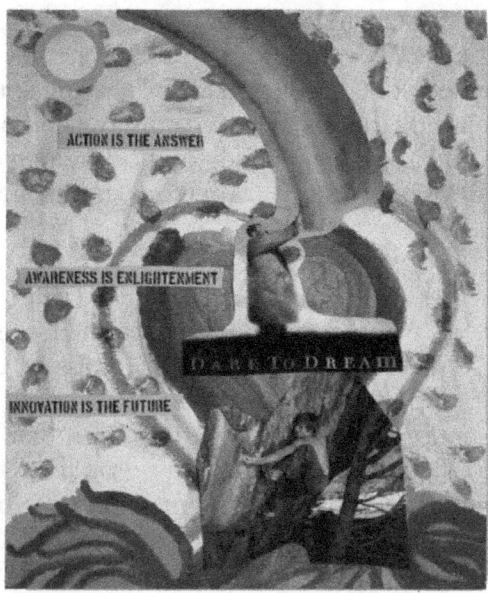

FIGURE 3 Collage by Emily. (Color figure available online.)

Becoming Untimely: Decolonizing CYC Practice—Nishad Khanna

Over the last decade, I have been working in the field of youth engagement, employing critical youth participatory action research and youth-engaged research to involve young people who have been marginalized from the means of (formal) knowledge production. As a visibly racialized settler and a queer transman, I am deeply disturbed by the continuous centering of White, Eurocentric, heteronormative, and neoliberal ideologies in various practices that often go unquestioned and that further marginalize certain young people and their experiences. It has been crucial—both personally and professionally—for me to bring a queer, feminist, anti-racist, postcolonial framework to my work, life, and activism. I also bring to this work a focus on decolonization as defined by Jacquie Alexander and Chandra Talpade Mohanty: that which addresses the traces of the hegemonic that mark us as we struggle against hegemonic power structures (Alexander & Mohanty, 1997; Mohanty, 2003).

This vignette depicts a feminist, anti-racist, intergenerational, girl-centered participatory action research program in the summer of 2009 in Victoria, BC.[6] I have also explored this study in greater detail elsewhere (Khanna, 2011). For Indigenous peoples and non-White/racialized settlers in Canada (particularly in predominantly White cities like Victoria), the invisible, normalized, hegemonic nature of Whiteness functions to denaturalize and (re)colonize non-White citizens (Lee, 2007; Razack, 2002; Thobani, 2007). The vignette shares possibilities and hopes for racialized and Indigenous girls and young women in this city to have a non-White space to share knowledge, critically politicize their social conditions, and be together in a different, generative way through decolonizing practices. By sharing some of our struggles and negotiations regarding the practices we employed in our program, I hope to demonstrate how we applied a transtheoretical framework to (temporarily and imperfectly) disrupt neocolonial formations in our practice.

Regulating Timely Conversations and (Un)timely Bodies

Among many goals, we wanted the program to deliberately open a space to explore sexuality in response to both the girls' expressed desire to talk about it and their lack of opportunities to do so. However, we struggled with dominant colonial notions of development-in-time that played out as we purposefully divided the girls into groups based on their age and experience with feminist anti-racist analysis. We assumed that younger girls were not capable of or interested in engaging in such analysis (or that it was inappropriate) and, alternatively, that older girls were interested and ready to do so. This practice risked reinforcing normative developmental discourses, through which girls who are "untimely"—behind or ahead of their timely development—are considered abnormal in particular gendered ways (e.g., "immature," "precocious," "hypersexual"; Lesko, 1996), and thus excluded from certain conversations.

With the older group, the discussion was initiated by a queer-identified facilitator and a girl co-researcher; it deliberately focused on the intersections of race, sexuality, and gender. This discussion opened up a space where "belonging" was not jeopardized by speaking about all three at once, as it is in many other spaces. Our intentional division of the groups, while re-inscribing problematic age categories, arguably enabled conversations about sexuality and set the stage for one of the girls to "come out."[7] Rather than focusing on queer-as-sexual-identity in the group (e.g., the visibly "out" facilitator/staff and girl co-researcher), which would locate queerness solely on practitioners' bodies and their visibility, we conceived of a space that was intentionally made to defy normative, White, straight, adult expectations (e.g., Driver, 2007, p. 2). We did this through discussion and activities that challenged fixed notions of identity and explored how girls' complex experiences of gender, sexuality, and race intersect and shift across the multiple contexts they navigate every day (e.g., at home, at school, with their White friends). By challenging these traces of the hegemonic, we hoped to decolonize our practices and deregulate (untimely) bodies.

Colonial Time and Indian Time

Our team of facilitators situated the research process in a deliberately anti-racist framework, listing labels and stereotypes that we hear, see, and speak every day. Labels were written on pieces of paper and taped to one another's backs; the 23 girl co-researchers (ages 12–19) and seven adult research facilitators hinted at the labels on each other's backs as we tried to guess our own. In a strange combination of familiar icebreaker—the likes of which you might see at a typical "youth" event—and a serious display of subaltern knowledge, we faced each other's labels with discomfort and curiosity: coconut, gangsta, terrorist, slut, dyke, drunk Indian, Indian time. We were opening up conversations that in many other places are avoided, prevented, ignored, or silenced because they are difficult and risky—because they are *untimely*.

"What's 'Indian time'?" asks one of the girls in the circle during the debrief. An Indigenous girl co-researcher responds:

> Like, the only time I really hear "Indian time" is if I'm late, like, they're like, "Oh, [you're] on Indian time" because like, back in the day, First Nations didn't have watches or times, they just got there when they got there. And like, I think people are getting to know that now, they're just like, "Oh, they're on Indian time, which is late." And then, like, I think it's frowned upon, like when people are late. They call it Indian time because I think that some people frown upon Natives.

An Indigenous facilitator adds:

> That's exactly what it was. It...dates back to contact time when they were starting the fur trading back and forth. So...our people, they would go out, but there were certain times of the seasons that you would go out and get certain animals and then we would bring them back to the trading posts, but the White man would be there for days waiting and waiting and waiting, wondering why First Nations weren't there at the time they had predicted...And eventually a couple of terminologies came into use. Indian time means that they are always late and never on time and never can follow a certain order...And when you look at any different terminology and different labels, they do have a history that comes from someplace.

This conversation about Indian time, while not intended to speak back to our program, could have easily been a response to the unquestioned ways we had constructed the research space. Before this conversation, we had been rushing through our scheduled activities; after it, we asked new questions that changed the program's pace: How can we attend to different durations in our practices? How does the timeliness described in the conversation—the possibility for us to "get there when we get there" rather than impose a linear progression of activities that does not have room for unexpected detours or shifts—become part of the responsiveness of our practices?

Despite dominant discourses that situate the colonization of Canada in the past, these girls and young women situated it as ongoing in the present by contributing this knowledge about "Indian time" and unpacking neocolonial regulation. We live in colonial time; it regulates our practices by assuming a common duration that applies universally to everyone, every process, in every context. This concept of time has been contested by Indigenous peoples whose world views conceive of durations that exceed human lives and require time frames of several generations, placing them at odds with Western capitalist time frames of stock markets, oil exploitation, and economic growth. Decolonizing calls for centering worldviews that have meaning to people who are typically marginalized from knowledge production/mobilization (Smith, 2012).

In many ways, I understood that our program intended to disrupt the "past tense"—not only of colonization, but also of Indigenous peoples themselves. Andrea Smith (2006) describes the "logic of genocide" of Indigenous peoples in North America as one of the pillars that work together to uphold heteropatriarchal White supremacy (p. 68). This pillar locates Indigenous peoples as always disappearing so that they cannot contest settlement and ownership of the land by White (and non-White) settlers. We wanted to prevent unintentional erasures, so we paid considerable attention during the planning stages and throughout the program by partnering with an Indigenous community-based organization and collaborating with Elders and other Indigenous members of the community who generously shared their time, knowledge, advice, and experience. This was not a strategy for "representation:" we aimed to ensure that the experiences of Indigenous girls would be kept at the forefront within our process. In the deliberate intergenerational space we created, these women and Elders, although they were unable to be present throughout the whole program, kept the space open to colonial histories and Indigenous knowledge.

Various postcolonial theorists refer to disruptions of this "past tense" in contemporary contexts of dominant Whiteness as "hauntings" (Bhabha, 1994, 1997; Chambers, 2001; Gordon, 1997, 2004; Spivak, 1999). Avery Gordon (2004) describes a haunting as

> an experience or a phenomenon in which the normal divisions between past, present, and future are not holding up because things and people and knowledge that were supposed to be gone or not-there are making their presence known and felt, almost always in disruptive and unsettling ways. Haunting is precisely what makes the present waver, what makes it not quite what you thought it was. (p. 24)

Bhabha (1994) suggests that a haunting "fractures the time of modernity" (p. 252), hybridizes the present, and connects memories of colonial conflict with subtle forms of neocolonialism that have become diffuse and invisible within globalized iterations of imperialism. In our program, although the girl co-researchers surfaced these hauntings over and over again, sharing their experiences of and resistances to neocolonialisms, for many, this was the first place these experiences were invited and recognized. This was why I came to this project, hoping to share analytical tools and ideas that I so needed when I was a teenager to understand the complexity of living at the intersections of race, gender, age, and sexuality. By withholding concepts and analytical tools from racialized and Indigenous girls because they seem too complex or too theoretical, we deny the complexity of their experiences, prevent generative ways to understand their social conditions, and fall back on problematic assumptions about age, capacity, and timely development.

Becoming Radical: "I'm Not Crazy for Being Mad at Society"—Elicia Loiselle

> *They would not be contained*
> *Their bodies and minds wanted to resist it*
> *even if they couldn't quite put their finger on what it was*
> *Why were they so fucking angry?*
> *Didn't matter*
> *No one seemed to care*
> *because education is a well oiled machine that stops for nothing and no one*
> *Not for poverty, not for sexism, not for racism, and certainly not for girls who want to learn*
> *Not for girls whose minds and mouths are too big, too loud, too open, too demanding, too much of a disturbance*
> *So they were—they are—bound involuntarily to labels that mark them liabilities,*
> *make them disposable:*
> *"at-risk" "high risk" "disordered" "delinquent" "uncontrollable"*
> *They are pushed out of the machine*
> *but it's their own damn fault right?*
> *For being girls who rebel, refuse, resist—dissenters, disturbers, disillusioned....*[8]

In this vignette I share moments from Project Artemis, the participatory action research study I undertook with nine co-researchers (ages 15 to 19) who had all been pushed out of the mainstream school system and were attending an alternative education program for "at-risk" girls. Our research was rooted in a critical, collaborative framework that we developed together and used to investigate, problematize, and address (through social action) the systemic injustices the girls were experiencing. As a CYC practitioner, this politicized approach to practice requires me to continually ask myself and those with whom I work: What framework(s) can enable us to account for the complexities of peoples' lives? What possibilities or openings for transformation and social justice are emerging? What are the limitations of these frameworks? Where/how can we access new or different frameworks that could address these gaps? How do we open space—and hold it open—for that which is not yet? I take up these kinds of questions, and the thinking/being/doing/imagining/hoping they engender, as an ethical commitment to doing social change *with* youth. And it's hard. As I've written elsewhere, some of the most difficult work of doing critical praxis is

> getting comfortable with discomfort—the uncertainty of and tensions within the process—in order to really engage with what is emerging. I found that after awhile I began to count on the messiness as an indication that we were... [doing] deep, collective work, and/or as a reminder that we were doing research within complex and often unpredictable lives and within powerful structural forces. These things needed to be honored for their importance, even if they did produce a perpetual knot in my belly. (Loiselle, Taylor, & Donald, in press)

The girls on the Project Artemis research team were/are negotiating complex contexts in complex ways on a daily basis. All were living in poverty, many had past or current experiences of foster care or being involved in the child welfare system, most were White, one girl identified as part Métis, and one girl identified as Indigenous. I located myself in our research as a queer, White, middle-class, woman-identified settler/feminist/activist/youth-worker/community-organizer/researcher/writer. Through our process I offered my shifting understandings of (feminist, poststructural, queer, decolonizing) theoretical frameworks as tools we could use to name, unpack, and create alternative knowledge about systems that have marginalizing, violent effects in the girls' lives. The girls contributed their own multiple, shifting theories about the uneven material conditions in which they live and the social and systemic responses to these realities (usually inadequate, individualizing interventions). So, our process of becoming radical together emerged through our collective digging into the complexities of girls' experiences of systemic poverty and gender-based violence. While I offer only a small piece of this work here, I/we have written in more depth about the resistance and desire—the transformative possibilities—that emerged through this process (Loiselle, 2011; Loiselle et al., in press). As Lizz, a 16-year-old co-researcher, expressed:

> I don't think that people really take girls like us seriously. They see it like it's our fault and we just have to conform to society. It hurts and it's really not accurate. It's stuck in people's heads that you change for society, society doesn't change for you. In Project Artemis, we were talking back to that, and I feel like we made people take us seriously.... We made that opportunity for ourselves, and it was really brave of us because we're not "supposed to" share our opinions, especially being young women in a patriarchal society. (Loiselle et al., in press)

Pictured in Figure 4, our research team created a "stereotypes wall" where girls wrote labels that are projected onto their bodies as they navigate different contexts. The activity provided openings for us to explore the systemic/systematic processes through which the girls are assessed, intervened upon, silenced, and excluded. In the conversation below we were unpacking the label "crazy":

> Elicia: Are there stereotypes here that girls experience because they're girls?
>
> Mary (17): There's more girls on medication than there are guys on medication. Like, you know, it's like, if girls are a certain way then they should be, like, I don't know, diagnosed with some kind of mental illness or, like, you know, they're crazy.
>
> Anna (18): I can relate to that just because I was diagnosed with bipolar and I was taking lithium and then I chose not to take it. And it's almost like the lithium messed me up more emotionally than anything just because I felt like there was no way I could change the fact that I had mood swings.... Only the medicine's controlling it. But then I flushed like 200 pills down the toilet. And, like, I don't think I'm bipolar, I just think I have a lot of stuff that's happened in the past and I think that has a lot to do with my mood swings because certain things trigger things that have happened in the past... I feel like that psychiatrist was so wrong to say that I was bipolar.... I think that just goes to show how quick psychiatrists are to diagnose and get patients out of their office and just cure it with a band-aid of medicine.

FIGURE 4 Stereotypes wall. (Color figure available online.)

This is a moment of collective knowledge generation in action. I'm asking the girls a question about the stereotypes that are coming from a feminist lens, which takes into account the specificity of how "girl" gets gendered and constructed differently (and in intersection with conditions of poverty that place girls in Project Artemis under heightened surveillance and intervention). Mary responds by theorizing some of her observations about how girls get diagnosed. Anna relates Mary's perspective to her own life, generating a powerful moment of resistance and desire. Collectively, we begin to render visible how the prevalence of mental illness diagnoses for young women who are "a certain way" is deeply embedded in dominant constructions of appropriate femininity and heavily linked to discourses of vulnerability and the "crazy" girl. Mikel-Brown (2005) states that it is this "relentless overpsychologizing of girls that has served to render invisible the social and material conditions of girls' lives" (p. 147). Sparks (2002) argues that the growing preoccupation with and treatment of young women's "aberrant" behaviors are bound to a long history of oppressive psychological interventions on women that are justified through colonial, patriarchal logics:

> The discourse of gender sheds additional light on why medical interventions appear appropriate for teenage girls.... Psychological theories of women as emotionally unstable, dependent on men, or "asking for" the abuse they experience at the hands of men are just a few of the stories spawned by gender discourse and historically influencing the treatment of women in clinical settings.... Women are assigned the greatest number of bipolar, depressive, eating, and borderline personality disorder diagnoses. (p. 30)

Anna clearly demonstrates resistance to both the diagnosis and the medication prescribed on/to her by the psychiatrist. She disrupts this coding of her "mood swings" and her gendered history ("stuff that's happened in the past") as "disorder." She refuses the discursive move that reduces her life's complexities and multiplicities to the colonizing categorization "bipolar." As an ethical move away from such categorizations of (girls') bodies, I find it useful to draw on Deleuze and Guattari (1987), who conceptualize bodies not for what they are, but for what they do in connection—assemblages—with other (human and nonhuman) bodies. The creative and productive force generated when bodies connect with other bodies is desire:

> We know nothing about a body until we know what it can do, in other words, what its affects are, how they can or cannot enter into composition with other affects, with the affects of another body, either to destroy that body or to be destroyed by it, either to exchange actions and passions with it or to join with it in composing a more powerful body. (Deleuze & Guattari, 1987, p. 257)

For Anna, the connection of her body with a "band-aid of medicine" cuts off flows of desire in that it limits rather than creates possibilities ("the lithium messed me up more emotionally than anything"). Swallowing the pills as complicity with the capitalist biomedical machine produces undesirable affects for Anna, so she flushes "like 200 pills down the toilet." Human and nonhuman bodies connect—hands, pills, toilet—to produce the flushing as an opening. The medication Anna does not want to swallow, when flushed down the toilet, becomes part of an assemblage of bodies that liberates the flow of desire—allows movement away from the categorical constraint of diagnosis toward something other/else. Sparks (2002) notes that "the voices of adolescent girls may fall on patronizing ears when there is little room for girls to legitimately question some treatment recommendations" (p. 31). This discursive silencing is ruptured, however, in the moment when pills are flushed down the toilet, and again as that moment is relived in our conversation, and again as it leaves traces on this page, and again as it reverberates in the words of our co-researcher, Laura (17), who powerfully asserts: "I'm not crazy for wanting something to change and I'm not crazy for being mad at society."

These and many other openings constituted our process of becoming radical together:

When I connects with Them
and fumbles toward
some ever shifting version of
We
Threaded together through
some common understanding of pain
common belief in love
common desire for change
We
move in and out of unison through cycles of knowledge production
bound to circles of lives
of girls' lives
We
endeavour to speak our individual and collective selves
into existence
through a critical language of resistance
that will give this moment the power
to revise the next

CONCLUSION

Across our vignettes, we have shown how we engage critical, transtheoretical frameworks to do collaborative practice with children, youth, and communities in order to name and challenge the dominant, colonial power structures that produce the social inequities they/we are living. Further, we have demonstrated how politicized CYC practice might open spaces for resistance, desire, creativity, and action that subvert pathologizing frameworks and enable vital alternatives. Even as we highlight these common praxis threads that we feel are at the heart of politicized caring, we also want to emphasize the inherent limitations of any proposed framework—particularly when such a framework is transtheoretical, deliberately emergent, and politically engaged. Some caveats are important at this juncture.

First, we describe several theoretical assemblages that come from vastly diverse fields and theoretical histories. A full exploration of the debates within and across fields of feminism, queer theory, poststructuralism, Indigenous and postcolonial epistemologies, and so on, exceeds the scope of this article, but is central to the difficulties of enacting these ideas in practice. It is important that we have opportunities in our field to keep abreast of debates about applications to practice, tensions, contradictions, and points of alignment and connection, within and among these different theories—otherwise we risk oversimplifying concepts, obscuring important distinctions, and reiterating universalizing models.

Second, the examples we provide are not meant as a prescriptive "how to" of critical praxis; they are deliberately and importantly evolving, situated, and context-specific. They come out of critical relational praxis with the communities, places, and issues at hand, and as such cannot be neatly exported and reapplied in other settings. Struggling and collaborating together in the specific locations and communities in which we work is vital to our approach—we take the time to produce this in each new context, to live with the tensions and productive possibilities in relationship, with all the intricacies this implies. We acknowledge that working together in this way brings to light the incommensurability of the many deep-seated historical issues we address. In other words, working collaboratively and transtheoretically does not resolve the central issue of the ongoing colonial occupation of Canada, for instance. Nonetheless, we refuse to take that complexity as justification for saying "this is too big for me." The micropractices we have shared—presencing, naming, taking up space, disrupting, reclaiming, producing, storying, acting, challenging, standing up, working together, advocating, and so on—are necessary and important. As our examples show, our communities want *more,* not less.

The vignettes we have shared speak back to a frequently voiced concern in CYC that critical theory and analysis are not useful for or relevant to frontline practice with young people, families, and communities. We find this perspective deeply problematic on many levels. It reproduces a false dichotomy between those who work with and those who think about children, youth, and families, as if *working with* and *thinking about* were mutually exclusive acts. Understanding them as such only maintains the historical silencing of minoritized voices and theories and the reproduction of Euro-Western privilege. This silencing negates practitioners' ethical responsibilities to respond effectively—justly—to the complex social and systemic injustices people are negotiating every day. What is perhaps most disturbing about the "anti-theory" argument, is that it erases what so many of the children, youth, and families we work with already know or have experienced at a most personal level. As 16-year-old Priya said in the quote that opens this article, "They don't give us ... credit that we understand and yeah, we need to talk about it!"

We call for a collective, politicized approach to CYC praxis that integrates collaborative theorization and practice, one that is rooted in working *and* thinking *with* (de Finney et al., 2012). As the feminist, anti-racist scholar and activist bell hooks (1994) states, "I came to theory because I was hurting... I came to theory desperate, wanting to comprehend what was happening around and within me. Most importantly, I wanted to make the hurt go away. I saw in theory, then, a location for healing" (p. 59). As if echoing hooks, the young people we work with are saying that dominant Eurowestern psychological models, with their focus on relational, developmental, individualizing practice, are too apoliticial, not critical enough, and therefore inadequate to address deep-seated structural inequities. In other words, if we do not name it, how will we work collectively to change it?

Our ethical approach to the practice of "care" speaks back to "relational practice" that negates the impact of systemic injustice in people's lives. We propose an expansion into politicized, socially engaged approaches to "care" and "relational practice" that take up critical practice and collective action as a vitally important ethic. This possibility of transformation is what draws us to Tuck's (2010) desire-based framework that is "intent on convoking loss and oppression, but also wisdom, hope, and survivance" (p. 639). Survivance is distinct from survival, Anishnaabe scholar Gerald Vizenor (1994) tells us; it is "moving beyond our basic survival in the face of overwhelming cultural genocide to create spaces of synthesis and renewal" (p. 53).

Thinking *and* embodying *and* doing CYC practice by interrogating structural inequities and affirming the survivance and presencing of communities and ecologies can be incredibly difficult, but not doing this is not an option. It is not "in the best interests" of children, youth and families to maintain a practice of convenient silence and inaction; assuming they do not want to have these conversations maintains our comfort with the status quo, not theirs. In becoming theoretically critical, Skott-Myhre and Skott-Myhre (2011) ask that "we not only theorize and reflect, but that our theories allow us new avenues of action that have the capacity to change the world" (p. 44). Hopeful practice requires radical, critical action—otherwise it reproduces the very things we hope to change.

I loved this program 'cause we, um, got to, we got to talk, we got believed. In the program they knew what we're going through. Plus we did something about it. (Diego, age 9)

NOTES

1. For more on minoritization in CYC, decolonizing practice, critical girlhood work, and youth-engaged participatory action research, see: de Finney, Loiselle, and Dean (2011); de Finney and Saraceno (in press); Khanna (2011); Loiselle (2011); and Loiselle, Taylor, and Donald (in press). For more on critical residential care work and Indigenous analysis, see: Corcoran (2012); de Finney, Green, and Brown (2009); and de Finney, Dean, Loiselle, and Saraceno (2011).

2. The examples we use in this article are largely drawn from arts-based, youth-engaged and/or action-centered research studies. This is because such moments in our research processes were more rigorously documented than in our other sites of practice *and*, more importantly, because we have explicit written and verbal consent from those involved to write about and publish their words, experiences, and interactions. While we all have many examples from our practice that were not part of research studies, we find it unethical to share such stories without going through explicit informed consent processes with the children, youth, and families involved.

3. Minoritized groups are positioned as outsiders to dominant norms and consequently seen to fall short of the standards of the dominant group. When difference is the basis for exclusion, a social context is created where certain groups are privileged and others subjugated or minoritized (i.e., seen as "less than" or "other") based on their positioning in a normative social hierarchy. These exclusions produce drastically unequal outcomes for certain groups of children, youth, and families (de Finney, Dean, et al., 2011).

4. This project was conducted through a SSHRC grant in partnership with *Antidote*, an award-winning grassroots network for/by racialized girls, young women, and women (http://www.antidotenetwork.org).

5. See http://www.photovoice.org.

6. This program was part of a larger SSHRC funded study focused on identity, belonging, and solidarity among Indigenous and racialized girls and women in Victoria, led by Dr. Jo-Anne Lee. I had the honor of working on this project with Antidote: Multiracial and Indigenous Girls and Women's Network, a community-based organization that strives to reduce the social exclusion faced by Indigenous and minority girls and women in this city.

7. "Coming out" has been celebrated as a self-actualizing moment of modernist identity development, assuming a coherent identity. However, it is important to note that coming out is not "an equal opportunity endeavor" (Tilsen & Nylund, 2010, p. 98). Coming-out narratives inscribe and validate privileged (white, male) GLBT liberal subjects, and function as a technology of Western "homonormativity" (Puar, 2005, 2007).

8. This excerpt is from a spoken-word piece that I wrote and performed for my co-researchers in Project Artemis so that they could better understand how I was making sense of the experiences they were sharing and the knowledges we were generating together through our research.

REFERENCES

Alexander, J. M., & Mohanty, C. T. (1997). *Feminist genealogies, colonial legacies, democratic futures*. New York, NY: Routledge.

Artz, S. (2012). Dis[s]curse[if] challenges: Professional conversations in child and youth care in fluid modernity. *International Journal of Child, Youth and Family Studies, 3*(2–3), 146–163.

Battiste, M., & Semeganis, H. (2002). First thoughts on First Nations citizenship: Issues in education. In Y. Héber (Ed.), *Citizenship in transformation in Canada* (pp. 93–111). Toronto, ON, Canada: University of Toronto Press.

Bell, S. J. (2012). *Young offenders and youth justice: A century after the fact* (4th ed.). Toronto, ON, Canada: Nelson Education.

Bhabha, H. (1994). *The location of culture.* New York, NY: Routledge.

Bhabha, H. (1997). The world and the home. In A. McClintock, A. Mufti & E. Shohat (Eds.), *Dangerous liaisons: Gender, nation, and postcolonial perspectives* (pp. 445–455). Minneapolis, MN: University of Minnesota Press.

Chambers, I. (2001). *Culture after humanism: History, culture, subjectivity.* New York, NY: Routledge.

Child Welfare League of Canada. (2003). Children in care in Canada: A summary of current issues and trends with recommendations for future research. Retrieved from: http://www.cecw-cepb.ca/publications/574

Corcoran, R. (2012). *Rethinking "foster child" and the culture of care: A rhizomatic inquiry into the multiple becomings of foster care alumni.* (Unpublished master's thesis). University of Victoria, British Columbia, Canada.

de Finney, S., Dean, M., Loiselle, E., & Saraceno, J. (2011). All children are equal but some are more equal than others: Minoritization, structural inequities, and social justice praxis in residential care. *International Journal of Child, Youth & Family Studies, 2*(3–4), 361–384.

de Finney, S., Green, J., & Brown, L. (2009). Towards transformational research for and with Indigenous communities: The new British Columbia Indigenous child welfare research network. *First Peoples Child and Family Review, 4*(2), 161–164.

de Finney, S., Little, J. N, Skott-Myhre, H., & Gharabaghi, K. (2012). Conversing on conversations in child and youth care. *International Journal of Child, Youth and Family Studies, 3*(2–3), 128–145.

de Finney, S., Loiselle, E., & Dean, M. (2011). Bottom of the food chain: The minoritization of girls in child and youth care. In A. Pence & J. White (Eds.), *Critical perspectives in child and youth care: Working the borders of pedagogy, practice and policy* (pp. 92–121). Vancouver, BC, Canada: UBC Press.

de Finney, S., & Saraceno, J. (In press). Warrior girl and the searching tribe: Indigenous girls' everyday negotiations of racialization under neocolonialism. In C. Bradford & M. Reimer (Eds.), *Girls, texts, cultures.* Waterloo, ON, Canada: Wilfrid Laurier Press.

Dei, G. S. (2000). Rethinking the role of Indigenous knowledges in the academy. *International Journal of Inclusive Education, 4*(2), 111–132.

Deleuze, G., & Guattari, F. (1987). *A thousand plateaus: Capitalism and schizophrenia (B. Massumi, Trans.).* Minneapolis, MN: University of Minnesota Press.

Downe, P. J. (2005). Aboriginal girls in Canada: Living histories of dislocation, exploitation, and strength. In Y. Jasmin, C. Steenbergen, & C. Mitchell (Eds.), *Girlhood: Redefining the limits* (pp. 1–14). Montreal, QC, Canada: Black Rose.

Driver, S. (2007). Introducing queer girls and popular culture. In S. Driver (Ed.), *Queer girls and popular culture: Reading, resisting, and creating media* (pp. 1–25). New York, NY: Peter Lang.

Fechter-Leggett, M. O., & O'Brien, K. (2010). The effects of kinship care on adult mental health outcomes of alumni foster care. *Children and Youth Services Review, 32*(2), 206–213.

Fine, M., & Ruglis, J. (2009). Circuits and consequences of dispossession: The racialized realignment of the public sphere for U.S. youth. *Transforming Anthropology, 17*(1), 20–33.

Foucault, M. (1982). The subject and power. In J. Faubion & P. Rabinow (Eds.), *Power* (pp. 326–348). New York, NY: New Press.

Gordon, A. (1997). *Ghostly matters: Haunting and the sociological imagination.* Minneapolis, MN: University of Minnesota Press.

Gordon, A. (2004). *Keeping good time: Reflections on knowledge, power, and people.* Boulder, CO: Paradigm Publishers.

Harris, A. (2004). *Future girl: Young women in the twenty-first century.* New York, NY: Routledge.

hooks, b. (1994). *Teaching to transgress: Education as the practice of freedom.* London, UK: Routledge.

Indian & Northern Affairs Canada. (2008). Treaty research report. Ottawa, Canada: Department of Indian and Northern Affairs Canada. Retrieved from http://www.ainc-inac.gc.ca/al/hts/tgu/pubs/t3/tre3-eng.asp

Irwin, R., & de Cosson, A. (2004). *A/r/tography: Rendering self through arts-based living inquiry.* Vancouver, BC, Canada: Pacific Educational Press.

Khanna, N. (2011). *Decolonizing youth participatory action research practices: A case study of a girl-centered, anti-racist, feminist PAR with Indigenous and racialized girls in Victoria, BC.* (Unpublished master's thesis). University of Victoria, British Columbia, Canada.

Lawrence, B. (2004). *"Real" Indians and others: Mixed-blood urban Native peoples and Indigenous nationhood.* Vancouver, BC, Canada: UBC Press.

Lee, D. (2011, August 30). Dibaajimowinan: Four stories of resurgence in Michi Saagiig Nishnaabeg territory. Retrieved from http://dibaajimowin.wordpress.com

Lee, J. A. (2007). Localities and cultural citizenship: Narratives of racialized girls living in, through, and against whiteness. In P. Gurstein & L. Angeles (Eds.), *Learning civil societies: Shifting contexts for democratic planning and governance* (pp. 59–88). Toronto, ON, Canada: University of Toronto Press.

Lesko, N. (1996). Past, present and future conceptions of adolescence. *Educational Theory, 46*(4), 453–472.

Loiselle, E. (2011). *Resistance as desire: Reconfiguring the "at-risk girl" through critical, girl-centered participatory action research.* (Unpublished master's thesis). University of Victoria, British Columbia, Canada.

Loiselle, E., Taylor, R., & Donald, L. (In press). When girls talk back: Learning through doing critical, girl-centred participatory action research. In C. Etmanski, T. Dawson, & B. Hall (Eds.), *Teaching CBR: Linking pedagogy to practice.* Toronto, ON, Canada: University of Toronto Press.

Lugones, M. (2007). Heterosexualism and the colonial/modern gender system. *Hypatia, 22*(1), 186–209.

Mikel-Brown, L. (2005). In the bad or good of girlhood: Social class, schooling, and white femininities. In L. Weis & M. Fine (Eds.), *Beyond silenced voices: Class, race, and gender in the United States schools* (pp. 147–162). Albany, NY: State University of New York Press.

Mohanty, C. T. (2003). *Feminism without borders: Decolonizing theory, practicing solidarity.* London, UK: Duke University Press.

Puar, J. K. (2005). Queer times, queer assemblages. *Social Text, 23*(3–4), 124–139.

Puar, J. K. (2007). *Terrorist assemblages: Homonationalism in queer times.* Durham, NC: Duke University Press.

Razack, S. H. (2002). *Race, space, and the law: Unmapping a white settler society.* Toronto, ON, Canada: Between the Lines.

Richardson, C., & Nelson, B. (2007). A change of residence: Government schools and foster homes as sites of forced Aboriginal assimilation. *First Peoples Child and Family Review, 3*(2), 77–83.

Schutte, O. (2007). Postcolonial feminisms: Genealogies and recent directions. In L. Martin Alcoff & E. Feder Kittay (Eds.), *The Blackwell guide to feminist philosophy* (pp. 165–176). Malden, MA: Blackwell.

Simpson, L. B. (2011). *Dancing on our turtle's back: Stories of Nishnaabeg re-creation, resurgence, and a new emergence.* Winnipeg, MB, Canada: Arbeiter Ring Publishing.

Sinclair, R. (2007). Identity lost and found: Lessons from the sixties scoop. *First Peoples Child & Family Review, 3*(1), 65–82.

Skott-Myhre, H. (2008). *Youth subculture as creative force: Creating new spaces for radical youth work.* Toronto, ON, Canada: University of Toronto Press.

Skott-Myhre, K., & Skott-Myhre, H. A. (2011). Theorizing and applying child and youth care praxis as politics of care. *Relational Child & Youth Care Practice, 24*(1–2), 42–52.

Smith, A. (2005). *Conquest: Sexual violence and American Indian genocide.* Cambridge, UK: South End Press.

Smith, A. (2006). Heteropatriarchy and the three pillars of white supremacy: Rethinking women of color organizing. In Incite! Women of Color Against Violence (Ed.), *Color of violence: The incite! anthology* (pp. 66–73). Cambridge, MA: South End Press.

Smith, L. (2012). *Decolonizing methodologies: Research and Indigenous peoples.* New York, NY: Zed Books, Ltd.

Sparks, J. A. (2002). Taking a stand: An adolescent girl's resistance to medication. *Journal of Marital and Family Therapy, 28*(1), 27–38.

Spivak, G. (1999). *A critique of postcolonial reason: Toward a history of the vanishing present.* Cambridge, MA: Harvard University Press.

Thobani, S. (2007). *Exalted subjects: Studies in the making of race and nation in Canada.* Toronto, ON, Canada: University of Toronto Press.

Tilsen, J., & Nylund, D. (2010). Heteronormativity and queer youth resistance: Reversing the discourse. In L. Moon (Ed.), *Counseling ideologies: Queer challenges to heteronormativity* (pp. 93–104). Surrey, UK: Ashgate Publishing Ltd..

Trocmé, N., Knoke, D., & Blackstock, C. (2004). Pathways to the overrepresentation of Aboriginal children in Canada's child welfare system. *The Social Service Review, 78*(4), 577–600. Chicago, IL: University of Chicago Press.

Tuck, E. (2009). Suspending damage: A letter to communities. *Harvard Educational Review, 79*(3), 409–427.

Tuck, E. (2010). Breaking up with Deleuze: Desire and valuing the irreconcilable. *International Journal of Qualitative Studies in Education, 23*(5), 635–650.

Vizenor, G. (1994). *Manifest manners: Post-Indian warriors of survivance.* Middleton, CT: Wesleyan University Press.

White, J., & Pacini-Ketchabaw, V. (2012). Introduction to the special conference issue. *International Journal of Child, Youth and Family Studies, 2&3,* 125–127.

Child and Youth Care To-Come

SCOTT KOURI

*School of Child and Youth Care, University of Victoria,
Victoria, British Columbia, Canada*

The intent of this article is to follow deconstruction as a way to think about the questions that are currently being asked in Child and Youth Care (CYC). As a graduate student in the School of Child and Youth Care at the University of Victoria (SCYC), I am challenged to think my position and identity in terms of my location within, or on the borders of, a CYC community. In this article I bring together deconstruction and contemporary issues in CYC to propose a way forward in terms of conceptualizing CYC identities. The first part of this follows deconstructive thinking through an analysis of CYC as a context and the practice of "contextualizing" in CYC. The second movement of the article weaves in the notions of community, community identities, tradition(s) and relationships to demonstrate how linguistic representations may limit our possibilities for theory and practice. I end by proposing hospitality (Derrida, 2000) as a way to negotiate the borders of CYC and open toward a "Child and Youth Care To-Come." This article is specifically engaged with the conversations sparked at the Child and Youth Care in Action III Conference and the subsequent special issue of the International Journal of Child Youth and Family Studies, 3*(2-3). I situate this critical analysis within the current conversations of my local CYC community and explore how deconstruction can help to open our community to its own future.*

This research was supported by the Social Sciences and Humanities Research Council.

Working with deconstruction and hospitality (Caputo, 1997; Derrida, 1976, 2000), this article applies pressure to the possibility of stable notions of Child and Youth Care (CYC) identities, contexts, foundations, and communities. I work at this project from within the very CYC context, community, and conversations that I seek to open up, and, as such, perform a doubling practice that is characteristic of all deconstruction. Lather (2001) describes doubling practices of this sort as a simultaneous working-within and troubling-from-within. Doubling practices recognize the need for intelligible and identifiable repetition on the one hand, while, on the other hand, push toward subversive repetitions that disrupt the overcoding of knowledge and identity. As such, the doubling practice performed here works to both (re)create CYC as a context while also troubling the very grounds and borders of that context.

Caputo, in commenting on Derrida's claim of being "a very conservative person" (Caputo, 1997, p. 8), explains that deconstructive transgression is a double gesture in that it depends on a shared horizon or frame to transgress, while, in turn, transgression gives new inclinations and twists to those shared lines: new life, movement, and vitality. This type of radical conservatism, in a sense, preserves tradition by opening it to productivity, difference, and otherness. In my view, this style of approach is important for CYC at this time because it emphasizes the dimensions difference and otherness which necessarily constitute all our notions of identity, context, and community. Deconstruction offers us a way to think about our community and context in terms of its boundaries, openings, possibilities, and limitations.

In this article, I venture a thought that some of the current movements in CYC can be read as a self-deconstruction, which has always-already been at work. Deconstruction, in this sense, is specifically not a method or critique applied from outside the CYC context. Rather, it is the attending to the immanent rumblings of instability within a context somewhat set toward stable identity and a firm knowledge base. To propel CYC toward boundary transgression, internal critique, and invitation to otherness, I take up recent articles from the *International Journal of Child, Youth and Family Studies* (IJCYFS), Volume 3(2–3) (hereafter IJCYFS Conference Issue) as a site for a situated deconstructive thinking. This article enjoins with the critical trends in the field which open toward difference, otherness, and alterity, and interrogates notions and practices of context, community, identity, relationships, and care. Throughout this article, deconstruction works to both critique conventional CYC while also producing spaces and possibilities for an unknown future-to-come. The welcoming and opening to the other and the future of CYC are explored in this article in terms of an ethics of hospitality.

CYC IN ACTION: A TRANSIENT CONTEXT

The specific context and literature which acts as the temporary space for my work in this article is the special IJCYFS Conference Issue. This recent issue documents and builds on conversations which took place at the Child and Youth Care in Action III conference in April 2011 at the University of Victoria. The CYC in Action III conference engaged many of us in questioning the field's identity markers, core practices, and foundational beliefs. Many of the articles in the Conference Issue further theorize CYC at its limits and provide a space for thinking about how the borders of CYC are patrolled and negotiated. A specifically engaging event at the conference that is continued in the IJCYFS Conference Issue was the Roundtable Conversation, an interactive exploration of themes related to CYC identities and language and theory use in the field. The themes of this conversation seemed to me to be enacted simultaneously in the position each person took in relation to one another and in the mode of dialogue that emerged. The conversations of the conference stimulated a deep questioning for me in terms of my location, identity, and position as a CYC theorist and practitioner. The IJCYFS Conference Issue has, in turn, offered me an opportunity to engage CYC with protracted purpose and deliberation.

Many of the papers in the IJCYFS Conference Issue (de Finney, Little, Skott-Myhre, & Gharabaghi, 2012; di Tomasso, 2012; Phillips and Cameron, 2012; Saraceno, 2012; Yoon, 2012) explicitly take up the notion of deconstruction, albeit not all specifically in the Derridian sense, while other papers seem to implicitly perform a deconstruction (H. Skott-Myhre, 2012; K. Skott-Myhre, 2012). For example, Saraceno (2012), specifically referencing Derrida and Caputo in her analysis of the colonial practices inhabiting CYC, calls for a mapping of existing horizons of practice and a deconstruction of "the theories, structures, and values that shape how we practice" (p. 248). Similarly, Yoon (2012) argues that "in culturally responsive pedagogy, we start off with deconstructing what is already known and held to be true" (p. 179). In his article "Escaping Purity: Lessons for Child and Youth Care from Religion," Daniel Scott (2012) invites us to think with Derrida (1988) and Caputo (2006) about CYC's history and development, with a particular focus on contexts and communities.

The Roundtable Conversation itself, in its willingness to engage with difference, ambiguity, and complexity, demonstrates, I think, a deconstructive movement which invites a transgression across CYC boundaries and welcomes the new and unfolding in the field. The structure of the conversation, as an open and critical dialogue between theorists and practitioners in our field, worked to create a space in which questions could both create community by bringing us together around them, as well as invite the differences and transgressions necessary to keep the community up to its own future. As a student of CYC at the time of attending the conference, the tensions, connections, and transgressions of the conversations inspired a thought that the indeterminacy of CYC is (and has always been) an opening for participation, creation, and engagement. In this sense, the event of the conversation felt like a gesture of hospitality extended through the stances and positions that the interlocutors took up in relation to each other, the audience and the field more generally. It is in these sorts of encounters with one another and those on the borders of CYC that I see the working through of an ethics or relational stance that can be extended into our pedagogical, theoretical, and practice milieus. It is in the spirit of an ongoing search and working-through of an ethical and relational CYC that I engage with deconstruction and hospitality as a way to invite a CYC to-come.

DECONSTRUCTION, HOSPITALITY AND THE IMPOSSIBLE

To use deconstruction as a frame for making sense of the happenings in CYC is at once an impossibility and a necessity. The impossibility of using deconstruction as an interpretive frame or analytic method is precisely borne in the fact that deconstruction is against all enclosures, simplifications, reductions, and final explanations. As a challenge to the stability of meaning, deconstruction actively works to deconstruct or open up any stable meanings. Placing difference, mutalibility, and play at the structural interstice of any seemingly stable system, deconstruction is in the impossible position of being against all formulations which begin "X is ___", it "is," in this sense, a method against methods, a rule to be against rules. Deconstruction (if such a thing exists) "is" against foundational terms which subsume difference to the same; hence deconstruction as a foundational or centering term is always under deconstructive pressure.

Turning to the articles in the IJCYFS, deconstructive critique prevents any final frames of reference or correct interpretation for the texts. To secure an interpretation or meaning for what has been said/written would require static significations to be secured through fixed relations with one another. Deconstruction, conversely, is a movement toward the future; it is the excess of the boundaries which things—institutions, conversations, practices—seem to presently occupy (Caputo, 1997). Deconstruction is an exposure toward undecidability, complexity, and affirmation of the yet to-come. This does not imply that deconstruction is against meaning, but rather that deconstruction is perpetually putting pressure on the limits of meaning making and the suppression of variable and multiple meanings. Deconstruction breeds in questions like those posed by de Finney and colleagues (2012):

> I wonder what gets lost when we become stuck in the familiar contours of normative theories and practices. What knowledge and ways of being flow outside the overwhelmingly EuroWestern perspectives that so define our field? What critical theories—specifically, anti and postcolonial, Indigenous, feminist, queer, and other analyses of resistance, hope, transformation—can contribute to these discussions, and to a more productive praxis of social change? How can we make room

for unanticipated, nuanced, previously silenced narratives of what counts and what is effective practice? (p. 130)

Conversely, as a necessity, deconstruction is always-already happening: the play of difference and the self-differentiation of any system which seems complete and stable (Derrida, as cited in Caputo, 1997). Deconstruction is not something applied to a thing, but rather the very opening and complexifying from the inside that any assemblage of elements takes, hence an auto-deconstruction or self-deconstruction. Deconstruction is not, as is commonly thought, a taking apart and deep reading of constructs from an outside critical perspective, a reading for the history and embeddedness of the construct (Caputo, 1997). Deconstruction is the very future of things, their very iterability, and it is the very capacity of words to be repeated in new contexts or in new relationships, which generates deconstruction. Deconstruction fully accepts that meanings necessitate a context, and Derrida (1988) went as far as to say "there is nothing outside context" (p. 136). But, it is the very impossibility of finding a stable context or explanatory meaning for that, which puts deconstruction into play. Macleod (2002), in this sense, notes that meaning is always achieved through "an infinite network of texts" (p. 18) or what Derrida calls intertextuality (Spivak, 1976). Deconstruction, therefore, is more a project of demonstrating how power structures stabilize the meanings of things through the suppression of alternative and freely flowing meaning. Furthermore, by questioning stabilized notions and opening contexts up to difference, deconstruction works toward movement, life, and possibility.

As an example from the IJCYFS Conference Issue, Saraceno (2012) takes up Whiteness as a previously secured notion related to progress, economic development, and care. Notions of Whiteness were previously secured, Saraceno argues, through the practices of subjugating "other" identities and normalizing the experiences of two seemingly homogeneous groups: White and Other. Saraceno historically situates these concepts of identity and begins to reinscribe them in new matrices of meaning with particular reference to CYC and notions of care. Whiteness is now, under a deconstructive impetus, becoming associated with colonialism, neoliberalism, and oppression, while Indigenous and other subjugated identities are being proudly reclaimed. Saraceno, however, does not stop at this deconstruction of Whiteness and critique of current helping practices: she insists that future helping relationships are not instituted as substituting new rules or codes for the old ones, but rather as practices of "mapping out new, engaged methods to uncover, track, and resist these hidden hegemonic normative values and practices" (p. 261). Understanding identity and the helping professions in this way opens practices, traditions, and institutions to their own future through a perpetual subverting of the hegemonic and normative (Caputo, 1997).

To embrace the possibilities of thinking CYC as a perpetually open future, I will expand on how deconstruction invites a way to think of tradition as enlivened through transgression, opening, and otherness. This form of opening to the other and to the future is articulated by Derrida (2000) and Caputo (1997) as an attitude of hospitality toward the unexpected coming of the unanticipated other. Contexts, communities, identities, and foundational knowledge seen from this perspective are demonstrated to be contingent on and responsible to the coming of the other through the definition and structure of their boundaries. An attitude of hospitality is demonstrated to be a relational positioning which compromises finality and security in the opening toward a future which is forever to-come.

DECONSTRUCTION OF CONTEXT

At the time of the CYC in Action III Conference and the publication of the IJCYFS Conference Issue, Daniel Scott was the director of the School of Child and Youth Care at the University of Victoria. Scott (2012) in his contribution to the IJCYFS Conference Issue, reflects on the "current (and perhaps permanent) identity-making process and the establishing of orthodox claims and beliefs in CYC" (p. 188). Scott begins his analysis of CYC as a context by invoking Derrida's (1988) claim that "there is nothing outside of context" (p. 136), which Derrida himself equates with his previous claim that "there is nothing outside the text" (1976, p. 158). Read either way, Derrida's (1976, 1988) argument is that anything experienced or thought to be real is known or represented through an interpretive process which is itself referencable to particular, yet unfixed, historical, social, linguistic, and material contexts. Scott suggests that CYC is a complicated context that is composed of carefully constructed shared ideas as well as more implicit gestures and "contextual traces" (p. 188). In this section I elaborate on what Derrida's "nothing outside of text" might mean for a complicated CYC context, while also providing the groundwork for a critique of practices of contextualizing so central to the CYC context.

To being with, it is important to grapple with the concept of intertextuality (Spivak, 1976), or the claim that any seemingly objective or stable position is always-already embedded in an infinite and dynamic network of texts and relationships. The impossibility of getting outside of context in order to experience or interpret a pure happening, in our case CYC, is exactly what makes talking about deconstruction on every occasion so very difficult: deconstruction resists a metacontextual definition that would be transcontextually representative. Caputo (1997) explains that context, as the very condition of possibility for meaning, is precisely what makes secure meanings impossible as all contexts are contingent in nature. Any seemingly coherent context is contingent and interwoven with innumerable other contexts (e.g., historical, social, economic, political, cultural, linguistic) and any seemingly stable context therefore depends on the suppression of conflicting interpretive schema. Said in another way, contexts deal with the differential nature of language by suppressing variable meanings and erecting centering concepts which can stabilize meaning through association to those terms.

If such a singular and centering thing as CYC were to exist, as a context or otherwise, it would depend on a system of stable and communally shared signs. This system of signs, or context, would operate by reducing the multiplicity of meanings attributable to the concept CYC and hence create a potentially threatening underbelly in the form of suppressed meanings. The idea of CYC, viewed from this perspective, would be open to multiple heterogeneous interpretations made from within the original context itself as well as from other interconnected contextual systems of meaning. In order to maintain the stability of the concept CYC, or any concept related to it, systems of power need to stabilize the play of traces (the potentially threatening underbelly) within the immediate context as well as boundary against all other contextual interpretations in which CYC could be read differently. The impossibility of such final suppressions and totalizing boundaries is exactly what provides the possibility for movement, life, and the continuation of tradition through its own transgression. The argument here is that CYC, as opening to difference, transgression, and mutability, ensures the continuance of its context and community through its very subversion.

Contexts allow for the possibility of meanings through the fixing of categories and, as such, operate by suppressing the play of different possible meanings of any concept or sign. The suppressed variants, however, can never be fully erased and therefore work as trace elements that inhabit all texts (Derrida, 1976). Traces are neither present or absent and act as a structural undecidability within every context. The presence or stability of any meaning is therefore always threatened by the trace living within the differential system and these traces are exposed by alternate readings within the original context and alternate uses in other contexts. For CYC, concepts such as care, practice, context, and even the notions of children, youth, families, and communities are inhabited from within and ultimately open to variable meanings. I propose that CYC, as with all contexts of interpretation, works to structure and secure meaning through the suppression of variable meanings and that deconstruction is a name for the interaction of these trace elements coming into contact with each other and exploding into unforeseen possibility.

Hans Skott-Myhre (2012) uses the ideas of social diagrams as a way of reading CYC in terms of its distribution of social norms, disciplinary practices, dominant ideas, values, ideas of normalcy and deviance, and coding systems such as conduct and language. In specific reference to linguistic coding, Skott-Myhre argues that CYC "facilitates the movements of certain ideas and beliefs across all the bodies in the field" (p. 319). Furthermore, he adds, renditions of the field that lack a historical contextualization make invisible tensions, struggles and contestations of such coding processes. Deconstruction, on the other hand, historicizes and troubles coding systems by applying pressure to seemingly stable contexts and meanings. To engage in the apparently always-already ongoing deconstruction of CYC as context, and to be more clear on the style of deconstruction particular to Derrida and Caputo, I will take a closer look at Derrida's twin claims that "there is nothing outside the text" (1976, p. 158) and "there is nothing outside context" (1988, p. 136). This exploration will provide the groundwork for a critical engagement with: (a) CYC as a context for making meaning; (b) contextualization as a central idea of CYC practice and theory; and (c) professionalization as a limiting force on the future of CYC.

TEXT/CONTEXT

A text, for Derrida (1976), extends beyond a written document to emphasize that all of our knowledge and actions rely on constructs that are embedded within interconnected and mutually referential systems. Texts, used here as anything which is constructed and open to interpretation—for example, a piece of writing, a child's behavior, a dream, a map, a practice—is in relation to an endless system of referentiality. In this sense, the statement "there is nothing outside the text" (Derrida, 1976, p. 158) is a critique of the idea that a construct, as constituted in language and a social context, is or was once somehow outside referential systems awaiting signification. An "outside context," if it existed, would be a space inhabited by all forms of fully present things like being, justice, objectivity, existence, and the like, which texts or constructs would then directly signify or represent through language. I am here reading Derrida as arguing that in opposition to the view that things exist first and are coded after, he contends that our constructions or representations bring things into being. Our constructs, signs, and representations therefore directly limit or provide possibilities for action.

Deconstruction moves beyond, while relying heavily on, Saussurean semiology and the structuralism of Levi-Strauss by insisting that not only are signs arbitrary and based on difference from other signs, but that all signs differ from themselves across time and context (Derrida, 1976, 1978). St. Pierre (2000) contends that poststructuralism "radically modifies de Saussure's theory by positing that the meaning of the signified is never fixed once and for all but is constantly differed" (p. 481). Meaning, in this case, no longer refers to specific things in the world but rather to other signs in a perpetually shifting landscape of semiology. The role of context in this regard is to temporarily fix meanings through the establishment of seemingly secure systems of concepts that depend on centering terms and the suppression of the play of difference. From this perspective, therefore, texts and contexts are neither stable nor innocent: they are interrelated systems of social practices that create, repress, and structure experience and action.

The deconstructive argument that there is nothing outside text implies somewhat of a reversal of the metaphysics of Western philosophy that places presence and essence before construction (Caputo, 1997). Tied to this understanding of "no outside text," deconstruction can never itself be outside text and therefore can never be applied to a text/context. Rather than some method, things or practice that is done to a text, deconstruction is the word given to a process that is immanent to every system of signification. Deconstruction, therefore, is not something that is applied to CYC but an always-already happening within CYC. The pragmatic value of thinking with deconstruction is that it provides an immanent critique of practice in terms of relationship to otherness, difference and the subjugated.

For an example close to CYC, take the thought that there is actually something out in the world called, say, "a boy" before our system of signification named it as such. This thought would be to suppose presence before construction, an essence or identity prior to the categories of human thought. To take a less obviously constructed (and deconstructed) term, take the more general signifier "human." The idea of "human" is both situated within a historical system of signification with a history including multiple meanings (and exclusions) as well as many different horizontal meanings. The term human, while possibly referring to something material and outside of language, cannot be applied without a fully constituted and shifting system of differential meanings. Any coherent use of the signifier "human" relies on the exclusion of all things which are related to but not defined as "human" as well as the suppression of all of the variable uses of the signifier "human" itself. Deconstruction, used as an analysis of language and context, is specifically the process of taking account of what structures are assembled and how power flows through them to attain material and linguistic consequences based on our constructions.

To move from using "there is nothing outside text" to "there is nothing outside context" offers a possible simplification that I would like to explicitly avoid. The use of the expression "nothing outside text" seems to play on the structuralist analysis of differential systems of language that understands that a text is always overrun by all the divisions and boundaries that a text may seem to have. A text is never complete, bounded, or secure; it is always open to reinterpretation, play of meaning, and the involvement of history, politics, the unconscious, and so forth (Derrida, 1978). There is no more a text that functions "in an immediate way, as the name of an intelligible textual object, counterposed to an extratextual outside" (Barnett, 1999, p. 284). The text is no longer a stable entity between stable entities, "but is given priority as a constitutive play of chance and necessity" (p. 284); it brings together a textured interweaving of differences. Without a clear border which lets in and keeps out certain interpretations, constructs, meanings, and readings, a text is no longer approachable from the outside; no longer situatable within a stable context. Deconstruction questions how the frames (contexts) of interpretation work to limit the otherwise unprecedented movement of the text and makes visible the power effects which seek to constrain intertextual movement.

Derrida's (1976) claim that there is nothing outside of text/context can be read as the impossibility of stepping outside language in order to validate truth claims. All language is inescapably referential and differential in that we can never speak of something without reference to its context and the entire differential system of signs which makes it intelligible. The word "professional," for example, does not refer directly to something in the world which was always there just waiting for its naming; neither does it correspond directly to a specific thing judged so by an interpretive community. The term "professional" becomes meaningful only in relation to other signs (e.g., paraprofessional, lay, amateur, rookie, untrained). The meaning of a word, for Derrida, "cannot stand on its own; its meaning is an effect of its differential relations within a system of referents" (Lucy, 2004, p. 143). Derrida applies pressure to the concept of context to emphasize the dynamism and slipperiness of language and blurs the distinction between text and context to the point of challenging the reduction of text to contextualized readings.

CONTEXTUALIZATION

Contextualization generally refers to the process of stabilizing the meaning or interpretation of texts/events by referencing them to the circumstances and relationships that they are thought to be interconnected with. To "put something in context" can help explicate the circumstances, meanings, and/or contingencies of texts/events. Practices of contextualization, such as historical or cultural, allow for more full readings which may challenge received or biased interpretations. Contextualization, as such, is a powerful tool of critique and interpretation. However, contextualizing practices may also work toward constrained, regulated, and stabilized interpretations which work toward final truths and secure meanings.

Contextualization challenges claims to essentialism and indeterminacy and provides a foundation for arguing that all meanings can be stabilized within an interconnected network of concepts and factors. As distinct from a contextualized interpretation, an essentialist position would advocate that the name and meaning of a text/event which achieves identity or Truth in an $A = B$ kind of way. To say "boy means this" (pointing to a boy or creating a dictionary-type description) is a correspondence theory which argues that language or signs refer directly to things in the world or the conceptual representation we carry of them. This type of theory of truth understands the human mind as a mirror of reality and believes that proper perception and clarity can deliver a true picture of the world outside of human consciousness. Not only does deconstruction argue that concepts and representations constitute what is represented (which can never be outside human consciousness or "outside context"; a truly present/transcendental signified), but that no signifier is identical to itself.

The differential nature of language perpetually differs any signifier's meaning to the point that it can never be fully identical to itself. Butler (2004) writes "If some readers thought that Derrida was a linguistic constructivist, they missed the fact that the name we have for something, for ourselves, for an other, is precisely what fails to capture the referent (as opposed to making or constructing it)" (p. 32). Similarly, Mason (2006) explains that Derrida's metonymical term différance (a misspelling of the French différence, translated "difference") has the structure of the impossible:

> For différance, like "the impossible," is in part about deferral, about things—in this case the full, or saturated, meaning of words—never arriving. Différance can be thought of as the process by which words are prevented from reaching full meaning that is perpetually active within discourse. Différance means that words are always deferred from reaching full meaning, and differed from their previous appearances. (p. 507)

Indeterminacy, as opposed to essentialism and contextualization, argues that the word "boy" can mean a potentially limitless number of meanings because the sound/writing "boy" is an arbitrarily chosen sign assigned to an indefinite event or conception of an event negotiated within a dynamic network of use. Indeterminacy is furthermore supported by the referential nature of sign systems which understand each sign as depend on other signs which in turn rely on others as infinitum. Signs cannot escape the looping effect which occurs when signs are referentially used achieve meaning. Imagine, for example, not knowing a word of English and trying to come to a determinate understanding of what the word "boy" means by consulting a dictionary. First you would need to find the entry "boy" and then look up all the words used in each definition offered. The definitions of the words used to define "boy" would then send you on another search for more definitions and the process would expand, loop, and repeat endlessly.

In one possible attempt at this project, the first round of searching for the definition of "boy" would yield "1. Often offensive: a male servant; 2. a. male child from birth to adulthood, b. son, c. an immature male, d. sweetheart; 3. a. one native to a given place, b. fellow, person, c. used interjectionally to express intensity of feeling" (Merriam-Webster dictionary online, 2012). The search would then move from this (already multiple) definition to a search for a definition of every term in the definition above. The process would move in loops which led back to earlier definitions which were not yet secure, as well as move outward toward even greater and more diverse possibilities of meaning. This process of referentiality would simultaneously run with the process of differal (understanding how "boy" differs from "man," "child," "woman," "girl," etc.). The meaning(s) of the word "boy," rather than being secured, would proliferate, including contradictions and inconsistencies (such as within the first-order definitions of "boy" as both an offensive degradation and the affectionate call of a sweetheart). For an example directly from CYC, Artz (2012), in her contribution to the IJCYFS Conference Issue, analyses the discourses and concepts related to girl's violence and writes:

> And those aspects of our human experience that we have for so long treated as "hard" concepts and even as trait variables—concepts like race, ethnicity, class, social position, culture, gender, sexual identity, personal identity—these are not merely fixed points or parts of an additive description of self, other and world, but fluid and emergent patterns, open to reinterpretation, to being lived in multiple ways at the same time. (p. 148)

Deconstruction, rather than living up to its reputation as completely siding with indeterminacy rather than essentialism, operates through an exposition of the tensions, exceptions and alternatives performed within governing context. Caputo (1997) insists that for deconstruction pure unity or pure multiplicities are both synonymous with death (lack of movement or future). Although always working to open heavily coded texts to the play of indeterminacy, Derrida (1976) also insists on good contextual readings. Deconstruction, rather than positing the hopeless relativity that indeterminacy seems to invoke, works within contexts, and good readings of contexts, to open them to the unexpected, the heterogeneous, and the play of difference which come from within any system. It is the exceptions and alternative understandings that deconstruction highlights, the stepping outside of the regulated contexts of meaning, the movement of meaning.

I am therefore not arguing for a limitless setting free of the differential play of meaning of CYC or its associated identities, concepts, and structures, but rather asking us to question of the forces which shape the particular, yet arbitrary, stabilizations of meaning. As a political act, therefore, deconstruction can work to uncover the instability of sharp conceptual divides or, conversely, to stabilize meanings where certain power relations work "through the recognition and explicit manipulation of instabilities of meaning" (Barnett, p. 285). Barnett (1999) contends that "deconstruction interferes with understandings of borders and boundaries by rewriting spatial categories according to a rhetoric of movement, tracking the ways in which conceptual closure is only ever constituted by regulating the play of opening and exposure" (p. 282). Deconstruction therefore calls us to notice the openings and closings, the movements and boundaries, the central and the exceptional. As an opening gambit in this project, I will now briefly look at two contemporary movements in CYC: the practice of contextualization and the professionalization of the field.

CONTEXTS AS OPENINGS AND CLOSINGS IN CYC

To work in context is to simultaneously extend intelligibility to include a more complex and full understanding of situations, while at the same time bordering off multiple meanings and stabilizing understandings within the play of indeterminacy. This takes place by way of suppressing the multitude of meanings that could be ascribed to a situation or term and reducing multiple interpretive possibilities to a few (or one). A contextualized reading of texts generally inscribes a correct/incorrect binary into interpretation which parallels the demarcation of correct and incorrect spaces within the static contextual grid into which the interpretations are fit. The interpretations "good student" and "professional" are assessable and rendered as correct or incorrect readings based on the communities interpretive system. Deconstruction, on the other hand, questions the operation of the borders and normative forces which stabilize context and therefore meaning, disrupting "the stable spatial order of categorical conceptualizations" (Barnett, 1999, p. 282). Deconstruction calls for a rigorous attention to the otherness of any system and "situates itself in the interstices of the no longer and the not yet" (Lather, 1993, p. 680).

To contextualize something is to put it back into a context, to make a something more intelligible, to understand it in terms of relationships. As a central tenet of CYC theory, contextualization, and "working in context" are accepted as frameworks for understanding individual development as directly related to, and interacting with, systems of relationships. Phillips and Cameron's (2012) article, for example, works with this central CYC tenet and recommend models for research and practice which capture the lived experiences of childhood "without decontextualizing their meaning" (p. 284). The authors explain that CYC practitioners must "enter into the complex and dynamic bio-ecological system from which they—the children and youth—construct meaning" (p. 285). Furthermore, they advocate for researchers to "cross multiple contexts" (p. 285) and investigate change as interaction and transaction. The models that the researchers propose move beyond the standard ecological model which is a cornerstone within our CYC program at The University of Victoria and promote Sameroff's (2010) unified theory which integrates personal, contextual, regulation, and representational change.

On one level, CYC seems to be trying to gain a more complete and complex understanding of how change and development occur. Ironically, however, this complete or holistic view only works by warding off many other meanings or contextual possibilities. The thought of moving toward more complete representation seems to be guided by an "outside text" ideal or a unified text philosophy in which all constructions will one day be stabilized, understood and rendered intelligible. Phillips and Cameron (2012) importantly warn against the decontextualization of meaning, which I understand as a counsel against simplified, singular or pathology-based understandings of childhood. On the one hand, these warnings are well deserved as they do respond to a closing down of interpretation sometimes imposed by organizational or governmental structures/contexts. However,

Phillips and Cameron seem to be arguing that the framework they are promoting is somehow more objective, true, complete, or adequate than other frameworks. The unified theory, for the authors, inevitably becomes "a model of how we *should* be conducting research within the field of child and youth care" (p. 296, italics added). Here we begin to see how the very practice of contextualization is situated within an intertexual matrix.

Phillips and Cameron (2012) admittedly subscribe to the view that no single lens can account for the lived experiences of children and youth, however, they do continue to search for a framework which can "capture lived childhoods without decontextualizing their meaning" (p. 285). The use of the word "capture" is particularly informative in its relationship with contextualization. Although contextualization is a seemingly indispensible tool for contemporary CYC practice and research, its underbelly, even while acknowledging the impossibility of comprehensive frameworks, is the warding off of simultaneous and multiple meanings, or at the very least ordering frameworks hierarchically or reductively in relation to each other. In this "context" it is the claim that some systems of interpretation render a more true, full or accurate representations than those of say medical, organizational, or governmental frameworks.

A deconstructive reading of the interaction between ecological systems theory, the unified theory model proposed by Phillips and Cameron (2012), and the demands of policy makers and employers for more "simplified" information, is to understand all of these frameworks as themselves intertextually vying for power and dominance. This is the sense of there being no outside text: the very practices of contextualization and meaning making are interconnected with the contexts of their emergence *ad infinitum*. The unified theory gains interpretive ascendency for particular communities within a contingent and situated context while pathology based descriptions gain in meaningfulness and legitimacy due to other circumstances. From a deconstructive perspective, it is the forces of constraint and the relationships between the seemingly stable and enclosed systems that are the focus of analysis rather than the truth claims that any one system produces.

Deconstruction situates itself in the intertextual matrix as a position among many, and owns that it is socially, historically, and economically situated. Importantly, however, a deconstructive perspective refrains from inserting a correct/incorrect binary into doing such things as contextualization and rather moves toward a proliferation of contextualizing practices (hence the earlier discussion regarding the impossibility of stabilizing deconstruction as a centering concept). Contextualization, as it is done in CYC, very much depends on the academic, social, historical, relational, and practice contexts in which we, as the ones doing the contextualizing, find ourselves. A contextualizing practice, therefore, remains contextualized itself and any critiques of such practices are again contingent, constructed and legitimated by a context. This interconnection without end prevents a stable foundation upon which to launch an "outside context" interpretation or critique, but does allow an analysis of the discursive power of vying contexts. In this sense, deconstruction sides with the marginal, silenced, subjugated, and the to-come.

Take the examples of "good children" and "professionals." The "good child" is no longer understood as essentially good (which would correspond to some ideal or transcendent fixed meaning of good) but neither good within a specific context defined by the specific and regulated history and normative standard of achievement, gender, ethnicity, economics, sociality, and behavior. Derrida takes the essentialism/contextual binary as a starting point of deconstructive analysis. A deconstructive analysis of the essentialism/contextual binary begins with a recognition that contextualization is an interpretive principle which buffers the effects of linguistic circularity, deferral, and indeterminacy (Barnett, 1999). As such, historical, social, linguistic, and material contextualizations have become inextricably linked to interpretive processes that seek to localize, frame, bound, and secure meaning. As with the example of the "good child," the stability of the academic environment becomes a seemingly stable context in which the meaning of "good student" could be ascertained. With professionalization, the field of CYC is brought to a halt; some voices are privileged while others suppressed, and a coded system emerges which seeks to determine the meaning of a professional worker in a seemingly stable CYC context. This sort of situating meaning contextually hinges on bordered and stable renderings of the context, which in turn relies on ordering and normalizing practices of language use and behavior.

CYC PROFESSIONALIZATION AS CONTEXT

Professionalization is perhaps one of the most potentially stabilizing forces within current conceptualizations of CYC as a context for practice. For example, the current CYC Competency Document (Mattingly, Stuart, & VanderVen, 2010) has emerged as a singular and unifying framework for defining, developing, monitoring, and assessing professional CYC work across North America. The framework employs normative conceptualizations of child and youth development, a clear definition of the field, and educational requirements and guiding principles for the development of professional practitioners. Although the movement toward competency-based professionalization in CYC is supported by numerous associations, councils, consortiums, and coalitions, a strong voice of critique also exists.

Beginning with Saraceno (2012) in her analysis of the ongoing colonialism which shapes and guides helping professions in Canada, we find that "the assumption that professionalized helping is better follows the natural logic of a Western ontology, with its inherent privileging of hierarchy, power, and a paternalistic stance" (p. 257). In this sense, Saraceno views professionalism in terms of its hegemonic tendencies and advances instead a CYC grounded in collectivism, decolonization, social justice, and the creative capacities of those generally constructed as the clients of professionals. This attitude of CYC praxis as affirmative and political seems to align well with Kathleen Skott-Myhre's (2012) critique of how, within the discourse of professionalism, "the call for professional boundaries becomes a political call for collusion in the ongoing project of defining the terms and conditions of what one can do and where one can go" (p. 305). Professionalization, through these critical lenses, can be seen as a mechanism evolved from systems of domination intent on the continued advancement of a project of stabilizing and fortifying structures and boundaries. Furthermore, discourses on professionalization in CYC are usually lacking in an account of the political dimensions of CYC work or the political agenda inherent in the very idea of professionalization itself.

This is not to say that the professionalization of CYC is automatically politically suspect, but rather that every position is political. Derrida (1988) writes that although there is always something political about attempting to stabilize contexts, it does not follow that such actions are politically suspect by necessity. He argues that an agenda is always implied in any contextual configurations but that contextual configuration, and hence politics, are always necessary. Deconstruction, following the logic of "always in context" argues that neutrality is impossible and that any process or critique issues from one context or another. The critique of professionalization, as with all else, is a political act which is intelligible from within a context of meaning. As a location from which to launch a critique of professionalization, some voices within CYC have taken up the notion of praxis as an attempt to politically situate all attempts at engaging with children, youth, families and communities, including the move toward professionalization.

PRAXIS AS CONTEXT

Saraceno (2012) calls for a deconstruction of CYC theories, structures, and values in an attempt to move from a practice steeped in coloniality to a praxis of social justice. de Finney et al. (2012) call for "a more productive praxis of social change" (p. 130), and Little (de Finney et al., 2012) is inspired by conversations which deconstruct "the dialect of CYC praxis with a focus on gender, identity, and social change" (p. 132). Although approximate to current understandings of practice, praxis involves the integration of theory and practice manifested in the application of self-understanding (White, 2007). White argues that praxis necessitates an ongoing, situated, dialogic, and emergent stance in relation to theory, practice, and conceptualizations. She defines CYC praxis as ethical, self-aware, responsive, and committed action involving dimensions of knowing, doing, and being. Furthermore, these dimensions of knowing, doing, and being are diverse, multiple, and "always get expressed within specific historical, sociocultural, political and institutional contexts" (While, 2012, p. 227).

In contrast to the movement toward professionalization exemplified in the CYC Competency Document (Mattingly et al., 2010), which White (2012) critiques as flat and informed by an instrumental/technical rational paradigm, a praxis framework resists standardization and highlights the complex situatedness of all CYC work. Rejecting the majority view that the complexities of human service can be conceptualized and measured in standardized forms and delivered by a homogenous group of practitioners, CYC praxis uses a web metaphor to appreciate the "active, intersecting, embedded, shifting and asymmetrical qualities of everyday practice" (White, 2007, p. 241). Contrasted to traditional ideas of practice, praxis is risky, free, and a more value laden form of action (Smith, 1999). For example, White uses verbs to linguistically transform knowledge to knowing; skills to doing; and self to being. This change in language reflects an active, dynamic, and situated perspective on CYC.

Intertwined with the emphasis on the contextual, active and situated nature of knowing, doing and being, praxis, for White (2012), highlights the political and sociocultural dimensions of theory and practice. In describing CYC praxis as political, Skott-Myhre and Skott-Myhre (2011) mobilize and promote the use of theories which allow the thinking through of practice choices that challenge the dominant social forces of society. Skott-Myhre and Skott-Myhre take up a Marxist reading of praxis to extend the political aspects of White's (2007) proposals and argue that praxis "requires that we not only theorize and reflect, but that our theories allow us new avenues of action that have the capacity to change the world" (p. 42). Skott-Myhre and Skott-Myhre suggest that professionalization and standards of competence draw on and sustain hierarchy, power and profit at the consequence of the revolutionary political potential in youth and youth-work. A praxis approach to CYC, on the other hand, is an active and creative political approach lived through the complex relations between youth and adults.

Praxis, however, under the pressure of deconstruction, does not move us toward a higher ground of practice where we as CYC, having successfully deconstructed our positions and acknowledged our political situatedness, now set out from an "outside text" position to help those still caught up in the web of text. Deconstruction, rather, seems to instigate what H. Skott-Myhre (de Finney et al., 2012) calls a "political project designed to constantly undermine the fundamental assumptions of our field..." (p. 134). He furthermore follows Marx in promoting contradiction and uncertainty as a means of making visible "the actual machinery of domination" (p. 134). Although in solidarity with a Marxist critique, deconstruction lacks the stability, realism, or objective "outside text" necessary for a comprehensive structural and materialist understanding of history or the means of emancipation from domination. Praxis, therefore, under conditions of post-structurality becomes a self-subverting opening onto the yet-to-come.

DECONSTRUCTION, MARXISM, PRAXIS

Lather (2003) works from a deconstructive perspective and challenges the notions that a deconstructive praxis can be conflated with Marxist ideological critique or that deconstruction can serve clear and useful purposes. Lather renders Derrida's "nothing outside text" as "nothing that is not caught in a network of differences and references that give a textual structure to what we can know of the world" (p. 258). In this reading of intertextuality, all cultural practices are delimited and inscribed by frameworks that are produced-by and productive-of networks of power. Intertextuality is a critique of logocentrism, a searching for the failures of language to provide stable meanings, and a working within the ruins of such failures. In terms of the "cultural constitution of subjectivity" which deconstructive textuality makes visible, Lather writes:

> Here the complexity of subject formation includes how various axes of power are mutually constitutive, productive of different local regimes of power and knowledge that locate subjects and require complex negotiations of relations, including the interruption of coherence and complete subordination to the demands of regulatory regimes. Engaging the real is not what it used to be. Different ideas about materiality, reality, representations, and truth distinguish different epistemological orientations where reality does not precede representation but is constituted by it. (pp. 258–259)

In terms of praxis, which is intractable and perhaps indistinguishable from subject formation, Lather places deconstructive efforts again in the wastelands beyond assured concepts and "in excess of traditional political agendas" (p. 258). This excess, on the one hand, moves beyond the dialecticism of Marx, most especially its dogmatic configurations; while, on the other hand, returns to a Marxist reading of justice which foregrounds the asymmetries in relationships. The task is no longer to uncover hidden material or structural injustice, but rather to set to work a different logic that "works against the leveling processes of the dialectic and for the excess, the nonrecuperable remainder, the different, the other/outside of the logic of noncontradiction" (p. 259). Deconstruction (if there is such a thing) demands the impossible and unanswerable in an engagement with the "other".

Lather (2003) argues that although the "posts" and Marxism share the task of understanding representational practices as socially and historically located, the two approaches differ in ontological positioning. Marxism, as an enlightenment and modernist project, poses a material real, whereas deconstruction is ontologically indeterminate, even in regard to its own existence. Deconstruction (if there is such a thing) is interested "in complicit practices and excessive differences rather than unveiling structures and illuminating the forces and relations of production" (p. 260). Deconstruction eschews notions of correct consciousness, categorical thinking, intentional agency, and reason more generally. Lather writes "indeterminacy and paradox become conditions of affirmative power by undoing fixities and mapping new possibilities for playing out relations between identity and difference, margins, and centers." Furthermore, "the deconstructive shift is from the real to the production of the reality effect" (p. 260). From this perspective, therefore, "praxiological engagements" (p. 260) open to difference and abide within the immanent sphere of which there is no outside. Deconstruction is complicit in its participation in reinscription; however, this participation is propelled by the respectful engagement with the "other." Lather describes this praxis as a getting lost in "an ethical relationality of non-authoritarian authority to what we know and how we know it" (p. 261), which again, to me, sounds like H. Skott-Myhre's (de Finney et al., 2012) call for CYC as a "political project designed to constantly undermine the fundamental assumptions of our field..." (p. 134). This relational ethics extends beyond theoretical conceptualizations of the field and is precisely the praxis of engagement, which I will later articulate as an ethics of hospitality.

The impossibility of how deconstruction cannot be applied while at the same time is always-already in motion, is deconstruction in a nutshell (Caputo, 1977). Lather writes "deconstruction is aimed at provoking fields into new moves and spaces where they hardly recognize themselves in becoming otherwise, the unforeseeable that they are already becoming" (Lather, 2003, p. 261). To be CYC for me, therefore, is to be within and against, to keep alive and transgress, to do and undue in the same movement. Deconstruction invites us to sustain our tradition through the engagement with the new and the other, that which exceeds our boundaries and lives on the far side of tradition and legitimation. Praxis, in this form, is now reinscribed as a shaping of a "future that must remain to come, in excess of our codes but, still, always already: forces already active in the present" (Lather, 2003, p. 262).

DECONSTRUCTION: AN IMPOSSIBLE APPROACH

Deconstruction happens from within a context by showing the workings and failings of the system in its attempts to remain stable and coherent. Deconstruction begins through a genealogy that pays close attention to the layers and constructedness of concepts both across time and in relation to other concepts within the system. Many of the IJCYFS Conference Issue articles examine the history and meanings of ideas of relationship, practitioner, context, colonization, theory, professionalization, and praxis within the context of CYC. The second movement of deconstruction, or rather the process through which the first movement is possible, is the juxtaposition of seemingly stable concepts with their trace: Whiteness and helping with colonialism and oppression (Saraceno, 2012); professionalization with limited agency and movement (K. Skott-Myhre, 2012); and community with fragmentation and exclusion (Scott, 2012). This second movement of deconstruction, rather than confounding meaning permanently, creates the space in which productive and critical readings are possible.

Barnett (1997) argues for a deconstructive epistemology of metonymy, a reading practice that displaces or puts off any attempt at stable interpretation based on identity or metaphor. Put positively, the stable and contextualized meanings of concepts are liberated through the supplemental invocation of alternative readings. The boundaries and relationships based on separations that are necessary for stable concepts are blurred and the ambiguous space in-between becomes a site for studying the limits and performances of reading and writing and their relations to power and social institutions. In sum, deconstruction is an analysis of boundaries in terms of their productive and restrictive textual force. While meaning is perhaps dependent on context for stability, the stability of context is thrown into question by deconstruction.

My claim for deconstruction as a process already at work in CYC is based on the double movement of contextualized readings and radical openness. On the one hand, I am making a strong call for a contextual reading of all of our practices; while on the other hand, this deep and situated reading is aimed at calling forth a radical openness which subverts the recapture of the to-come within the previously established. In a seemingly similar movement, de Finney (de Finney et al., 2012) calls for immediate attention to the historical and ongoing colonial practices which directly position Indigenous children and youth as "the ethno-cultural group that is most represented yet receives the least funding" (p. 129) while simultaneously resisting theories, languages and services which will reinscribe helping within the dominant EuroWestern norms. de Finney is calling for an openness to the unanticipated and the disregarded through a questioning of "the encumbered, malfunctioning machine of social services" (p. 131). Importantly, however, de Finney also levels a critique of nomadic and hybridic philosophies, such as deconstruction, for their movement toward uprootedness and dilution. As an ongoing challenge to think our ways out of dominant practices and theories, de Finney asks us to "understand how active coloniality operates" and "seriously and humbly interrogate our own complicity/embeddedness in its inner workings" (p. 131) even when employing critical and poststructural approaches.

As a second example from the Roundtable Conversation, H. Skott-Myhre (de Finney et al., 2012) levels a scathing critique of the workings of capitalism which underwrite all contemporary CYC practices while also calling for contradictions, difference, ambiguity, deviance, and uncertainties which can challenge any other dominant constructions in our field.

Skott-Myhre, in a similar warning call to de Finney's, alerts us to the re-appropriation of human service work by capital and asks us to rid ourselves of our addictions to global capitalism. I understand both Skott-Myhre and de Finney (de Finney et al., 2012) as reading the CYC context for its genealogical and productive forces, while also seeking to destabilize the foundations of our practices rather than propose a new platform or foundation for our work.

Without stable boundaries or foundations, or even the ability to state a CYC identity through an "X is Y" type statement, I will approach the question of "what 'is' Child and Youth Care?" through two parallel questions: "how can we conceive of CYC as a community to-come?" and "what relational stances are made possible for CYC by reading deconstruction as an engagement and ethics of hospitality?"

COMMUNITY IDENTITY AND TRADITION

Moving from the question of contextualized definitions or meanings to questions of communities and traditions seems to signify a movement from the discursive to the material. However problematic a discursive/material binary may be (especially for deconstructive activity which is always at work in the overflowing space between seemingly dichotomous binaries such as material and discursive), it is nevertheless productive to ask how discursive practices, such as contextualization, legitimation, and signification, act to mark and produce relationships between bodies. As categories and signifiers such as "child and youth care practitioner (or professional)," "counselor," "theorist," "revolutionary," "at-risk," "criminal," "professor," "youth," "child," "minority," and the like work to position, produce, and restrain the movement and connection of bodies, and bodies work to produce and reproduce such abounding discursive categories, the questions of how we define ourselves and the "other" who is by definition not-us, are directly constitutive of our relational possibilities. Working again with the deconstruction of context, I will in this section ask how our ideas of CYC as a context are enacted in our conceptions of a CYC community or tradition. Simultaneously I will explore how our relationships to difference across and within these community boundaries reflect and produce possibilities for relating. This investigation will then lead to the proposition of an ethics of hospitality as a way of relating: a proposition which circles back to the beginning of the article in the sense that it demonstrates how hospitality is another word for deconstruction.

Scott (2012) works with Caputo's (2006) etymological investigation of the word community to explore the potentials for inclusion and exclusion under the CYC community banner. Communities, from the Latin *communis*, seem to be historically established on terms of shared identities, similarities and commonalities (Caputo, 1997). Two important questions, therefore, are "what of difference within and outside the community borders?" and "how are the community borders managed?" The tail end of the word community gives us some of the answer: from the Latin *munis*, it refers to defense or fortification, and in this sense is related to the word munitions (Caputo, 1997). So for one, we must contend with the intra-communal fusion of identities (some sort of essentialism which would define a common root, tradition, function, identity, or distinctiveness to CYC), and second, it seems necessary, in the name of community, to have an outside or other which is not CYC and borders between us and them. The deconstruction of the word community performs an excellent example of how warm and welcoming concepts such as community open up to alternative readings and transgressions. Community is at once a homestead in which the peace of the community depends on its munitions and readiness for war, or as Caputo (1997) states "if a community is too welcoming, it loses its identity, if it keeps its identity, it becomes unwelcoming" (p. 113).

Derrida maintains that either pure unity or pure diversity are impossible and would amount to death if achieved (Caputo, 1997). As an alternative to purity and multiplicity, deconstruction advocates for "highly heterogeneous, porous, self-differentiating quasi-identities, unstable identities, if that is what they are, that are not identical with themselves, that do not close over and form a seamless web of the selfsame" (Caputo, 1997, p. 107). With a gesture of responsibility toward the incoming of the other, the internally differentiated community is always already open to the coming and play of difference. This internal self-differentiation Caputo (1997) calls a "we" who cannot settle into being at home with themselves, a "we" who cannot finally say "we."

The self-identical community, however, is impossible, and if it were possible, it would be death, that is, it would be without movement or future. Languages are spoken variously and subject to a variety of uses and transformations, the moment it would be otherwise the language would be a dead and finally susceptible to a complete and stable analysis. Similarly, psychoanalysis has shown us that the individual subject is composed of a myriad of selves and the point at which self-differentiation ended so to would the subject. Again, a political party has factions and dissenters, without which it would be totalitarianism. Difference is necessary to identity and therefore the politics of difference is paramount. Difference is the movement and possibility of a future which allows concepts, communities and identities to continue. The specific example of children and youth is an exemplar of the dependence on difference for future, movement, and hence survival.

In reference to the relationship between a community and the children and youth who we find in care, H. Skott-Myhre (2012) writes "They cause us trouble because when they are with us in community, they produce holes in the fabric of *our* lives, *our* habits, *our* comforts, and *our* commonality. Their difference must be secluded away and not missed except in the solitude of those who know they also do not really belong to the commonality of the social" (p. 327). Difference, from the perspective of a self-identical or stable community, is a rupture. Our particular community, intent on engaging the marginalized and excluded of the normal and comfortable community, is therefore a ripe location for investigating the politics that informs our relationship to inter-communal and extra-communal difference.

COMMUNICATIVE COMMUNITIES

The idea of communication as the context, language practices and shared meanings of a community is challenged the play of difference. Rather than view communities as homogeneous groups of language users secured in their meanings by a shared context, "deconstruction exposes difference, chance, disjuncture and uncertainty as necessary conditions of communication" (Barnett, 1999, p. 286). It is the spaces of disjuncture, contradiction and tension, rather than consensus and mutual understanding, which provide for us in CYC the possibility of opening to our future. Communication mediates between a "space-between that gathers up and separates speakers and listeners, writers and readers in a non-reciprocal ethical relationship of responsibility that exceeds calculation" (Barnett, 1999, p. 286). Commonality, in this reading, is precisely the shared limits and impossibility of homogeneity and identity that communication is thought to demand. Alterity and difference therefore share in a new ethics of community and relationship. Artz (2012) writes:

> New turns of phrase, new ways of employing words that for many of us have had fixed meanings, now force us to meet these words again in different guises, and so create the need for a re-acquaintance, for hearing and seeing again in a different way, what we thought we knew.... (p. 146)

CYC: TRADITION IN TRANSGRESSION

Caputo (1997) argues that contextualized readings and stabilizing interpretive communities are the guardrails within which interpretation and meaning to take place. The necessity of these guardrails is invaluable to the conservation of a tradition, but may also be the end of any communal project if transgressive readings are actively suppressed. For a tradition to thrive, Caputo argues, the possibility of reading otherwise must always be kept alive. To be truly concerned about a tradition, a text, a community, new renditions and performances are necessary. Transgressive readings with the power to transform, however, do not move from outside the text, but always move through a thorough reading to open onto new possibilities.

Caputo advises taking "whatever the masters of legitimation can hand out" because transgression "requires first the conventions of the same in reference to which one sets out to find something contravening and counterconventional, something transgressive of the horizons of legitimation" (p. 81). Transgressive readings and subversive performances, which arise from within as acts of self-differentiation, opens the conventional, traditional and reproductive to productive otherness. This internal self-differentiation, furthermore, destabilizes the center and boundaries of the community and allows for greater opening toward the more radical otherness outside the community walls.

I am arguing here that contemporary CYC is in an always-already position of opening to an array of internally inhabited heterogeneous interpretations and performances, as well as challenged to account for its relationship to the others outside its community boundaries. The ideas of CYC as context or community may work to stabilize this heterogeneity into a seemingly coherent and intelligible whole, but I propose that the idea of a Child and Youth Care To-Come opens to productive relationships within and across community borders. The IJCYFS articles described thus far evidence a rumbling of differential meanings of some of our more established axioms: strengths-based, relational, helping, contextual, professional, and pluralistic. For meaning to happen at all, there needs to be some gathering up: a shared identity and intelligibility of some sort. The call from deconstruction, however, is for a self-differentiated identity which is perpetually on the move and opens to the yet-to-come. Once we take responsibility for own inner differences, our own self-differentiating identity, we can realize that our identity is not exclusive of another identity and we can open to difference and the future: as Derrida states "dissociation is the condition of community and relation to the other" (Caputo, 1997, p. 15).

In this regard, it is interesting to note that the Roundtable Conversation itself was sparked by an online debate provoked by the question "why are people speaking about the field in ways I don't understand?" (de Finney et al., 2012). This question seems to me to reflect both the question of CYC identity and the parallel question of the relationship between practice and theory. The authors of the Roundtable Conversation (de Finney et al., 2012) take up these questions in mutual respect and attention to difference. Before engaging with these questions and responses, however, it is important to note that a deconstructive reading is vastly more than appreciating difference across two options. Binary thinking, such as that which underlies theory/practice arguments, is very different than the intertextual, differential, and to-come notions of difference that are being proposed here. Although the theory/practice divide demonstrates some internal self-differentiation, the deconstructive process works to closely read the genealogy of these two concepts, demonstrate their mutual dependence and supplimentarity, and open both up to their own trace or intertextual features. I read Little (de Finney et al., 2012) as moving toward this in her argument that the theory/practice dichotomy is untenable although unavoidable, and in her invitation for:

> More conversations around theory and common sense that ground our current perspectives of how dominant and non-dominant discourses merge and counter-merge with the process of helping children, youth, and communities. (p. 132)

In response to this perspective, Gharabaghi (de Finney et al., 2012) defends the theory/practice divide and adds a number of categorical divides between "groups" or types of CYC contributors. Gharabaghi seems to be calling for a clear reading of the terms and categories and their associated relationships in the field while also calling for a container that can sustain such differences. In response to the question of CYC identities, he is little perturbed by the field's seeming crisis as for him "identities in crisis are really the only authentic identities to begin with" (p. 137). On the question of identity and relating across identity categories, H. Skott-Myhre (de Finney et al., 2012) emphasizes "the importance and value of deviance and difference" (p. 133) and challenging the dominant construction of truth regarding youth and adults, and specifically their relationship to each other.

From a deconstructive perspective, identities, either at the individual or community level, are constructed through practices, performances, and coding systems (Barnett, 2005). Furthermore, identities are constructed in relations to other identities through processes of either identification to same or differentiation from other. Relational identity formation, from a post-structural perspective, therefore "works primarily by excluding some element that takes on the role of the Other, setting up an image of non-identity that confirms the identity of the self or the collective community" (Barnett, 2005, p. 7). All relating, from this perspective, becomes a process of boundary maintenance and "territorial integrity of communities or selves" (p. 7). The question of identity, community, and meaning, therefore becomes a question of maintaining boundaries, relating across them, and moving with direction.

THE DIRECTION OF THE COMMUNITY

While the questions of community and identity leads to the question of direction, the orientation, movement and direction of the "other," whether inside or outside our community borders, calls for a thinking through of our relationship to those headed otherwise. Derrida's (1992) expression "the other heading" explored in a book by the same name, "suggests a mindfulness of the heading of the other, which forces us to be a little more accommodating about those who are headed otherwise, headed elsewhere, than are we" (Caputo, 1997, p. 116). A strong *teleos*, or goal orientation, requires a repression of the headings of the other and can subsume the other's identity in the form of unity-in-difference. Caputo (1997) argues that Derrida's idea of difference works to deconstruct a Hegelian notion that all differences or oppositions gather themselves together in an ever expanding and differentiated unity. This deconstruction of Hegel helps to see what Derrida is actually up to: he avoids (as best has been possible in language up to now) any essentialism and argues for "a certain contingent assembly of unities subject always to more radical open-endedness that constantly runs the risk of going adrift" (Caputo, 1997, p. 117). This drift or heading otherwise takes the place of a direction or program in terms of history and destiny. Deconstruction moves against accumulation and the dominant heading: identified in our times as neoliberalism, neoconservatism, colonialism, and global capitalism (de Finney et al., 2012; Saraceno, 2012; Yoon, 2012).

In the mid 1990s Derrida was highly concerned with the pervasive directional sway of international movements by European headings: an accumulation of less-powerful nations under the planned destiny of the few and the gradual squeezing out of difference (Derrida, 1992). Today, in CYC, "we" are being asked to relate to the traces of our history and the processes of our present (colonialism, neo-liberalism, capitalism) that can undo a seemingly coherent community or clear intent and purpose, while also subsuming the radical project of praxis to a new dominant form. We are being asked to relate across theoretical divides, we are being asked to relate to those headed otherwise. The stances we take up in relation to our internal self-differentiations, I argue, reciprocally affect our relational capacities to receive the yet-to-come: the future of CYC.

DECONSTRUCTION IS HOSPITALITY

To be open to the heading of the other, to affirm the different, new, and the yet-to-come, to be open and responsible, and to do so in the name of community is difficult. Derrida acknowledges an irrepressible desire for community but seeks a community who can know its boundaries and allow its boundaries to be its openings (Caputo, 1997). A community as such is impossible, yet necessary: a community without the munitions, a "weak community" as Caputo (1997) calls it, a community frayed at the edges resisting unity and opened to the coming of the other. The deconstruction of community is very much the impossibility of hospitality. Derrida (2000) writes "to take up the figure of the door, for there to be hospitality, there must be a door. But if there is a door, there is no longer hospitality" (p. 14).

H. Skott-Myhre (2012) brings up "the problem of the door" (p. 324) in terms of its capacity to not only operate as an entrance, "but as an active piece of machinery that signals certain practices, beliefs, and even forms of identity." H. Skott-Myhre argues that entrances shape the ideological belief systems of those who cross the borders and marks the identities of those on the inside. He is specifically discussing the physical institutions in which CYC practitioners have historically operated, however, his analysis of contradiction and antagonism as possible means of "destroying the logic of the door" (p. 328) are particularly relevant to the current analysis of CYC as a context or community in its own right. In his analysis, the doors of institutions are material production of a community "built on a framework of exclusion" (p. 327). In this sense, doors provide an outside to the community that can be inhabited by those who upset the seamless form of the dominant structures. H. Skott-Myhre argues that exposing the contradictions and antagonisms inherent in the machinery of the institution are possible avenues for destroying the logic of the door. Without explicitly using deconstruction, H. Skott-Myhre seems to be proposing a community without doors. Caputo (1997) explains that hospitality is the open door that prevents the at-homeness necessary for concentrations of power and control. Hospitality, in this sense, is a not-being-at-home, a movement to the sway and headings of the other. Put otherwise, hospitality is the open door through which the other disrupts the accumulation of the self-same.

Hospitality, as the welcoming of the other, is the more socially palatable way to state what deconstruction is (Caputo, 1997). From the linguistic through the material, personal, communal and social (if there are such divides), hospitality is a yes-saying to the coming of the other. In deconstructing the word hospitality itself, Caputo, not-surprisingly, finds the etymology of the word carries its own opposite. He explains that the Latin *hostis* originally meant stranger but came to mean enemy or hostile over time, while *pets* means to have power. The extension of welcome, therefore, "is a function of the power of the host to remain master of the premises" (p. 110). This inward tension of hospitality, or rather its own auto-deconstruction, and therefore its impossibility, is precisely its possibility. Deconstruction is an opening to the future, to hospitality to come, never self-same, never contained, hospitality, like all else, "is inhabited from within" (p. 112).

Westmoreland (2008) takes up Derrida's question of how hospitality is an interruption of the self. To begin to answer the question, Westmoreland contrasts pure unconditional hospitality to the hospitality of rights and laws that are conditional and co-extensive with established relationships. Based on the laws of the state, individuals are identified, divided and categorizes, with legal and economic consequences, into "citizens and non-citizens, citizens and foreigners, hosts and guest" (Westmoreland, 2008, p. 2). A host, in this sense, demands something of the guest (name, origin, intent, etc.) and applies a system whereby the guest is recognizable, restricted and owes a debt for the hospitality extended to them. Barnett (2005) describes conditional hospitality as an exchange for something, such as good conduct, respect, obedience or repayment. This type of hospitality is offered from a place of self-possession, an unabandoned mastery, colored by overtones of paternalism and tolerance (Barnett). In other words, conditional hospitality is the door of the institution. H. Skott-Myhre (2012) connects this institutional door to CYC as a social diagram, a social diagram which:

> maps the relations of children and adults. It inscribes sets of values, codes of conduct, definitions of childhood and adulthood, trajectories of social competence, and deviance. It distributes these maps in the forms of codes, both linguistic and material. At the level of linguistic code, the diagram facilitates the movements of certain ideas and beliefs across all the bodies in the field of child and youth care. At the material level, the diagram enables the spread of practices and forms of discipline. That is to say, it promotes certain usages of the body and mind as preferable or ideal. (H. Skott-Myhre, 2012, p. 319)

Unconditional hospitality, as contrasted with the hospitality of the law, would efface any law that conditioned or limited the absolute openness to the other. Derrida (2000) pushes further than to think of unconditional hospitality as the duty to give all that one has or be without restriction, which again would inscribe hospitality within the law, but as a complete break with laws, duties, concepts, politics, and rights. In this sense, then, hospitality is involved with the singular, the event, ethics, and the impossible. We can only know the absolute in terms of limits, such as giving without return and welcoming without restriction, but absolute unconditioned hospitality exceeds such formalizations (Westmoreland, 2008). As such, absolute hospitality cannot be conditioned by any debt, invitation or necessity, including the necessity to give without debt. To welcome unconditionally, therefore, means to be rid of security and open to the unexpected, including the incoming of violence and disruption. Westmoreland explains that Derrida is pointing toward a stance in which sovereignty and authority gives way to benevolence and the overturning of power; the repositioning of the guest as the host's host. The host has now become the hostage of the other, the subject of the other, which is an impossibility within the laws of conditional hospitality and an interruption of the self.

Barnett (2005) similarly argues that the impossibility that hospitality must go through provides an immanent critique of practice in which "any ordered discourse of responsibility, organised infrastructure of laws and rights or regulated arrangement of boundaries is thought to contravene a principle of unlimited responsibility towards otherness by introducing a degree of calculation into the practice of care" (p. 14). This question opens CYC up to some of its fundamental premises regarding the seemingly apolitical and generous practices of care and responsibility practitioners are supposed to deliver. It further destabilizes the homogeneity within the

CYC context by asking who, within our community, is served by particular practices, structures, and approaches to care.

Barnett (2005) argues against the mapping of the ethics of absolute hospitality against the politics of hospitality for two reasons: (a) it implies that self or community could be extracted from existing positions, relationships and commitments in favor of new ones; and (b) it implies an always-already accepted acceptance of responsibility and welcome by an abstract other. Barnett summarizes that in Derrida's later work, he himself begins to deconstruct the binaries between conditionality and unconditionally and moves toward singularities in which hospitality requires that a guest be greeted as a singular somebody. This moves hospitality beyond indifference and to a recognition of particular, and necessarily not all, guests. Butler (2004) writes in reference to Derrida,

> he drew critically on the work of Emmanuel Levinas in order to insist on the Other as one to whom an incalculable responsibility is owed, one who could never fully be "captured" through social categories or designative names, one to whom a certain response is owed. (p. 33)

Although deconstruction submits that meaning and action depend on boundaries and contexts as conditions of possibility, the important questions remains of how boundaries are reinforced to protect against the coming of the other. Furthermore, questions have now been raised as to our invitations and exclusions: who is the other who we are responsive to? How are those invited received differently from those who visit us unexpectedly? How can we refrain from the capture that turns the other into the same? How do we position ourselves in relation to that which is our perpetual undoing?

KEEPING QUESTIONS IN MOTION

This article has proposed that openness toward a CYC To-Come is one possible way of keeping our traditions, communities, histories and identities alive. Deconstruction has been offered as a way to move with the current questions being asked in our field and following deconstruction I have argued that stable understandings of context, relationships, community, practice, and CYC more generally may limit relational capacities. The question of who we are, and the similar question we ask of others, needs to be perpetually asked, needs to be extended indefinitely into the future, needs to avoid foreclosure. In this sense, I have proposed a relational ethics of hospitality as the impossible gesture of a community which can never know itself fully: as a stance that is always to-come and open to the future. It is with gratitude to my mentors and the leaders of my community that I offer this as a thought toward our forever indefinite future.

REFERENCES

Artz, S. (2012). Dis[s]curse[if] challenges: Professional conversations in child and youth care in fluid modernity. *International Journal of Child, Youth and Family Studies, 3*(2–3), 146–163.

Barnett, C. (1999). Deconstructing context: Exposing Derrida. *Transactions of the Institue of British Geographers, 24*(3), 277–293.

Barnett, C. (2005). Ways of relating: Hospitality and the acknowledgement of otherness. *Progress in Human Geography, 29*(1), 5–21. doi:10.1191/0309132505ph535oa.

Butler, J. (2004). Jacques Derrida. *London Review of Books, 26*(21), 32. Retrieved from http://www.lrb.co.uk/v26/n21/judith-butler/jacques-derrida

Caputo, J. D. (1987). *Radical hermeneutics: Repetition, deconstruction, and the hermeneutic project*. Indianapolis, IN: Indiana University Press.

Caputo, J. D. (Ed.). (1997). *Deconstruction in a nutshell: A conversation with Jacques Derrida*. New York: Fordham University Press.

Caputo, J. D. (2006). *The weakness of God: A theology of the event*. Indianapolis, IN: Indiana University Press.

de Finney, S., Little, J. N., Skott-Myhre, H., & Gharabaghi, K. (2012). Pre-conference roundtable discussion. *International Journal of Child, Youth and Family Studies, 3*(2–3), 128–145.

di Tomasso, L. (2012). More equal than others: The discursive construction of migrant children and families in Canada. *International Journal of Child, Youth and Family Studies, 3*(2–3), 331–348.

Derrida, J. (1976). *Of grammatology* (G. C. Spivak, Trans.). Baltimore, MD: The Johns Hopkins University Press.

Derrida, J. (1978). Structure, sign and play in discourse of the human sciences. In *Writing and difference* (A. Bass, Trans.) (pp. 351–370). Chicago, IL: University of Chicago. (Original work published 1966)

Derrida, J. (1988). *Limited Inc*. Evanston: Northwestern University Press.

Derrida, J. (1992). *The other heading: Reflections on today's Europe*. Bloomington, IN: Indiana University Press.

Derrida, J. (2000). Hospitality. *Journal of the Theoretical Humanities, 5*(3), 3–18.

Lather, P. (1993). Fertile obsession: Validity after poststructuralism. *Sociological Quarterly, 34*(4), 673–693.

Lather, P. (2001). Postbook: Working the ruins of feminist ethnography. *Journal of Women in Culture and Society, 27*(1), 199–227.

Lather, P. (2003). Applied Derrida: (Mis)reading the work of mourning in educational research. *Educational Philosophy and Theory, 35*(3), 257–270.

Lucy, N. (2004). *A Derrida dictionary*. Oxford, UK: Blackwell Publishing.

Macleod, C. (2002). Deconstructive discourse analysis: Extending the methodological conversation. *South African Journal of Psychology, 32*(1), 17–25.

Mason, M. (2006). Exploring 'the impossible': Jacques Derrida, John Caputo and the philosophy of history. *Rethinking History, 10*(4), 501–522.

Mattingly, M. A., Stuart, C., & VanderVen, K. (2010). Competencies for professional child & youth work practitioners. Retrieved from http://acycp.org/2010_Competencies_for_Professional_CYW_Practitioners.pdf

Phillips, L., & Cameron, C. A. (2012). Investigating the multimodality of children and youth. *International Journal of Child, Youth and Family Studies*, *3*(2–3), 284–299.

Saraceno, J. (2012). Mapping whiteness and coloniality in the human service field: Possibilities for a praxis of social justice in child and youth care. *International Journal of Child, Youth and Family Studies*, *3*(2–3), 248–271.

Scott, D. (2012). Escaping purity: Lessons for child and youth care from religion. *International Journal of Child, Youth and Family Studies*, *3*(2–3), 187–197.

Skott-Myhre, H. (2012). The question of doors. *International Journal of Child, Youth and Family Studies*, *3*(2–3), 316–330.

Skott-Myhre, K. (2012). Nomadic youth care. *International Journal of Child, Youth and Family Studies*, *3*(2–3), 300–315.

Skott-Myhre, K., & Skott-Myhre, H. A. (2011). Theorizing and applying child and youth care praxis as politics of care. *Relational Child & Youth Care Practice*, *24*(1/2), 42–52.

Smith, M. (1999). Praxis: An introduction to the idea plus an annotated booklist. Retrieved from http://www.infed.org/biblio/b-praxis.htm

Spivak, G. C. (1976). Translator's preface. In J. Derrida, *Of grammatology* (pp. ix–lxxxvii). Baltimore: The Johns Hopkins University Press.

St. Pierre, E. A. (2000). Poststructural feminism in education: An overview. *Qualitative Studies in Education*, *13*(5), 477–515.

Westmoreland, M. W. (2008). Interruptions: Derrida and hospitality. *Kritike: An Online Journal of Philosophy*, *2*(1), 1–10.

White, J. (2007). Knowing, doing and being in context: A praxis-oriented approach to child and youth care. *Child & Youth Care Forum*, *36*(5), 225–244.

Yoon, J.-S. (2012). Courageous conversations in child and youth care: Nothing lost in the telling. *International Journal of Child, Youth and Family Studies*, *3*(2–3), 164–186.

Stories of Another Kind: Engaging in Generative Conversations in Pedagogical Spaces

MARIE HOSKINS

*School of Child and Youth Care, University of Victoria,
Victoria, British Columbia, Canada*

Many of us from what are referred to as "dominant cultures" are reluctant to speak because of fear of offending those who are marginalized and perhaps making matters worse. Over the last several years, I have attended talks on various kinds of discrimination, especially when racialization is the main focus. As a White woman of privilege, I often have the experience of being the target of difficult accusations. In essence, I often feel myself being positioned as the problem. And these kinds of allegations are not easy to bear. In response, there are times when I find myself grappling silently while secretly yearning for conversations that could be more generative and insightful. By revisiting some of these experiences, I hope to deepen understandings of the kinds of responses that seem to prevent us from working in more relational ways. Further, I hope that by doing so, I might also understand some of the reactions and difficulties our White (majority) as well as our marginalized students tend to experience.

On this earth there have been many diasporas, many refugees, and many living, hence subtle and intricate, communities torn apart that were once whole. There is a way that we are all connected. Even through the eyes of science we can see it. One need not be a mystic to know this. Common sense gives us a daily taste of our union with all kinds of beings and phenomena which we have imagined, in other moments, to be separate from us (Susan Griffin, 1993, p. 75).

As a member of the dominant culture[1] in Canada, I begin this article with a certain amount of trepidation. I am not alone in my apprehension. Many of us with origins in what are called *dominant cultures* are reluctant to write about issues related to diversity because we worry we might offend those who are marginalized and perhaps make matters worse.

During the last decade I have tiptoed into the topic of cultural diversity[2] by examining teaching and learning contexts and what is required of educators in order to be culturally attuned to difference (Hoskins, 1999, 2003). My efforts have been well received by some and this has been reassuring. But I have also felt that something was missing and that ultimately I may have minimized the complexity of what is really required to engage with difference. For the most part, I have written about how only one group, that is, the dominant group, needs to engage. In many ways, I have lapsed into individualizing discourses when it comes to something that is so fundamentally relational. My hunch is that if we continue to think in binaries and reified categories, we may end up repeating colonizing practices and limiting our full potential to, in Helen Veron's words, "get on together." This, no doubt, will not be good for any of us whether marginalized or not.

Over the years, I have attended presentations on various kinds of discrimination, especially when racialization is the main focus. I am fully aware that I need to learn more. But while listening to various speakers, I have sometimes felt the weight of being a target of difficult accusations. Put simply, because of my "Whiteness," I often feel myself being positioned as *the problem*. Although completely understandable and a necessary step, these kinds of allegations are not easy to hear. In response, there are times when I find myself grappling silently with my discomfort while secretly yearning for conversations that could be more generative. By generative I mean more insightful, empathic, and generous toward each other (see, e.g., Caputo, 1987, 1993, 1997, 2000; Gergen, 1994, 2000, 2006, 2009; Pelias, 2011).

By reflecting on my own experiences and, I confess, my limited exposure to recent literature on the topic of diversity—in particular, colonization— I hope to expand understandings of conversing across differences. By doing so, I also hope to understand some of the reactions and difficulties our students, both White as well as marginalized, tend to experience in classroom settings. Over the years there have been too many times that an uncomfortable silence is all I have to offer. It is pedagogical spaces about which I am particularly concerned.

Before going further, however, I want to acknowledge that this is a personal exploration that enters the topic through experience. I am fully aware of the limitations of taking such a micro approach to what is not only relational but also structural and discursive. Experience itself does not occupy an omnipotent position on truth; it is merely an entry point.

Although issues related to diversity are widespread, I focus this discussion on Aboriginal[3] people in North America and our collective struggles as we attempt to work together. There are many similarities that pertain to discrimination in general, particularly the injustice that underlies the term, *racialization*, but I also believe there are important distinctions that need to be considered when acknowledging the effects of colonization. Colonizing comes in many guises but in this article I take up the blatant attempts in Canada to not only indoctrinate people into one way of being, but to also strategically attempt to eliminate a segment of the Canadian population, in other words, to commit genocide.

There are two parts to this article. The first is an exploration of the difficulties that some may experience when confronted with difficult labels. The second part examines in more depth some of the issues that arise given the current complexities of trying to get on together. By reflecting on my own reactions, I hope to provoke others to consider the complexities and not run from them (or scramble out, as I suggest later) but rather to stay with the difficulties as painful as they are, in order to engage in more generative conversations. My hope is that this article will be useful for students, educators, and various helping professionals such as counselors, child and youth care practitioners, social workers, and psychologists.

TROUBLING AN EVENT

Sitting in a large auditorium, I begin to listen to the speaker's words that are no doubt chosen in order to make critical points about how we understand diversity, especially when it comes to ethnicity and racialization: *Eurocentric! Hegemony! Racialization!* The words ring through the large auditorium, begging for attention. Listen. This is important. But soon after they have been introduced, they seem to lose their effect. For me, they are beginning to fade into the background. More words are brought into the presentation: *Marginalization! White privilege! Colonization!*

These words are frequently used in these kinds of talks. I know I'm supposed to *feel* something, but sometimes I'm not sure what. I've attended talks on these difficult issues several times before. Am I in denial, I wonder? Have I distanced myself in order to deal with the discomfort? In psychological terms, am I splitting off or dissociating?

I start to squirm. I'm beginning to feel itchy now, aware of the rough fabric of the chair prickling the back of my legs. It is as if the chair, too, is prodding me to pay attention. I carefully glance down at my watch knowing that the speaker might catch me. How much longer will I feel like I'm under siege, I begin to wonder?

These are common reactions that people experience when listening to the treatment of one segment of society imposed on another. Students often do not know what to do and sometimes they sit quietly in their discomfort. It is well documented that acknowledging one's privilege due to class, gender, race, or any other cultural or social marker can be uncomfortable (see, to name just a few, Brodkin, 1998; Fine, Powell, Weis, & MunWong, 1997; Giroux, 1997; McIntosh, 1989, 1995). But by not acknowledging our privilege, even though it is uncomfortable, we run the risk of it being taken for granted and our acquiescence mistakenly attributed to personal characteristics instead of "Whiteness." Put simply, white is a color that has real effects.

Recently, a flourishing body of research has emerged that explores what it means to be White[4] in today's society. But this is a relatively new endeavor. Race theorists in the past tended to focus on the experiences and developments of minority communities, their struggles with racism, and their hopes of one day creating more inclusive communities. Unfortunately, minority communities have been problematized and pathologized by doing so. In *The Souls of Black Folk*, for example, Du Bois (1904/1989) posed the question to African Americans: "How does it feel to be *a* problem?" (emphasis in original). Although intended to be provocative in the sense that African Americans were on the receiving end of racism, the question was troubling when one is perceived to be *a* problem. Now the turn to Whiteness studies decades later asks White people the same question but with an ironic nuance: How does it feel to be *the* problem? A different subject is now being interrogated.

I'm jolted back to the speaker's words as if someone has just elbowed me out of a deep sleep. Wake up. Listen. This is important: *Mothers! Children! Abuse! Poverty!* The talk has a different emphasis now as it begins to focus on issues that affect a marginalized segment of Canadian society, that is, Aboriginal people.[5] And now, as I listen once more closely to these kinds of intricately woven stories, they are beginning to sting, like ripping off a band-aid on a scab that has yet to heal.

The auditorium is almost full although it's only nine o'clock on Saturday morning. I become acutely aware that I am a member of the oppressor group, the settlers who came to Canada to claim territory that was never meant to be theirs. As usual, I find myself vacillating between feelings of guilt and denial. *Are you sure*, I want to cry out! *Are you sure they (we) were that cruel?* I can feel my chest begin to tighten. Discomfort is mixed with resistance; resistance is mixed with discomfort. I want to protest! *Is this what my people did to your people? Are you sure? But they didn't mean to. We didn't know.* I *didn't know.*

The talk is evocative. I know the speaker wants me to *feel* the pain in order to understand at a much deeper level. This is necessary. But I really don't want to. I sense my jaw tightening and the knot at the back of my throat is beginning to feel uncomfortable. I resonate with Tuck's (2010) words: "I experience this complicatedness as a knot, a hulking knot with many strands, each with their own knots contributing to the tangle" (p. 646). I make a feeble attempt to get in touch with my emotions. But there seems to be too much at stake. My mind begins to wander as I try to grasp the processes involved in colonizing others.

Several emotions surround the issue of colonization for all involved. Those who are positioned as colonizers (the offenders) have much to learn (and feel) in order to stay open to difficult accusations. This is, unfortunately, our settler legacy. Particularly troubling is that reactions to these historical facts can result in emotions such as guilt, denial, avoidance, and shame. And these are not helpful responses. The danger, according to Ridley (1995), is that these feelings can also lead to dysfunctional rescuing, paternalism, and a reluctance to use confrontational skills when necessary. Unfortunately all of these responses can also lead to quietly brewing resentment for everyone involved, those who are privileged and those who are marginalized.

Getting in touch with the emotionality of it all (the pain and suffering as well as the hope and potential) is what I consider to be a useful and necessary approach. But not everyone agrees. There are debates in the literature about the utility of focusing on one's emotions. Leonardo (2004), for example, contends that feeling guilty is not a helpful response. Particularly problematic, he argues, is that it actually blocks critical reflection and ends up being overly personal. In his words, "whites end up feeling individually blameworthy for racism. In fact, they become over concerned with whether or not they 'look racist' and forsake the more central project of structural racism" (p. 140). This seems to be the case particularly in classroom settings. However, without an emotional connection to an issue, I contend that it risks becoming merely a cognitive exercise and it may lack an embodied understanding. Feeling, according to Artz (1994), is a valuable way of knowing and I agree. As an entry point, feelings can lead us toward other modes of knowing that have the potential to expand and deepen understanding.

At the same time, it is important to note that emotions are not "natural." They are socially constructed. Emotions such as sadness, guilt, anger, shame, and resentment (see, for example, Ahmed, 2004; Gergen, 1996, 2009; Nussbaum, 2001) all come out of a set of social, cultural, and political relations, and for these reasons, are not fixed. Just because we get in touch with our feelings and they seem authentic, does not mean that they are resistant to change.

While continuing to listen and attempting to *feel* what the speaker is saying, I get a sense that an apology may be needed as a first step. I imagine saying I am sorry for all of the injustices that have happened, but then I postpone the inclination to do so.

Am I really sorry? Will saying *I'm* sorry help? And who will really be helped by it? Is it so we, the colonizers, can be free of guilt and abdicate further responsibilities? It is painful to apologize and yet equally painful to hold back. And this kind of pain has physical manifestations. I begin to feel an annoying tightness in my chest as if the apology itself is trapped between my head and my heart. And then I move to another place commonly referred to as "denial." I feel my jaw begin to tighten which seems to have the uncanny effect of trapping the apology.

I begin to wonder about the kinds of apologies that need to be given, to whom and how. As I listen to the speaker describe more stories of the effects of colonization, I recall a photograph of my grandmother taken when she was a young girl. It was 1915. There are other figures in the photo, obviously all related. Ten family members are all wrapped heavily with scarves, hats, and herringbone tweed overcoats. They dutifully pose for the camera in order to document their arrival. Their expressions are lifeless and I am left with more questions than answers. Why did they choose to leave Brighton and make the long journey across the Atlantic? What was it my great-grandfather hoped for when he decided to sell everything they had in order to come to an unfamiliar place where he knew no one?

My mind zooms in on the face of my grandmother. She's 15 and has just lost her mother to cancer. I recall more images in the photograph. No one is smiling. This frail, tired, frightened cluster of people, like so many thousands of families at that time, will now be categorized as *landed immigrants*. Landed immigrants. Settlers. Colonizers.

I will never know what really prompted my great-grandfather to come to Canada, whether it was unresolved grief regarding his wife's death, the weight of having to provide for his large family, the seduction of imagining a better life, or any number of other reasons. Our family, unfortunately, has impoverished stories from which to draw.

The presentation continues. I try to imagine. I try to make links between my life and the stories of discrimination that permeate the cruelty that is really what this talk is now about. In keeping with Artz's recommendation to use my emotions, I try to connect by remembering my own instances of emotional pain, by recalling the teasing and ridicule that I experienced growing up with a French Canadian name on the west coast of Canada. I felt such a strong desire to conceal my differences. The pain, however, is distant, it's now a dull sadness as I recall being called a "frog" and being repeatedly told I must really excel at the French language. No, I wanted to protest. I'm British.

Context matters when it comes to discrimination. French Canadians were considered to be troublemakers at that time and when the Front de Libération du Québec (FLQ) kidnapped and murdered provincial Labor Minister, Pierre Laporte, anti–French Canadian sentiments were at an all-time peak. But this is as far as I can go when it comes to actually feeling discrimination due to my cultural background. And I know that this is so trite in comparison to what others have to endure. I recall some of my students who often attempt to understand by describing experiences of discrimination. I assume they see these disclosures as being empathic. Experiences of racism— the degree and frequency— all matter to students and frequently become integrated into classroom discussions and assignments. Unfortunately these kinds of discussions tend to result in comparisons of who has been hurt the most, when, where, and by whom[6].

I return to my earlier question: Is taking an apologetic stance a good beginning? And is *feeling* the guilt actually helpful? If I truly grasp (cognitively, emotionally, and spiritually) that I have played a part in the living conditions of Aboriginal people in Canada, for example, how do I respond to this sad history, presence and perhaps future? What is my responsibility other than carrying the burden of guilt and blame?

I tune in again to the presenter who continues to speak of the pain levied by the dominant culture. For me, something I react to when listening to presentations on colonization is how the dominant culture is scripted as if it is homogenous, unified, and stable. But it may be that positioning one as dominant and another as subjugated based on an assumption of reified characteristics may contribute to the tangled knot when attempting to put things in motion and getting on together. As Tuck (2010) reminded us earlier, there are many knots and strands all tangled up. Transnational feminist efforts have focused on the complexities of layered subjectivities, highlighting the intersections between and among several categories of experience: race, gender, class, ability, and so on. By resisting binaries, they have emphasized that we all occupy multiple positions at various times (see, e.g., Hoskins, 2004; Lee & de Finney, 2004; de Finney, Loiselle, & Dean, 2011). But for those who have been repeatedly marginalized, this way of conceptualizing human experience may not be embraced. More about this tension will be discussed later.

I return again to feeling that I need to atone for all of the past wrongs that have been committed. But how would I apologize for my ancestors? This is a common argument so I am not alone in my lament. For example, how do I reconcile that although my grandmother was privileged in many ways, she lived a life of hardship due to losing a son to war, a husband to an early death, and constant economic struggles. How do I think of her as an oppressor when she had little formal education and struggled financially?

These are common responses for those of us on the privileged side of the binary. Human suffering is not only because of discrimination we argue. But there are important distinctions.

The emotions in the auditorium begin to feel overwhelming. Although a non-Aboriginal person, the presenter is now speaking about her own personal discrimination as a minority woman. A blanket of sadness covers the room. Those who have similar experiences of racism appear to know this pain so well. I glance at the young woman beside me but try not to make eye contact. She, too, is nodding in solidarity with the speaker. Tears are shed by many. I want to be there too, to be thought of as a supportive ally, as one who "gets it." But my physical body betrays me. I am White, middle-aged, English-speaking. Unfortunately, I only speak the language of the colonizer.

WORKING TOWARD GENERATIVE DIALOGUES

Despite all of the emotional knots I have identified, the ultimate challenge is how to move forward together (to act in the meantime, as Caputo [2000] points out) so that we can offer a critical pedagogy that does not incite less than helpful responses. As repeatedly mentioned throughout this article, such responses serve no one and do not lead to generative conversations. Instead, we need to consider how we could have conversations about learning and living together that are life sustaining rather than demoralizing regardless of positionality. How can we as educators respect the kind of personal and political work that needs to be done by all of us, not just those who are marginalized and/or oppressed? What does this ultimately require of us as students and educators?

So far, I have reflected on my own reactivity so that I could understand more fully how we might get on together in more generative ways. My experience tells me that when emotions and reactions simmer just below the surface, it is easy to become walled off and retreat, especially when hearing difficult accusations. This is what Leonardo (2004, 2009) warns us about. And even more alarming is that these kinds of responses can result in what Fanon (1961/2004) describes as "violence rippling under the skin" (p. 31). What I have learned so far is that intense reactivity or retreating in silence never seems to move any of us forward, at least not in the ways that the speaker and many of us in the audience quietly hope for.

There are several issues that come to the surface for me when I reflect on this recent experience, especially when considering pedagogical spaces. Now that I have "felt" my way through it again, I discuss in more depth some of the strands that emerged. Ultimately, I hope to disentangle some of the knots related to discussions of colonization in classroom settings.

Degrees of Suffering: Conflating Differences

The issue of competing over who has suffered the most is one that frequently comes into the learning environment; see Dulwich Centre (n.d.) for fuller discussions. I am convinced that as educators we need to find ways to respect expressions of difficulties no matter how inconsequential (or perhaps trivial) they may seem at the time. Students need to find ways to connect emotionally and reflecting on their own pain is a valuable starting point. What is also important is for educators to avoid being dismissive when students disclose their experiences and to carefully include these disclosures in a non- competitive way. Having said this, it is also important to juxtapose these situations against more pervasive structural forms of racism, sexism, ageism, and so on in order to move students beyond their own subjective experience. The danger in having them dwell for too long on their own pain is that it tends to minimize larger, more oppressive structures found in institutional policies and practices. In this sense, I certainly concur with Leonardo's concerns mentioned earlier. Also, it is important to juxtapose experiences of what Joanne Lee (2012) refers to as "ambient hatred" against the horrific effects of colonization on Indigenous peoples locally and globally.

The Danger of the Single Story

As I reflect on my own heritage as a settler, I am aware of the tensions that underlie certain versions of history and how individuals are scripted and trapped within words, images, and metaphors. The danger of the single story, highlighted so poignantly by Nigerian novelist Chimamanda Adichie does not only apply to those who are marginalized but to those whose identities are tied up with oppressor, colonist, racist, and other similar descriptors. Gordon (1996) says it clearly when he emphasizes that we all possess "a complex and oftentimes contradictory humanity and subjectivity that is never adequately glimpsed by viewing [one another] as victims or, on the other hand, as superhuman agents" (cited in Tuck, 2010, p. 639). Gordon's words prompt some questions when we develop curriculum. For example, if we continue to use rigid categories such as colonizer and colonized, oppressor and victim, racist and racialized, are we not perpetuating the same kinds of stereotypes that many have found harmful? How might we all resist these less than helpful categories and narratives and still work toward an affirmative ethics (Braidotti, 2009) that is both sustainable and life enhancing for everyone? How can we hold ourselves accountable and responsible to each other without lapsing into harmful singular and impoverished stories? What are the advantages and disadvantages of breaking free from single stories?

Relevant Indigenous Contributions

While reading in the area of Indigenous scholarship, I encountered an interesting trend regarding these kinds of questions. Many scholars are actively resisting singular and unified accounts of history that only emphasize problems, especially when it comes to their own people. Tuck's (2010) recent article on research, for example, provides a poignant example that sheds light on the issue (and danger) of shallow accounts of human experience. In particular, she offers ways of revising what have often been problem-saturated, or in her words, damage-centered stories. Although her focus is research, her ideas have much broader relevance for how we could relate to each other in classroom settings, how curriculum could be developed and in the end, how we could promote more socially just professional practice. What she proposes is that more scholars could adopt a "desire-based research framework" that would seek out complexity in lives and avoid "one-dimensional analyses of people, communities, and tribes as flattened, derelict, and ruined" (p. 639). This kind of research would provide holistic accounts of human experience that are otherwise absent when it comes to minority populations. In the end, Tuck argues, we could deepen our understanding if we also included accounts that emphasize survivance[7] as an "active repudiation of dominance, tragedy, and victimry" (Vizenor, 1998, p. 15).

From a pedagogical perspective, Tuck and Vizenor's ideas are significant. Aboriginal students often resist narrow accounts of their lives and not surprisingly, so do students from the dominant culture. Although these writers focus on Aboriginal issues, I believe the same strength-based approach could apply to all. We need to engage generatively in new ways. Vizenor plays with words, metaphors, and images in order to stretch our perspectives. For example, *survivance*, one of Vizenor's many neologisms, combines the words survival and resistance to make his point. The experiences of American Indians are often full of survival and resistance accounts, especially when told from their perspective. Vizenor further explains by saying that survivance also emphasizes "a sense of presence over absence, an innate or cultural philosophy, and a strategic resistance to extreme situations. Survivance literature creates a sense of presence, not historical absence or victimry" (Vizenor & Lee, 2010, p. 278).

Bringing survivance stories to light paints a very different picture of Indigenous cultures from the frequent portrayal as problem saturated and pathology driven. Indigenous people, it is argued, "need to write their own history because whites either demonize them or, worse, use them as sticks with which to beat other whites by emphasizing the Indian's poverty, despair, and alcoholism. No people deserve to have its history reduced to a litany of failures, disasters, and humiliations" (Velie & Vizenor, 2010, p. 278). It is well-written survivance stories that have the potential to promote change and strengthen communities.

This brings me back to the issue of the danger of the single story. Vizenor's perspective, consistent with Adachie's does not advocate for a singular, unified version of Indigenous "reality:" nor does he subscribe to romantic tales of resistance. He argues instead that a singular, unified identity for any group operates on the assumption of sameness that is doomed to failure because it lacks the ability to represent the whole array of identity positions. This can be problematic as Griffin (1993) also reminds us:

> Tradition gives one the feeling that life is predictable. Yet, in a period of rapid change, tradition can be like a plank of wood, one part of a bridge extending over the water, but now connected to nothing, an illusion of solidity moving randomly in the rushing stream. (p. 194)

There is a fragile balance that needs to be struck between the collective identities found in certain cultural groups and the need for individual subjectivities. Nationalism (or nation building) itself has a tendency to reify tradition and naturalize a myth of purity; there are dangers in treating people or the nation as a unitary force or indivisible essence.

From Vizenor's perspective, there is much freedom and potential for change within Aboriginal communities and rather than promoting nation building, he argues instead for a relational approach found in micro contexts in individual tribes or bands. Attention to moment-to-moment encounters, although they remain embedded in macro discourses of power and identity, would mean that relations are more malleable than some might think. It follows that we have the capacity to negotiate with each other through conversations that avoid hierarchical relationships and that may be bound to an identity politics that serves no one in the end. Ultimately we can consider a different kind of consciousness, one that is relational in every sense.

Returning to my beginning questions, how can we work with the multiplicity discussed above when we think not only of those who are marginalized but those who have been scripted as colonizers and oppressors? How can we stay open to the complexity and multiplicity of people's lives in classroom settings? Are there other stories that could or should be told?

As a case in point, for many years Canadian journalist Terry Glavin has been a strong advocate when it comes to alternative versions of Aboriginal and non-Aboriginal relations. He emphasizes that in certain communities on the west coast of Canada, for example, English, French, and Aboriginal people lived in harmony. They even created a synthesized language, *Chinook*.[8] This is an important and hopeful history.[9] At the same time, as Vizenor, Tuck, and others argue, naïve, romantic narratives are hopeful alternatives but not the only ones. Once again, the intent is not to position them as binaries but rather as good friends, complementing each other. It is the co-creation of new, multilayered stories that can possibly lead to more generative conversations and a sustainable affirmative ethic.

Multiplicity and Recognition: Cautions

Before going further, a few cautions are in order because it is not as simple as just creating new hopeful stories. We need to tread lightly into these textured narratives with a different kind of consciousness. Particularly noteworthy is the fact that not everyone agrees with recent postmodern conceptualizations of subjectivity and multiple storylines. People who have experienced the effects of colonization have concerns over fluid conceptualizations of human experience given they are just now being recognized as distinct with their own sets of beliefs, values, customs, traditions, and Indigenous knowledges. Accentuating, not minimizing, differences has its benefits for those striving for recognition and justice that is long overdue (see, for example, Gergen, 1999). Consequently, fluid and hybrid identities expressed through multiple storylines are highly contested ideas within some Indigenous communities, despite newer postcolonial arguments.

Shohat (1992) sheds light on these controversies by arguing that "for communities which have undergone brutal ruptures, now in the process of forging a collective identity, no matter how hybrid that identity has been before, during, and after colonialism, the retrieval and re-inscription of a fragmented past becomes a crucial contemporary site for forging a resistant collective identity" (p. 99). Despite the inherent advantages of the need for collective identities in order to gain long overdue rights, she suggests that memories of the past could be negotiated differently so that there is not an effort to literally reproduce a time and place, but to think of history "as fragmented sets of narrated memories and experiences on the basis of which to mobilize contemporary communities" (p. 99). Some communities need these kinds of alliances in order to gain long overdue rights, but it is also important to be aware of the agendas of such a perspective.

What is significant about this discussion and associated tensions surrounding difference is not whether one approach is better than another (this would be impossible to conclude) but that these issues need to be considered before they erupt in classroom settings. They are raw and emotional issues that exacerbate the fragility of relationships between students and educators and many students (and educators) have not had opportunities to reflect on them. For example, I once had the experience of showing a very positive video of an Aboriginal community in Northern British Columbia and the response from non-Aboriginal students was outright disbelief. When one student expressed her skepticism, an Aboriginal student was justifiably offended.

THE POLITICS OF RELATIONSHIPS: SYSTEMS AND INDIVIDUALS

Stories do not just come out of the blue; they are nested within contexts and those contexts consist of what Adele Clarke (2005) refers to as "objects." Policies, procedures, and structures are the hard materiality or objects that underlie understandings of experience, consequently influencing relationships as much as face-to-face or moment-to-moment interactions. Examples affecting Aboriginal peoples include the reservation system, the Indian Act, the legacy of residential schools, Indigenous governance, third party surveillance,[10] the federal control of funds to those living on reserve, and more. The list is extensive. One of our challenges as educators is to remind students (and ourselves) that policies are not neutral by any means. In fact, they can be the very opposite. For example, there are growing efforts to improve Aboriginal and non-Aboriginal relations in Canada. In British Columbia, *The New Relationship Document* created in 1995 was an attempt to renegotiate how Aboriginal and non-Aboriginal people engage with each other while working together on challenging issues. This was a good beginning according to some, but Chief Alice Thompson of the Leq'á:mél council on the lower mainland makes a cautionary and important point. When asked how the document has shaped relationships with government, she responded in disappointment by saying: "I think it's dissipating before it even reaches the ground. The words in the New Relationship document, they're shiny, they look good on paper, but unless they're in motion they don't mean anything" (Shields, 2007). Instead of it being helpful, the report states that Chief Thompson finds herself trying to build capacity while grappling with Indian Affairs programs that fail to meet the needs of her community. Several knowledgeable Canadians, both

Aboriginal and non-Aboriginal, also agree that the Department of Indian Affairs needs to be dismantled or, at the very least, reconfigured because under the present system First Nations are drowning in paper. According to the same reporter for the *Tyee Newsletter*, when Attorney General Sheila Fraser conducted a review, she was shocked to discover that the "average First Nation, which is 500 people with probably five to 10 leaders doing all the work, has to prepare 162 different reports every year to the federal government" (Shields, 2007). This example suggests that damage-centered stories continue to affect how Aboriginal people are ultimately treated despite recent efforts. When we claim to treat people with dignity in daily encounters, knowing that certain injustices continue to exist, we have to question what we are standing in solidarity for and against.

Sadly there are other similar examples. Several policies lack basic dignity when they are implemented. It is important to remember these societal and political injustices. Leonardo (2004) provides an extensive list of such policies as they pertain to current American policies that affect several minority groups. Unfortunately these discriminatory policies have far-reaching effects at both local and global levels in various countries, including Canada.

This is where things become very bumpy or in Tuck's words, very tangled. To lapse into a neoliberal attitude lamenting "can't we all just try harder and be friends," without an understanding of the policies that have real effects and constraints on people's lives risks repeating colonizing practices, as I have mentioned throughout this article. We have to step forward, or lean in as Pelias (2011) says, but there are times when we all may feel like we're walking on shards of glass. None of us want to intentionally do more harm than good when it comes to acknowledging painful experiences. As educators we need to find ways to engage with difficult conversations as risky as they are. Taking the easy way out but cloaking these difficulties through the "safe space" terminology such as tolerance for differences and acknowledging White privilege, as Leonardo also reminds us, may not be the safest way to proceed for anyone, not just those who are marginalized. Further, safe spaces or safe learning environments are not transformative in and of themselves, as de Finney, Loiselle, et al. (2011) so aptly point out in their work with minoritized girls. In fact, if left unproblematized, the perpetuation of safe space discourse risks further reifying the status quo. *Critical* space, not *safe* space, is what is needed if we want to move forward.

Some questions remain. How might we keep knowledge alive and fluid (consistent with the etymology of the word *curriculum*[11]) so that we can struggle together on these kinds of issues? How can we foster a kind of relational ethics (Gergen, 2009) or affirmative politics (Braidotti, 1994) in our learning environments, especially when conflicts related to race, racism, and White privilege surface? And returning once again to the main thesis of this discussion, how can we stay with the difficulties I have highlighted without lapsing into less than helpful responses?

Leaning In Instead of Scrambling Out

To summarize and to reiterate what has been touched on earlier, stories about people, whether featuring the colonizer or the colonized, need to be multifaceted and multidimensional. It is problematic on many levels if we continue to reduce people to perpetrators and victims and ignore the multiplicity that all people embody within and between us. As educators, this can only happen if we are willing to learn to engage in challenging and critical conversations with all of their associated risks. We also need to remember that each of us embodies survivance and victimhood stories, often simultaneously. White privilege or White supremacy (Leonardo, 2009), although pervasive, is not the only cultural narrative. Although we tend to speak of groups as homogeneous, they are in fact, multiple in almost every way; they are full of contradictions, inconsistencies, ambiguities, and mythologies. The same is true for individuals. At the same time, we need to be respectful of the need for some people to emphasize their unique identities within smaller groups of affiliation in order to work toward social justice and unities of purposeful action. As Gerald Vizenor (1998) reminds us, this cannot be done in advance; such negotiations need to be contextually and temporally mediated. In other words, this requires continual moment-to-moment negotiations taking into account that politics are always at play in micro and macro contexts.

In addition, Shohat (1992) and several others remind us that, as members of the dominant culture, we cannot short-circuit our culpability when it comes to colonizing practices. Multiple wrongs have been committed and to *not* acknowledge this history is to maintain a cloak of ignorance and denial that serves no one. Hearts and minds need to open. Impoverished communities continue to exist and in the name of assimilation, those of us identified as the dominant culture have made terrible mistakes. In order to move forward, we as a whole society, regardless of cultural membership, need to work together as we all heal from both the shame of committing cruel acts and the pain of being on the receiving end. There is healing to be done within and between.

WHERE TO STAND AND HOW: PREPARING FOR ENHANCED PEDAGOGICAL SPACES

The issue of where to stand in relation to the ideas mentioned above comes to the forefront. As educators we also need to figure out how to stand in relation to each other (with all of our historical and current complexities) and this requires ongoing negotiation and dialogue. One place that we surely cannot stand is on the sidelines. In academia, we can no longer be silent and passive armchair readers of marginalized writings and eavesdroppers on difficult conversations. We must actively engage in multiple ways through our curriculum design, teaching, and writing, and be willing, as the speaker who became the impetus for this article said, to face conflicts, and yes, painful accusations. The speaker said that we need to face the elephant in the room but my hunch is we can see it very clearly. We all now need the moral courage to touch it, feel it, respond to it, and know it emotionally and cognitively so that we can get on together in more generous and generative ways. Students from the dominant culture have sometimes expressed concerns over feeling categorized and stereotyped in the same ways that those who are marginalized have been. Although it is critical to avoid minimizing the pain and suffering those who have been oppressed have had to endure, perpetuating single, problem-saturated stories of either dominant or marginalized groups will not get us where we need to go. We have to be more creative and flexible than that.

Braidotti (2009) also reminds us that transformations will not come without pain and suffering. Similarly, Leonardo and Porter (2010) argue that a risk discourse is necessary, one that does not "assume safety but contradiction and tension" (p. 141). Further, they argue that anger, hostility, frustration, and paring are characteristics that are not to be avoided under the banner of safety, which only produces, in Freire's (1993) words, a "'culture of silence'" (p. 149). Leonardo and Porter continue to say that "a comfortable race dialogue belies the actual structures of race, which is full of tension" (p. 153).

Perhaps it comes as no surprise that much of the safe space discourse and cultural competence training is based on the assumption that making students comfortable is the best way to proceed. Couched in terms of respect, dignity, and appreciation of differences, it conceals deep crevices of power that continue to support the status quo. Course content often trumps relational processes when this occurs. Much curriculum focuses on this kind of knowledge acquisition without considering the messy and difficult aspects of getting on together. Affect or emotionality is critical if we are going to move forward in generative ways. According to Braidotti (2009) ultimately we need to adopt a dynamic perspective of all affects "even those that freeze us in pain, horror or mourning" (p. 50). Transformations will not happen without pain and suffering, she cautions us, but if we can move from being trapped in binaries (good versus evil) and move from negatives to potentials, we will be getting closer to an affirmative ethics.

It is the fusion of both (ontology and epistemology), in essence, an embodied and generative pedagogical space that needs to be offered so that we can all be more responsive to each other. And just because it is messy and difficult does not mean that we have to throw up our hands up in despair. There are avenues of hope amidst the frayed edges of the knot. Along a similar and hopeful thread, Braidotti (2009) writes about the need for an affirmative politics, not one based on negativity and opposition. She states:

> Affirmative politics rests on a time-continuum that indexes the present on the possibility of thinking sustainable futures. The sustainability of these

futures consists in their being able to mobilise, actualise and deploy cognitive, affective and collective forces which had not so far been activated.... These driving forces concretise in actual, material relations and can thus constitute a network, web or rhizome of interconnection with others. We have to learn to think differently about ourselves. To think means to create new concepts. (p. 45)

If we can think in networks, matrices, or webs, perhaps we could avoid the kinds of conflicts that arise when being trapped within binaries. As mentioned at the beginning of this article, the focus on those who are marginalized and what the dominant culture can "do" has perhaps missed the relational aspect of how we might think and act differently together. Some questions that may be helpful to consider are:

- What do we include in our curriculum that promotes a politic of living together?
- How do we promote discussions that explore what it means to not only acknowledge one's positionality but how it affects the kinds of conversations and relationships we are all able to have with each other and our students?
- If we fully acknowledge our multiplicities, how could we converse differently?
- What kinds of skills, knowledges, and attitudes can be fostered with our students and our colleagues so that we can avoid single stories of all groups of people whether marginalized or not?
- In what ways do we introduce students to survivance stories, spatial justice, relational being, hospitality, and generosity?
- How might we avoid less than helpful responses on everyone's part?

Although there are no simple recipes for constructing enhanced pedagogical spaces, these questions can help to guide us. We can keep these kinds of questions in mind as we continue to create generative learning environments built on an affirmative ethic so that when we and our students encounter the rub of differences that might seem insurmountable, we can avoid responses that minimize differences, invoke denial and resentment, and/or a desire to scramble out. Leaning into difference with all of its complexities (material conditions, political injustices, multiple stories, survivance and victimization narratives) can be painful but can also result in hopeful possibilities yet to be imagined. Living a relational politics, according to Gergen (2009), is precisely the attempt to put this ontology in motion. Instead of staying within the confines of identity politics, he suggests that a relational politic may move us further as a society. Over a decade ago, Gergen (1999) also wrote the following related to the challenge before us:

I am not proposing...that we abandon previous traditions of identity politics, the discourses of oppression, justice, equality, rights and so

> on, nor the in your face activism that we have come to know so well. . . .
> The point is not to eradicate existing vocabularies of action. Rather, my hope is that we are now participating in the generation of a new vocabulary, a new consciousness, and a new range of practices—a relational politics that will be incorporative, pervasive, collaborative, and unceasing. (p. 5)

Keeping Gergen's words in mind, I return once again to Vizenor's work, primarily because I believe he has so much to offer when he proposes a holistic understanding of history, the present and the future. He advocates for the adoption of an "imagistic gaze" which I find to be intriguing and, once again, hopeful. The gaze, he argues, is much more than visual. It consists of more than mere pictures, mirror images, or representations; it is a visionary perception of narrative scenes. He explains: "Native storiers, the best oral storiers, were visionary. So the most memorable, creative, and ironic stories are holovisionary" (Vizenor & Lee, 2010, p. 271). And in concert with the recommendations put forward by the speaker to whom I am grateful and have repeatedly referenced, we as educators have much work to do if we want to live the imagistic gaze more fully and more ethically.

I recall the presentation again, especially how it ended. Audience members enthusiastically clapped and stood in appreciation. Emotions filled the room. There were many reactions. Many responses will be helpful in that they will mobilize people to take steps, some larger than others. The lecture provoked much discussion and people were eager for more. My hunch is that many strands of the tangled knot were beginning to loosen. Hopefully there will be stories of another kind as we try to get on together while creating a generative learning environment that moves us closer to life sustaining practices and relationships. One can only hope…

NOTES

1. According to Wikipedia, "The *dominant culture* in a society refers to the established language, religion, behavior, values, rituals, and social customs. These traits are often the norm for the society as a whole. The dominant culture is usually but not always in the majority and achieves its dominance by controlling social institutions such as communication, educational institutions, artistic expression, law, political process, and business. The concept is generally used in academic discourse in fields such as sociology, anthropology and cultural studies. In a multicultural society, various cultures are celebrated and respected equally. Dominant culture can be promoted with deliberation and by the suppression of other cultures or subcultures."

2. It is important to note that although the White population is often thought of as the majority culture, it is in fact the minority.

3. In this article I use the term *Aboriginal* to refer to those people who are indigenous to Canada and the United States. When I use the term *Indigenous*, I am referring to others throughout the world who are the original inhabitants and have usually been colonized. When the term *Indian* is used, I am using the author's words. I am aware of the history of this descriptor in that it was a term applied by colonizers and settlers to the Indigenous peoples of Canada and the United States.

4. See for example, *Towards a Bibliography on Critical Whiteness Studies*, Center on Democracy in a Multiracial Society at the University of Illinois, for an excellent overview of current studies.

5. "First Nations experience disproportionately high rates of tuberculosis, diabetes, injuries, suicide and cardiovascular disease, although this is not necessarily the case in all communities. There is a high level of diversity among different nations and communities (Reading 2009; Assembly of First Nations/FNIGC 2007; Health Canada 2005, 2009). In addition to health outcomes, First Nations also experience disparities in the heath determinants. Based on the Community Well-being Index, a composite measure that includes education, income, labor force participation/employment and housing indicators, First Nations communities lag far behind compared to the general Canadian population on all indicators, and have experienced a decline in housing conditions from 2001 to 2006 (INAC April 2010). Nearly one-third of First Nations communities consider their water unsafe to Drink, and from 40% to 49% of homes have mold or mildew (First Nations Centre 2005)" (Jackson Pulver et al., 2010, in their World Health Organization Background Paper, "Indigenous Health—Australia, Canada, Aotearoa, New Zealand, and the United States—Laying claim to a future that embraces health for us all").

6. During a classroom discussion of racism, a student voiced her pain over her body size and was dismissed quite quickly by others in the group. The argument was that racialization is not temporary or all that malleable. Inscriptions on the body cannot be erased. Yet it is through these kinds of disclosures that students try to understand. Empathy requires an emotional connection of some sort.

7. *Survivance* is a term used in Quebec nationalism and one that has been also taken up by Vizenor in several of his works. Among his many other neologisms, "survivance"—a cross between the words "survival" and "resistance"—carries with it an implication of an ongoing, changing process, rather than the simple continuance of old ways into the modern world. Vizenor also points out that for tribal peoples, the act of survival is based in resistance.

8. "A common misconception about Chinook," Glavin writes, "is that it was simply an argot, invented by fur traders, in order to facilitate communication with and among aboriginal trappers associated with the maritime fur traders." A Great Voice takes pains to rebut this contention, one most notably voiced by historian F. W. Holway, by citing research by University of Victoria linguist Barbara Harris, who claims Chinook arose prior to the influx of Europeans.

9. Nicholas Klassen, in a January 10, 2006, article on the blog, *The Tyee*, stated: "Chinook served as a tangible bridge between all groups—whether aboriginal, European, Chinese, Japanese, even Hawaiian—and as a foundation for a syncretic culture where no single identity had to be dominant. Carryl Coles, whose Neskonlith forebears in the Shuswap region spoke Chinook, sees how the jargon would have connected cultures: 'Language is an obvious barrier for communication and Chinook seems to have brought different people together. So there's a lesson in that.'"

10. At the time of conceptualizing this article, there was a debate occurring over the crisis in Attawapiskat in Northern Ontario. The Assembly of First Nations collectively argued for increased funding in order to address a severe lack of housing. Third party monitoring instituted by the federal government in order to monitor funds was not welcomed by the community. For a CBC report see: http://www.cbc.ca/news/canada/story/.../pol-attawapiskat-court-ruling.html.

11. I am grateful to Dr. Alan Pence for introducing the term, "generative curriculum" in the School of Child and Youth Care when working with Aboriginal communities. I would like to use this term for all students in our programs.

REFERENCES

Adichie, C. The danger of a single story. *Ted Talks*.
Ahmed, S. (2004). *The cultural politics of emotion*. New York, NY: Routledge.
Artz, S. (1994). *Feeling as a way of knowing: A practical guide for working with emotional experience*. North Cumbria, UK: Trifollium Books.
Blackstock, C. (2010, May 19). Child welfare talk on discrepancies in funds to aboriginal children. Retrieved from http://sig.uwaterloo.ca/feature/cindy-blackstock-innovators-in-action-speaker-series
Braidotti, R. (1994). *Nomadic subjects*. New York, NY: Columbia University Press.

Braidotti, R. (2009). On putting the active back into activism. *New Formations, 68*(3), 42–57.

Brodkin, K. (1998). *How Jews became white folks and what that says about race in America*. New Brunswick, NJ: Rutgers University Press.

Caputo, J. (1987). *Radical hermeneutics: Repetition, deconstruction and the hermeneutic project*. Bloomington, IN: Indiana University Press.

Caputo, J. (1993). *Against ethics: Contributions to a poetics of obligation with constant reference to deconstruction*. Bloomington, IN: Indiana University Press.

Caputo, J. (1997). *Deconstruction in a nutshell: A conversation with Jacques Derrida*. New York, NY: Fordham University Press.

Caputo, J. (2000). *More radical hermeneutics: On not knowing who we are*. Bloomington, IN: Indiana University Press.

Clarke, A. (2005). *Situational analysis: Grounded theory after the postmodern turn*. Thousand Oaks, CA: Sage.

de Finney, S., Dean, M., Loiselle, E., & Saraceno, J. (2011). All children are equal but some are more equal than others: Minoritization, structural inequities, and social justice praxis in residential care. *International Journal of Child, Youth and Family Studies, 2*(3–4), 361–384.

de Finney, S., Loiselle, E., & Dean, M. (2011). Bottom of the food chain: The minoritization of girls in child and youth care. In A. Pence & J. White (Eds), *Child and youth care: Critical perspectives on pedagogy, practice and policy* (pp. 70–94). Vancouver: UBC Press.

Du Bois, W. E. B. (1989). *The souls of black folk*. New York, NY: Penguin Books. (Original work published 1904)

The Dulwich Centre. (n.d.). An invitation to narrative practitioners to address privilege and dominance: A document created from conversations between Salome Raheim, Maggie Carey, Charles Waldegrave, Kiwi Tamasese, Flora Tuhaka, Hugh Fox, Anita Franklin, Cheryl White and David Denborough. Adelaide, Australia: The Dulwich Centre.

Fanon, F. (2004). *The wretched of the earth* (R. Philcox, Trans.). New York, NY: Grove Press. (Original work published 1961)

Fine, M., Powell, L., Weis, L., & MunWong, L. (Eds.). (1997). *Off white: Readings on race, power, and society*. New York, NY: Routledge.

Foucault, M. (1980). *Power/knowledge*. New York, NY: Pantheon Books.

Frankenberg, R. (1993). *White women, race matters: The social construction of whiteness*. Minneapolis, MN: University of Minnesota Press.

Freire, P. (1993). *Pedagogy of the oppressed*. New York, NY: Continuum.

Gergen, K. J. (1994). *Realities and relationships: Soundings in social construction*. Cambridge, MA: Harvard University Press.

Gergen, K. J. (1996). Technology and the self: From the essential to the sublime. In D. Grodin & T. Lindlof (Eds.), *Constructing self in a mediated world* (pp. 127–140). Thousand Oaks, CA: Sage.

Gergen, K. J. (1999). Social construction and the transformation of identity politics. In F. Newman & L. Holzman (Eds.), *End of knowing: A new developmental way of learning*. New York, NY: Routledge.

Gergen, K. J. (2000). *An invitation to social construction*. London, UK: Sage.

Gergen, K. J. (2006). *Therapeutic realities: Collaboration, oppression, and relational flow*. Lima, OH: Fairway Press.

Gergen, K. J. (2009). *Relational being: Beyond self and community*. New York, NY: Oxford Press.

Giroux, H. (1997). White squall: Resistance and pedagogy of whiteness. *Cultural Studies, 11*(3), 376–389.

Gordon, A. (1996). *Ghostly matters: Haunting and the sociological imagination*. Minneapolis, MN: University of Minnesota Press.

Griffin, S. (1993). *A chorus of stones*. New York, NY: Anchor Books.

Hoskins, C. R. (2004). *Transnational political activity and host state policy: Canada's Sikh and Tamil diasporas*. Vancouver, BC, Canada: University of British Columbia.

Hoskins, M. L. (1999). Worlds apart and lives together: Developing cultural attunement. *Child and Youth Care Forum, 28*, 73–85.

Hoskins, M. L. (2003). What unites us, what divides us? A multicultural agenda within child and youth care. *Child and Youth Care Forum, 32*, 319–336.

Jackson Pulver, L., Haswell, M. R., Ring, I., Waldon, J., Clark, W., Whetung, V., ... Sadana, R. (2010). Indigenous health—Australia, Canada, Aotearoa, New Zealand and the United States—Laying claim to a future that embraces health for us all. *World Health Report Background Paper, 33*. Geneva, Switzerland: World Health Organization.

Klassen, N. (2010, January). Can we still speak Chinook? *The Tyee*. Retrieved from http://thetyee.ca/Life/2006/01/10/StillSpeakChinook

Lee, J. (2012, January). Public presentation. Diversity workshop, University of Victoria, Victoria, BC.

Lee, J., & de Finney, S. (2004). Using popular theatre for engaging racialized minority girls in exploring questions of identity and belonging. In M. Hoskins & S. Artz, (Eds.). *Working relationally with girls: Complex lives/complex identities* (pp. 95–118). New York, NY: Haworth Press.

Leonardo, Z. (2004). The color of supremacy: Beyond the discourse of "white privilege." *Educational Philosophy and Theory, 36*(2), 137–152.

Leonardo, Z. (2009). *Race, whiteness, and education*. New York, NY: Routledge.

Leonardo, Z., & Porter, R. K. (2010). Pedagogy of fear: toward a Fanonian theory of "safety" in race dialogue. *Race, Ethnicity and Education, 13*(2), 139–157.

McIntosh, P. (1989). White privilege and male privilege: A personal account of coming to see correspondences through work in women's studies. Working paper 189. Wellesley College Center for Research on Women.

McIntosh, P. (1995). White privilege and male privilege: A personal account of coming to see correspondences through work in women's studies. In M. L. Andersen & P. H. Collins (Eds.), *Race, class, and gender: An anthology* (2nd ed., pp. 76–87). Belmont, CA: Wordsworth.

Nussbaum, M. C. (2001). *Upheavals of thought: The intelligence of emotions*. New York, NY: Cambridge University Press.

Pelias, R. (2011). *Leaning: A poetics of personal relations*. Walnut Creek, CA: Left Coast Press.

Ridley, C. R. (1995). *Overcoming unintentional racism in counseling and therapy: A practitioner's guide to intentional intervention*. Newbury Park, CA: Sage.

Roediger, D. (1991). *The wages of whiteness*. New York, NY: Verso.

Shields, S. (2007, April 27). At the table: A 'new relationship' perhaps, but Stó:lō frustrations are mounting. *The Tyee.* http://thetyee.ca/News/2007/04/27/Reconciliation.

Shohat, E. (1992). Notes on the "post colonial." *Social Text 31/32* (pp. 99–113). Durham, NC: Duke University Press.

Tuck, E. (2010). Breaking up with Deleuze: Desire and reconciling the irreconcilable. *International Journal of Qualitative Studies, 23*(5), 635–650.

Velie, A. (2010). Pacifists, tricksters, writers, and victims in Hiroshima Bugi. In D. Madsen & A. R. Lee (Eds.), *Gerald Vizenor: Texts and contexts* (pp. 30–45). Albuquerque, NM: University of New Mexico Press.

Vizenor, G. (1998). *Fugitive poses: Native American scenes of absence and presence.* London, UK: University of Nebraska Press.

Vizenor, G., & Lee, A. R. (2010). Praise the Ravens: A literary interview. In D. Madsen & A. R. Lee (Eds.), *Gerald Vizenor: Texts and contexts* (pp. 268–288). Albuquerque, NM: University of New Mexico Press.

Journeying With Youth: Re-Centering Indigeneity in Child and Youth Care

DAWN ZINGA

Department of Child and Youth Studies, Brock University,
St. Catharines, Ontario, Canada

It is difficult, given the societal and systemic realities within Canada, to have open and frank discussions about social inequalities and impacts of equity and diversity in lived experiences. In this article, I offer a frank discussion about re-centering Indigeneity within Child and Youth Care. The discussion focuses on the challenges associated with re-centering Indigeneity and is illustrated by personal reflections and the reflections of Indigenous individuals involved with a mentorship program for First Nations youth, By drawing upon Indigenous theorists (Alfred, 2009; Archibald, 2008; Black Elk, 1953; Ermine, 2004; Smith, 2012; Wilson, 2008) and grounding the discussion in lived realities, I provide readers with both a theoretically based and practical understanding of how Indigeneity can be re-centered within CYC and well as a consideration of whether this should be done and by whom. Particular attention will be paid to how mainstream Child and Youth Care can support such efforts while operating within a colonial state.

Canada's approach to multiculturalism tends to fall largely within conservative multiculturalism and as such triggers surface changes that do not disturb

---

I would like to thank the First Nations community, the mentors and mentees for sharing their journeys with me. Thank you to the community members for their insightful comments on drafts of this article. The comments from the anonymous reviewers were also very helpful in strengthening this article—thank you. I would also like to thank the many Indigenous colleagues and scholars who have been so generous with their time and their sharing of their own stories. I have gained so much from the intersections between our journeys.

the mainstream or dominant core of society. Tiffany (2010) has likened conservative multiculturalism as being similar to a cappuccino as it offers a "sprinkling of the Other on the dominant, essentially resistant, core" (p. 72), much like one might add a sprinkling of chocolate to cappuccino. This metaphor works well within Child and Youth Care (CYC) as many programs give a nod to multiculturalism and may have diversity policies, but do not change the essentially mainstream core of the organization and its fundamental operating procedures that shape the experiences of youth clients (Jones, 2010; Lavergne, Dufour, Trocmé, & Larrivée, 2007; Leclaire 2007; McKenzie, Seidl, & Bone, 2005; Skott-Myhre & Skott-Myhre, 2011). More specifically, Skott-Myhre and Skott-Myhre reported that "in the settings in which we have worked and in the multiple agencies we have consulted with over the years, we seldom encountered self-reflection or theoretical investigation as an institutionalized practice." The embodiment of self-reflection and theoretical investigation within CYC workers is a necessary precursor to engaging non-hegemonic approaches to CYC.

It is essential to understand that while ground up or grassroots approaches may be effective in addressing how to embody non-hegemonic ways of engaging CYC practices for individuals and specific organizations, these approaches will come into conflict with hegemonic structures. These hegemonic structures exist within individuals as internalized majoritarian or dominant discourses (see Henry & Tator, 2005; Ortiz & Jani, 2010; Solórzano & Yosso, 2002), that both inform and constrain those individuals and organizations (Dell et al., 2011; Downey, Gibson,& Dini-Paul, 2011, Hand, 2006; Jones, 2010; Lavergne et al., 2007; Leclaire 2007; McKenzie et al., 2005; Skott-Myhre & Skott-Myhre, 2011; Tator & Henry; 2002). Regardless of cultural background, gender or class, individuals within Canada are exposed to liberal democratic ideologies and to the mainstream core through education and by living within society (Henry & Tator, 2006; Tator & Henry, 2002; Zinga & Davis, 2006). Foucault's (1977) discussion of how power operates through a system of relations is helpful in understanding how power and privilege operate within society such that individuals may be subjugated to power while also acting as consenting vehicles of power.

As CYC practitioners have experienced formal education and daily life within Canada, they are indoctrinated to the hegemonic approaches embedded within society and the associated relations of power and privilege. The mainstream core acts to influence every level of society whether through acceptance of the approaches as "normal" or by being the object that is resisted or rejected. Henry and Tator (2005) discuss how democratic discourses can simultaneously uphold the ideals of multiculturalism, while effectively undermining any attempts to cause deep changes to the dominant core through multicultural initiatives. Democratic discourses such as "equal opportunity" allow for the appearance of structural and systemic progress towards an ideal of multiculturalism while ignoring and actively denying systemic inequalities that would reveal the flawed basis of the equal opportunity discourse (Henry & Tator, 2006; Tator & Henry, 2002). These discourses also strangle attempts to discuss diversity and equity by providing prescribed language terms such as multiculturalism, diversity, and cultural competency that have meanings so tangled within democratic discourse that individuals and groups are unable to have or may choose to avoid having meaningful conversations that directly address systemic inequalities and their impacts. The power and privilege relations can be seen to be operating when we consider who is in a position to choose not to engage in such conversations and who is silenced by democratic discourses.

Canada's colonial history and the imposition of the Indian Act adds significant layers of complexity when one is seeking to employ non-hegemonic approaches and draw upon Indigeneity.[1] The discussion of First Nations sovereignty and the tangled history of colonialism from the perspectives of the colonizer and the colonized is beyond the scope of this article (see Alfred, 2009; Haig-Brown, 1988; Haig-Brown & Nock, 2006). However, there are layers of this complexity that are important to understand in terms of re-centering Indigeneity in CYC. Specifically, when considering the importance of Indigeneity within the context of Canadian CYC one must understand that Canada is a colonial state that has adopted multiculturalism. As stated earlier, this adoption of multiculturalism continues to be problematic. In addition, multiculturalism is layered on top of a long history of conceptualizing the first peoples of Canada as the "other" in specific ways that have been legislated through the Indian Act and have developed within Canadian culture. Francis (1992) has described this othering as the creation of the "Imaginary Indian." Thus, in many ways the majoritarian discourses in the Canadian context embody and impart these ways of othering and conceptualizing the First Peoples of Canada. It is against this backdrop, that I explore the idea of re-centering Indigeneity within CYC practice together with the associated challenges and tensions.

Within this article, I have taken the approach of conceptualizing the discussion about re-centering Indigeneity within CYC practice as a journey. This journey is contextualized by the societal and systemic realities and inequalities within Canada that frequently complicate attempts to have open and frank discussions about inequality, equity, and diversity. I draw upon personal reflections as a White researcher working with Indigenous colleagues and communities as well as reflections from Indigenous youth and community members involved in a particular mentorship program for First Nations youth. The discussion also draws upon the work of several Indigenous theorists (Alfred, 2009; Archibald, 2008; Black Elk, 1953; Ermine, 2004; Smith, 2012; Wilson, 2008) and provide a theoretically-based and practical understanding of how Indigeneity can be re-centered within CYC. Most importantly, the discussion will explore questions of whether Indigeneity should be re-centered within CYC and by whom that work should be done.

CONTEXT

Language and Positionality

The use of language within this article is an important contextual consideration as language is politized and pregnant with multiple meanings and interpretations. The term Aboriginal is a political and contested term (see Alfred & Corntassel, 2005) as well as a federal and legal designation in Canada, and will be used only where necessitated by an original source. I prefer the terms Indigenous and Indigeneity as these terms are more common globally and reflect "natural, tribal, and traditional characteristics of various peoples" (Alfred, 2009), these terms will be used throughout unless different terminology is necessitated by source material. The term First Nations is also used due to original usage in source research and to recognize the community and the agency associated with the Youth Mentorship Program. When speaking of First Nations, I do not use the term "reserve" as First Nations community members have expressed their thoughts about how politicized the term is and how it fails to capture Indigenous concepts of community, and so to honor that I refer to First Nations communities. Similarly, I use the term re-centering rather than centering to recognize that among Indigenous peoples, Indigeneity has always been part of the care of children and youth. The term centering implies a newness that can be seen as appropriating Indigeneity while also erasing or discounting its historical influences. These are two examples that emphasize the importance of language use and interpretation. Furthermore, as this article is written in English it is essential to emphasize that concepts and teachings drawn from Indigenous thought will be discussed within this article and English does not adequately capture the associated nuances.

There similar cautions are associated with my positionality as a White researcher. As the sole author of this article, my positionality is very important. When I speak of the Canadian education system and how it serves to further disseminate and perpetuate liberal and majoritarian discourses, I am speaking from personal experience as one who was a student in the system and who now is a professor in higher education. Regardless of what point I am in my own journey of struggling with and against colonialism, colonialism influences my understandings of the world around me. Given that I have not been raised in an Indigenous community nor do I speak an Indigenous language, I am a learner in the context of Indigenous thought.

Social Realities

Prior to considering the youth mentorship program, it is important to contextualize the program. This contextualization involves looking at the history of child welfare services for First Nations children and youth within Canada to gain a small appreciation of the complex histories of colonialism that serve as a backdrop to the journeys of current First Nations children and youth. These histories act to inform understandings and misunderstandings around the role of First Nations children and youth in their communities, in their schools, and in mainstream society. The multiple impacts of colonial histories may be passed down through the generations often shifting traditional understandings and distorting knowledges that have been passed down orally through language and cultural traditions of sharing. The children and youth involved in the mentorship program were often resisting and acting out against colonialism and the resulting modern realities that attempted to shape and inform their journeys.

There is a long history of assimilation targeting First Nations children and youth. From the earliest recorded times of first contact there is a tangled history of imposing majoritarian norms and understandings onto First Nations children and youth. A pattern that many would argue has not changed sufficiently with the advances in child and youth work in the twentieth century and the adoption of multicultural policies and cultural sensitivity training and protocols (Bell & Libesman, 2005; Blackstock, 2007, 2011; Blackstock & Trocmé; 2004; Galley, 2010). Durst (2002) organizes First Nations child welfare into three periods: the assimilation period (1876–1960s), integration period (1960–1980s) and the current period of local control (1980–present). While it is beyond the scope of this article to provide a detailed understanding of how these periods operated and the varied impacts of the associated structures and policies, it is important to have a basic understanding of how these periods influence current realities. It is important to note that Durst has the period of local control beginning in 1980, the last residential school closed in 1996.

Durst's (2002) assimilation period begins with first contact and concludes during the height of the residential school period. The strategy of removing First Nations children from their families was fully implemented with residential schools and then exacerbated during the integration period with the Sixties Scoop approach of the child welfare system. The next change as outlined by Durst has been the period of local control marked by the devolution of responsibility for child welfare to First Nations agencies. However, many of these agencies must operate under the umbrella of the province adhering to the provincial guidelines and often operating as a "child" or branch of the larger provincial child welfare system. Those First Nations workers who operate in "child" branches frequently have to go above and beyond what is expected of their mainstream counterparts and are still mired in paternalistic relations with agencies of federal oversight. Thus, local control is more illusion than reality. The complexities of funding arrangements further complicate matters as the federal government retains control of the purse strings for "locally controlled" agencies and the provincial and federal bodies have frequent protracted negotiations around responsibility and jurisdiction that have devastating consequences for individual First Nations children who require quick and decisive action.

Within the literature, First Nations children have been repeatedly identified as being over represented within child welfare across Canada. In 2003, Farris-Manning and Zandstra reported that First Nations children represent 40% of the 76,000 children in care in Canada. Based on data from the Canadian Incidence Study of Reported Child Abuse and Neglect (CIS-1998), Blackstock and Trocmé (2004) found that First Nations children continued to be over-represented. According to more recent Canadian Incidence Study of Reported Child Abuse and Neglect (CIS-2008) findings, the rate of investigations involving First Nations children was 4.2% higher than non-Aboriginal with higher incidence rates across almost every category (Sinha et al., 2011). In 2009, Blackstock reported that there were more First Nations children in care than at any other point in history, including the residential school years. Galley (2010) also documented that First Nations children were 6–8 times more likely to be in care than non-Aboriginal children. The involvement of some form of child welfare services is a reality for many First Nations children.

First Nations families residing in First Nations communities experience higher levels of social, cultural, and economic risk than other Canadian families, but have significantly fewer resources to employ to address these risks (Blackstock & Trocmé, 2004). Blackstock and Trocmé call into question how much First Nations families are being called to account for systemic and structural factors such as poverty and poor housing that are considered to put children at risk and to what extent child welfare services are committed and able to support community development efforts that would address the causal agents of child risk. Furthermore, they stress the need for these community development approaches to be rooted in cultural ways of knowing that call upon ancestral approaches to parenting and child rearing that have sustained First Nations children through the continued impacts of colonization.

Indigenous ways of knowing and the resulting ways of addressing risks to child safety are distinctly different from western ways. Allowing for variations through different First Nations groups in Canada, Blackstock (2009) described the fundamental ontological differences between western and Indigenous ways of knowing. She sees western ways being more individually based and firmly rooted within specific linear timeframes whereas Indigenous ways are more collective and consider a broader concept of time that reaches back to benefit from ancestral knowledge and considers the impacts ahead for seven generations. While both are focused on keeping children safe and addressing risk factors, they use different ways to perceive, evaluate and address those risk factors.

Several researchers (Blackstock, 2011; Blackstock & Trocmé, 2004; Galley 2010; Jones, 2010; Sinha et al., 2011) have pushed for the adoption of an Indigenous epistemology in First Nations child welfare. However, the fundamental stumbling block to implementation (practical funding and jurisdictional issues aside) remains the western perception of the Indigenous epistemologies as "approaches" that must fit in the western framework as a special program. Furthermore, the western perspective tends to view these 'approaches' as "new" when they draw upon ancient knowledges that have been passed down through generations and also perceives Indigenous epistemologies as a singular entity that fills in gaps not covered by western knowledge rather than as another dimension on knowledge. Thus, western knowledge is frequently used to subjugate and control other knowledges and understandings in much the same way that western approaches were used to subjugate and control First Nations children in residential schools and through other forms of colonization.

This tendency to subjugate and control information is also seen in news coverage of First Nations child welfare. The news coverage tends to minimize any structural or complex issues and deliver messages of blame and the perceived inability of First Nations peoples to self-govern. These messages are consistent with the majoritarian discourses found throughout Canadian culture (Francis, 1992) and are not contextualized by a consideration of how provincial and federal governments have compromised and undermined First Nations sovereignty (Harding, 2010). The struggle for First Nations sovereignty and the battles to hold Canadian government to its promises to First Nations (see Alfred & Corntassel, 2005; Alfred, 2009; Blackstock, 2011; Harding, 2010; Hughes, 2012; St. Denis, 2011; Valverde, 2012) influences the lives of First Nations children and youth. The systematic inequalities and discriminatory practices of the child welfare institutions (Blackstock, 2011) continue to be pervasive influences on the lives of many First Nations children and youth. First Nations children and youth live in a world that perceives their histories through a colonial lens that is reproduced within the school system. It is a society that denigrates and questions their Indigenous identities while legislating and articulating back to them who is and who is not "Aboriginal". Despite these challenges many young people are able to draw support from their families, their communities, and their culture. They frequently resist these majoritarian influences and conceptualizations of their identities and histories and insist on developing their own visions for their future, understandings of current contexts, and their cultural histories (see Bergstrom, Cleary, & Peacock, 2003; Hare & Pidgeon, 2011).

Some First Nations youth resist colonial influences by dropping out of school (Hallett et al., 2008; Statistics Canada, 2006; Zinga, Styres, Bennett, & Bomberry, 2009), getting into trouble with the legal system (Canadian Centre for Justice Statistics, 2005; Corrado, Cohen, & Watkinson, 2008; Indian and Northern Affairs Canada, 1996), struggling with self-esteem (St. Denis & Hampton, 2002; Neegan, 2005; Whattam, 2003), and turning to substance abuse (Ghelani, 2010; Whattam, 2003). Many of these youth would benefit from early intervention programs such as mentorship programs, but all too often they only have access to mainstream programs that continue to problematize their behavior according to majoritarian norms, fail to adequately appreciate their identities, cultures, and contested histories. Programs that have been designed with the best of intentions to help youth, become yet another venue in which Indigenous youth are exposed to hegemonic structures and discourses that continue to discount and often denigrate their identities and cultures.

THE YOUTH MENTORSHIP PROGRAM

To maintain the anonymity and confidentiality of the Indigenous youth and community members associated with the Youth Mentorship Program (YMP), the First Nations community will not be identified other than as being a First Nations community located within Canada. What will be shared are the reflections of the youth, their families, and the mentors associated with the program. These reflections articulate the internal and external challenges that were experienced in embodying Indigeneity within the program.

I became aware of the YMP through my collaborative research with various groups within the community. I was approached by members of the community agency about conducting an external review of the program. The members of the community agency felt that given my familiarity with the community and Indigenous approaches, I would "get" their program and that as a White researcher, I would be able to provide the kind of validation that the mainstream funding agency was seeking. The program reflections by First Nations youth and community members were shared as part of the research through individual and group interviews. Following Smith (2012), Aboriginal ways of knowing took precedence over Western paradigms of understanding in the research and the research was done with the youth and community members not on or about them. Individuals choose whether their reflections were to be used only as part of the review or could be included as research data. All participants opted to be included in the research. Ethics clearance was granted by the Research Ethics Board of the First Nations Community and as well as by Brock University.

The YMP was developed by a First Nations community service organization to serve the youth and their families in a sovereign First Nations community located within Canada. The motivation for the program was twofold. There were concerns that youth and their families needed more support to change behavioral patterns associated with risk for involvement with the legal system. In some cases, these were intergenerational patterns that included dropping out of school, substance abuse, criminal behavior, and limited options. The program was designed to help youth disrupt these behavioral patterns and assist them in pursuing other activities that would provide more life options. The second motivation was rooted in a belief that available mainstream approaches did not serve the needs of the community's youth. In developing the program, the organization drew upon the cultural knowledge of the community and a model provided by the Panyappi Indigenous Youth Mentoring Program from Australia.

The Panyappi program was designed to serve Indigenous youth and their families with a focus on individual needs, rebuilding family connections, and working from a developmental perspective (Stacey & Associates, 2004). The program supports youth who experience various issues that may lead them to be hanging out in one or more known inner city or suburban youth hangouts that places them at risk for being victimized or engaging in criminal behavior (Australian Human Rights Commission, 2008; Richards, Rosevear, & Gilbert, 2011; Stacey & Associates, 2004). Some of the key features of the program include: (a) having a formal case management approach to mentoring; (b) focusing on individual needs; (c) "mentoring beyond the trouble zone"; (d) having paid mentors with professional training; (e) utilizing a developmental perspective; (f) culturally appropriate practice with a focus on strengthening family connections; and (g) collectively addressing issues faced by Indigenous youth through partnerships with other stakeholders (Australian Human Rights Commission, 2008; Bell & Libesman, 2005; Richards et al., 2011; Stacey & Associates, 2004). It has been recognized as a successful program for Indigenous youth (Stacey & Associates, 2004) and identified as being a best practice (Australian Human Rights Commission, 2008; Bell & Libesman, 2005; Higgins & Butler, 2007; Richards et al., 2011).

The First Nations organization customized their mentoring program incorporating relevant aspects of the Panyappi program and making modifications to suit community needs. The resulting program had a strong focus on individual needs and was customized to each client and his/her family where relevant. The program was a small pilot program with limited external funding. It included two First Nations staff members who organized the program and conducted all of the mentoring. One staff member focused on the young adult populations and generally employed an individual-focused mentoring style that acted to support the young person in setting and obtaining positive goals. The other staff member primarily worked with younger mentees who required a combination of individual-focused and family-based mentoring. Some youth were referred to the program in fulfillment of a youth diversion initiative (mentorship instead of criminal charges), while others were identified by their families or referred by other social service agencies.

The program was designed to serve Aboriginal youth and their families within a culturally relevant framework. It was based on a set of core values, namely: intense focus on individual needs and self-actualization on the part of the mentee; rebuilding family connections; building relationships; culturally appropriate mentoring; and maintaining a community-based focus.

Thus, there is a marked difference in the approach of the program if one were to compare it with mainstream mentorship programs. In particular, the YMP has a strong relationship orientation with less formal interactions. This allows the mentor to build a relationship with the individual and the family (where appropriate) that extends into the community. For example, while there are specific meetings and consultations the relationship between mentor and mentee is not restricted to those times but may include encouragement and spontaneous conversations should the mentor come into contact with the mentee at community events or locations.

Given its highly individualized focus, the program does not employ specific program durations, but tailors the arrangements for each mentee based on his/her specific needs. The mentors draw upon a strong philosophy of community-based outreach with a set of core values (as described above) that guide the program. Furthermore, the program follows the Panyappi model of "mentoring beyond the trouble zone" (Stacey & Associates, 2004) as the mentees may come into the program due to a crisis or an acute trouble stage but the mentoring continues after the initial crisis/trouble has been resolved or managed. The idea is not to establish a reactive pattern of support but to model and teach mentees how to secure and maintain support so that they can avoid crises. Youth are mentored until they feel comfortable on their own and often a graduated system is employed whereby fewer meetings are required during times of progress and the mentor-mentee meetings may be focused on progress updates, sharing, and future planning. This regular contact provides opportunities for the mentee to discuss potential problems and difficulties before they become seemingly insurmountable.

The YMP continues to be an exceptional program that reflects both the commitment of the community service agency's approach to service provision and the dedication of the mentors to providing highly individualized mentorship experiences within a culturally relevant context. While the program is resource intensive, it is also highly effective as evidenced by participant interviews, and has great promise to continue to develop and serve the needs of more youth and their families.

At this point it is important to point out how the program differs from mainstream CYC approaches. Certainly, some might find similarities or connections to other CYC approaches such as Relational CYC. This is a case where language plays a very important role. While it is true that Relational CYC as described within the research (see Fulcher, 2003; Garfat & Fulcher, 2011; Skott-Myhre & Skott-Myhre, 2011) seems to be similar to the YMP approach, there are some marked differences. YMP's culturally relevant framework is based on community understandings of traditional teaching. In this way, "self-actualization" is helpful in describing, but fails to adequate capture, the nuances of what is meant. Within YMP, "self-actualization" refers to the importance of a young person coming to know and appreciate the gifts the Creator has bestowed on him/her and to start on the path s/he was meant to follow. Furthermore, the term "culturally relevant framework" cannot adequately capture the richness and diversity of the teachings that are drawn upon.

According to the World Health Organization (2007), there are approximately 370 million Indigenous peoples living in over 70 countries and offering an incredible diversity of cultures, languages, histories, customs, and religions. First Nations communities within Canada also offer great diversity within their languages, cultures, and traditions. While communities share common understandings, there are also nuances of difference within and between communities. Many communities would resonate with the five ethics that Ross (1992) describes as shaping Ojibwe parenting: (a) the ethic of non-interference; (b) the ethic of not showing anger; (c) the ethic of conservation; (d) the ethic of expecting excellence; and (e) the ethic of acting when the time is right. Understandings of these ethics would shape the design of a mentorship program in an Ojibwe community in ways that may be similar and yet distinct from another First Nations community (Hand, 2006). Thus, the YMP approach described in this paper is very much in keeping with the community's cultural understanding and while it may offer insights that are useful to other Indigenous communities and agencies—Indigeneity should not be seen as a once size fits all term.

JOURNEYING WITH YOUTH

In the context of this article, I am drawing upon a conceptualization of journeying (Styres, 2011; Zinga, Styres, Bennett, & Bomberry, 2009) articulated as:

> the passage from one place to another; is initiated by questioning, meanings, interpretations, and identity; is begun by making a conscious decision to move into unfamiliar territory while maintaining an observing and reflective frame of mind. Journeying is a place where spirituality is infused into the mind, body, and emotion states of our being; where our stories intersect and become interconnected with other stories. Journeying without intent is nothing more than aimless wandering. Purposeful journeying leads us to shift and transform the landscape of our previously held assumptions and paradigms. (p. 35)

In many ways, the mentors were teaching the youth about journeying through life by stressing the importance of self-reflection and journeying with intent. They modeled the interconnected nature and centrality of relationships identified by many Indigenous scholars (Archibald, 2008; Black Elk, 1953; Blackstock, 2009; Wilson, 2008) and helped the youth shift from aimless wandering to journeying with purposeful intent. The community aspects of the program were essential to showing the youth how stories intersect and become interconnected with each other. All of this was done in ways that honored the journeys of the mentors and mentees by tailoring the program to the skills and contexts of each mentor–mentee pair such that each pairing was unique and reflective of the journeying that they engaged in together and separately.

Mentees

It became evident during the research that there were two distinct types of mentoring being used within the program. The first type was individual-based mentorship that focused on providing encouragement and support for older youth in setting goals and taking positive steps toward those goals. The youth engaged in supportive mentoring were fourteen years of age or older and had experienced difficulties with the police and engaged in problematic behaviors at school or within the community. They come into the program as an alternative to being charged with a misdemeanor or due to identification by police, school, or other community personnel as youth at risk. The second type tended to involve younger youth and blended the individual-focused approach with family-based mentoring. These younger youth were between thirteen and five and could not easily establish goals. They were often identified by family and school/police personnel as being at-risk and at times out of control. Often they had very difficult experiences in their backgrounds that involved a lot of change in their living situations at a young age and\or older siblings who already exhibited a strong tendencies for risky and illegal activities. Family involvement was key in establishing regular routines to address behaviors, to encourage and reward positive behaviors, and to provide structure within the young person's environment. Individualized approaches were designed to incorporated community supports to systematically address areas of concerns such as school performance (e.g., tutoring, homework support), socializing (e.g., extracurricular programs, art therapy), and regular routines (e.g., bedtimes, mealtimes, school attendance). Regular intensive contact with the mentor involved home visits, transportation to supportive programs identified by the mentor, and regular reinforcement of progress. These two types of mentoring were not just a reflection of the specific skills sets and approaches of the two mentors but were also reflective of the distinct needs of the young people involved in the mentorship program. I refer to these two types of mentoring as supportive mentoring (older youth) and intensive mentoring (younger youth).

The mentees and their families were very clear on the importance of the program. As one parent stated, "I don't know what I would have done without [names mentor] she really cared about us and it may a difference that I could call with any question not feel stupid," and another family member stated, "I wish this program had been around when my older sons needed it and there are so many families in the community who could benefit from being involved." One youth commented, "I don't like having to meet at [names location] but the program really helps and I can always call if I need to and she cares how I'm doing." while another suggested, "It really should be expanded—there are more youth who could use it." All of the youth talked about how knowing that someone was there for them and cared about their actions made them think twice because they did not want to disappoint that person. As one youth shared, "Sometimes, I'd be about to do something...like you know I used to do but then I would think about having to tell her that I messed up so I just wouldn't do it." Another youth described telling his mentor about a mistake, "I told her my old friends came around and I should have said no but I didn't. She still cared and told me not to beat myself up about it but helped me focus on getting back on track."

They also talked about the ways that the mentorship relationship helped them understand their own importance and worth. All participants indicated that they highly valued the individual-based approach and relationship-based context. They spoke of knowing many other individuals and families who would benefit from the program and of how well it addressed needs within the community. They liked that the mentors understood their cultural backgrounds and experiences. As one youth said, "I've been in other programs and they just didn't get it—didn't get me. Here I don't have to explain why I hate the high school or what the White kids say. She just gets it. She understands the community and has helped me." Another youth stated, "It's not like we talk about culture all the time—it's more that we don't have to cause she gets it"; and a third said "there are things you just know because you live here and people from outside just can't know and I don't want to explain." One youth made a particularly strong point about the program in saying, "other programs are White. They are not me, they don't care about me. They just want to make me into something else and that's why I dropped out of school in the first place."

In terms of weaknesses, participants commented on how the program was not well advertised and some did not like needing to call the community agency or have their mentorship meetings at the community agency. Overall, the participants spoke very highly of the program's effectiveness with many families in the intensive mentoring indicating that they had been at their wits end prior to the program and did not know how they would have made it through without the program. Youth in the less intensive mentoring also indicated how essential the program was in helping them establish a positive pathway and in staying on the path or recovering it when they were challenged. Participants also appreciated being connected to additional culturally appropriate programming and supports as well as receiving help navigating supports and programming outside the community.

Mentors

The mentors generally agreed with the comments of the mentees and their families about the program's strengths and weaknesses. They also believed that the community-based program was more effective than other mainstream programming that the youth had experienced. What was most interesting about the mentors' comments during the interviews was how they talked about their work, what they were trying to accomplish, and the ways they worked with the youth.

As previously mentioned, the two mentors differed in their approaches to mentoring the youth. One mentor, who will be referred to by the pseudonym Terri, tended to work with the older youth using a supportive mentoring approach. The other mentor, who will be referred to by the pseudonym Linda, tended to work with the younger youth and their families through the use of intensive mentorship. Both individuals had received professional training and had prior experience working with youth. While some of their training had Indigenous elements, much of their training and work experience had been heavily influenced by mainstream organizations and agencies. Both mentors lived in the community and were very familiar with the political situations and overall functioning of the community.

During the interview Terri spoke about the program and described how she conducted her work. She spoke about how important it was to establish a relationship with the youth but that it was also important to maintain a professional distance and establish boundaries. For example, she would call the youth at home if necessary and if the youth had agreed to home calls but she would not conduct home visits. While Terri did refer to her knowledge of the culture and the community as being assets in understanding the youth, there was nothing else in her interview that set her apart from a mentor in any other mainstream mentoring program. Her focus during the interview was on demonstrating the ways youth made progress and explaining how she structured her mentoring to ensure professional distance and proper protocols. Terri stated,

> I know the expectation is that we will chat with our mentees if we meet them at events in the community but I am not entirely comfortable with that—for me. I think it can impact the professional relationship that I am establishing. So sometimes I will avoid events or if I do meet one of my clients at an event, I make sure it is a brief professional chat. Maintaining the boundaries is important.

Boundaries were not Linda's primary concern. In her intensive mentoring approach, she stressed the need to break down some of the boundaries and indicated that often mainstream programs had difficulty working with Indigenous youth because of their focus on the professional relationship. Relationships are central in Indigenous contexts and seen to be interconnected so in Linda's opinion youth would not connect when they thought that you were just another person paid to "care" about them in a specific way. She believed that the youth needed someone to really care about them in all their contexts and to develop a relationship with them that went beyond an hour consultation each week. This is not to say that she was unconcerned about professional distance but that she saw it as being secondary to establishing a relationship with the youth and family. She was very concerned about determining the line between support and enabling and spoke about how she was constantly trying to determine whether an action she was about to undertake was supportive or just enabling certain behaviors.

While Linda did not refer to what she was doing as "re-centering Indigeneity" in her work with youth, a large component of her interview focused on this theme. Linda spoke about how she sometimes felt that she was "just a brown face pushing White policy" in some of her work and that she was determined not to do this in the mentoring program. When discussing the external review process for the program she spoke about a tendency that she had seen in her community and other First Nations communities. According to Linda,

> We have skilled individuals within our communities but when it comes time to solve an issue or evaluate something it seems as if we have to look outside the community. If someone White says that one of our programs is effective or that we should implement program X then that is what is considered. It's like we constantly need external validation. I think it's the effects of colonialism and internalized oppression. The community feels as if something is not valuable unless it has been validated by someone mainstream. Yet, at the same time the community resists the mainstream and blames mainstream education for some of the problems youth experience. It is a constant tension between seeking external validation and resisting mainstream influences. Why is it that what we do is not enough? That if someone native validates a program the community still looks outside.

She also spoke about how personnel from programs other than the Panyappi program would not understand how and why she engaged in intensive mentoring. She described her approach to mentoring as doing what needs to be done and not defining the process by boundaries. If several home visits were needed then that was what she did. If one of her youth needed tutoring then she set it up and if that youth could not get transportation to the tutoring then she drove him/her or arranged for transportation. Linda described herself as looking at the whole child and his/her relationships when helping the child and caregivers to set goals and put routines in place. As she indicated, "helping is an important part of our culture in this community and the only limit I put on helping is enabling because if you enable then you are not really helping."

It was interesting that the two mentors viewed their mentorship roles quite differently but were able to work together very closely and effectively.

Terri's interview provided evidence of strong mainstream influences that informed how she structured her mentoring with the inclusion of cultural understanding as a secondary concern. This may have been due to the fact that she was not engaged in or chose not to share any personal introspection on the tensions around mainstream and Indigenous ways of approaching mentoring that were shared by Linda. In contrast, the excerpts shared from Linda's interview clearly demonstrate a high level of personal introspection and engagement with the challenge of re-centering Indigeneity within the mentoring program. Linda is grappling with important questions about what she does, how she does it, the ways it impacts the youth, and the ways it might be viewed and evaluated by an outsider.

RE-CENTERING INDIGENEITY IN CHILD AND YOUTH CARE

We have now come full circle in our consideration of re-centering Indigeneity within youth work. According to Archibald (2008), Black Elk (1953), Wilson (2008), and many other Indigenous theorists, the centrality of circularity in Indigenous ways of knowing inherently lends itself to circularity in thought wherein one journeys around the circle deepening one's knowledge in each revolution. In our journey, we have discussed how Canada's approach to multiculturalism is conservative and has tended to result in surface changes that do not disturb the mainstream core. Many researchers (Blackstock, 2007, 2009; Blackstock & Trocmé, 2004; Findlay, Hardy, Morris, & Nagy, 2010; Jones, 2010; Leclair, 2007; McKenzie et al., 1995) have argued that within Indigenous contexts, CYC has followed this model of surface enhancement, consciously or unconsciously, by adding diversity training or designing programming that incorporates Indigenous names and concepts without substantively impacting the agency's mainstream structure, policy, and procedures.

Often agencies and their staff have good intentions but fail to ask the most important questions. Too often, the focus is on "how we can incorporate Indigeneity in child and youth work" when it should begin with questioning whether or not it is possible for mainstream agencies and personnel to do so and further whether or not they should do so by giving full consideration to the appropriateness of such an action. Skott-Myhre and Skott-Myhre (2011) have stressed the danger of trying to have genuine encounters with youth if "you feel that you can interpret their behavior through a lens of superior expertise" (p. 43). Due to being bombarded by images and stereotypes about what Francis (1992) terms the "Imaginary Indian" through the majoritarian discourses, non-Indigenous individuals are at great risk for consciously and unconsciously interpreting the behavior of Indigenous youth through a colonial lens of superiority.

Skott-Myhre and Skott-Myhre's call to ensure that critical reflection is part of CYC and that it is recognized as being politicized is a step forward.

As they define their conceptualization of postmodern praxis as being, "critical reflection on the ways that the current dominant regime of power, postmodern global capitalism, disciplines and controls all of us living in today's world" (p. 44). Drawing upon Basaglia's (1987) work, Skott-Myhre and Skott-Myhre (2011) talk about "class traitors" as being those individuals who "identify with the needs and aspirations of those within their circle of care and who are willing to betray the rules of the dominant social or the institution" (p. 46). These ideas lay important groundwork for the future of CYC and open the door to more possibilities, but fall short of addressing the complexities of Indigeneity within CYC. This is not surprising given that addressing Indigeneity was not their focus. However, it is a helpful progression of thought. Consider, what would be necessary for mainstream CYC workers to begin to appreciate the complexities associated with attempting to re-center Indigeneity within CYC. It would be necessary go beyond being a "class traitor" to being someone who is willing to identify with the needs and aspirations of Indigenous people and who actively interrogates and resists colonialism within themselves and others while seeking to decolonize. According to Smith (2012), "decolonization is a process which engages with imperialism and colonialism at multiple levels. For researchers, one of those levels is concerned with having a more critical understanding of the underlying assumptions, motivations and values which inform the research process" (p. 21).

The mentors of the YMP are both Indigenous and within their shared reflections, evidence of the influences of colonization can be clearly seen. They have struggled to re-center Indigeneity within CYC and Linda clearly talks about her struggles with internalized oppression as a "brown face pushing White policy" and her work at decolonizing. In my work with Indigenous communities and colleagues, I constantly struggle to be critically aware and interrogate my thoughts and actions for colonial influences. My process of decolonization is a painful struggle that involves critical reflection, careful consideration of word choice and the meaning of words, and the acceptance of Indigenous ways of knowing and my associated role as a novice learner. These experiences have led me to offer a caution. Those of us who have been raised within mainstream society and with the mantle of mainstream privilege should be honest about the associated limitations and our own abilities to challenge our mainstream privilege. We must be careful not to compound the damage through misappropriation or co-optation. As Smith (2012) states, "Under colonialism, indigenous peoples have struggled against a western view of history and yet been complicit in that view. We have often allowed our 'histories' to be told and then have become outsiders as we heard them being retold" (p. 34).

I have been privileged to be invited into the First Nations community and to have had many opportunities to listen to what Indigenous colleagues and scholars have shared with me. Through those experiences, I have developed a deep appreciation for other ways of knowing and the need to question the ways my own background, experiences and exposure to dominant culture has shaped and continues to influence my thinking and patterns of interaction. Through this learning, I have come to realize that we are at a critical juncture and if Canada is to move forward in a positive way that honors and recognizes the histories and culture of the First Peoples—it is time for mainstream individuals, agencies and levels of government to question their understandings of the contested histories and to acknowledge and actively work to recognize and support the sovereignty of First Nations communities. We need to question our mainstream privilege at every level and resist the western knowledge system's position that there is a legitimate knowledge. It is through our questioning that we contribute to opening space (Ermine, 2004) for First Nations community-based programming and approaches.

The First Nations youth mentoring program provided excellent examples of how grassroots approaches may successfully embody non-hegemonic ways of engaging in CYC while coming into conflict with hegemonic structures that both inform and constrain those individuals and organizations. This was clearly evident in an organization and community that is Indigenous and has complex relationships with mainstream influences that has resulted in a pattern of tensions between the constant pressure to conform to or seek validation from the mainstream and the simultaneous ongoing process of resisting and rejecting mainstream influences. There are other programs working to re-center Indigeneity (e.g., Dell et al., 2011; Pazaratz, 2005) as well as promising new partnerships between Indigenous communities and mainstream agencies (e.g., Downey et al., 2011; Findlay et al., 2010). Downey et al. (2011) speak to the heart of the matter in describing the work of Gibson as an Indigenous partner in an Indigenous program that has mainstream partners, "Bruce describes this as 'walking between two cultures', which involves the constant switching between languages and ways of talking, body language, and awareness, skills that are quite impossible for non-Indigenous people to develop" (p. 143). Consider then how the difficulty increases exponentially if one were attempting to embody these non-hegemonic approaches within a mainstream CYC agency.

At present Canadian society indoctrinates its citizens in hegemonic approaches and the associated relations of power embedded within society. Canadian institutes are designed to actively expose every individual to liberal democratic ideologies and to the mainstream core regardless of an individual's culture or race. One of the most utilized terms for the First Peoples of Canada is Aboriginal. This term is regularly used within Canadian society but rarely with any consideration of its origins or implications. Alfred and Corntassel (2005) have described the term as "a powerful assault on Indigenous identities" (p. 599) as well as being part of a legal and political framework that both defines identity and positions Indigenous peoples according to a colonialist agenda that does not allow for any true reconciliation or acknowledgement of historical truths. As Wane (2008) has indicated, Canadians have difficulty engaging in conversations about equity and diversity issues and these conversations when they do happen are often full of platitudes and theories while lacking frank and honest considerations of the impact of equity and diversity.

Within this context, I argue that it is possible to re-center Indigeneity within CYC but that mainstream agencies and personnel not only lack the ability to do so at this point but also lack the understanding that it is not their place to do so. There are conversations that Indigenous individuals need to have among themselves and that mainstream people need to respect. There may be times when mainstream individuals are invited to listen to these conversations and there may be times when they are asked to provide support in specific ways but for the most part re-centering Indigeneity within CYC lies within the purview of Indigenous peoples. Mainstream agencies and personnel can better serve the Indigenous children and youth who utilize their services by questioning their own preconceived notions and engaging in deep introspection about why they do what they do within their work and what that means for the youth with whom they interact. It is time to have frank and honest discussions about equity, diversity and what we as agencies and individuals are prepared to do to actively engage the issues in our work with Indigenous children and youth.

NOTE

1. It is important to discuss language use within this article. As the term Aboriginal is a political and contested term (see Alfred & Corntassel, 2005), the terms Indigenous and Indigeneity are used throughout unless use of the term Aboriginal is necessitated by an original source. The term First Nations is also used due to original usage in source research and to recognize the community and the agency that developed the mentorship program.

REFERENCES

Alfred, T. (2009). *Peace, power and righteousness: An Indigenous manifesto* (2nd ed.). Don Mills, ON: Oxford University Press.
Alfred, T., & Corntassel, J. (2005). Being Indigenous: Resurgences against contemporary colonialism. *Government and Opposition, 9,* 597–614.
Archibald, J. (2008). *Indigenous storywork: Educating the heart, mind, body and spirit.* Vancouver, BC, Canada: University of British Columbia Press.
Australian Human Rights Commission. (2008). *Preventing crime and promoting rights for Indigenous young people with cognitive disabilities and mental health issues.* Sidney, Australia: Australian Human Rights Commission.
Basaglia, F. (1987). Peace time crimes: Technicians of practical knowledge. In A. Lovell & N. Scheper-Hughes (Eds.), *Psychiatry inside out: Selected writings of Franco Basaglia* (pp. 143–160). New York, NY: Columbia University Press.

Bell, T., & Libesman, T. (2005). *Aboriginal and Torres Strait Islander Child Protection Outcomes Project: Report on national and international child protection frameworks for Indigenous children*. Melbourne, Australia: Secretariat of National Aboriginal and Islander Child Care. Retrieved from http://www.amsant.org.au/documents/article/143/110523Child%20Protection%20Outcomes%20Project%20Report.pdf.

Bergstrom, A., Cleary, L. M., & Peacock, T. D. (2003). *The seventh generation: Native students speak about finding the Good Path*. Charleston, WV: Appalachian Regional Laboratory.

Black Elk (with Brown, J. E., Ed.). (1953). *The sacred pipe: Black Elk's account of the sacred rites of the Oglala Sioux*. Norman, OK: University of Oklahoma Press.

Blackstock, C. (2007). Residential schools: Did they really close or just morph into child welfare? *Indigenous Law Journal, 6*(1), 71–78.

Blackstock, C. (2009). Why addressing the over-representation of First Nations children in care requires new theoretical approaches based on First Nations ontology. The Journal of Social Work Values and Ethics, 6(3), 1–18. Retrieved from http://www.socialworker.com/jswve/content/view/135/69/

Blackstock, C. (2011). The Canadian Human Rights Tribunal on First Nations child welfare: Why if Canada wins, equality and justice lose. *Children & Youth Services Review, 33*(1), 187–194. doi:10.1016/j.childyouth.2010.09.002.

Blackstock, C., & Trocmé, N. (2004). Community-based child welfare for Aboriginal children: Supporting resilience through structural change. In M. Ungar (Ed.), *Pathways to resistance: A handbook of theory, methods and intervention*. Thousand Oaks, CA: Sage.

Canadian Centre for Justice Statistics (2005). *Collecting data on Aboriginal people in the criminal justice system: Methods and Challenges*. Ottawa, ON, Canada: Canadian Centre for Justice Statistics.

Corrado, R., Cohen, I., & Watkinson, A. (2008). The over-representation of Aboriginal youth in custody: Policy challenges. *Horizons, 10*(1), 79–82.

Dell, C. A., Chalmers, D., Bresette, N., Swain, S., Rankin, D., & Hopkins, C. (2011). A healing space: The experiences of First Nations and Inuit youth with equine-assisted learning (EAL). *Child and Youth Care Forum, 40*, 319–336.

Downey, L., Gibson, B., & Dini-Paul, K. (2011). The Cape Kids service. *Relational Child and Youth Care Practice, 24*(1–2), 142–147.

Durst, D. (2002). Self-government and the growth of First Nations Child and Family Service (FNCFS). Regina, Saskatchewan, Canada: Social Policy Research Unit, Faculty of Social Work, University of Regina. Retrieved from http://www.pinkcandyproductions.com/portfolio/conferences/state_of_federation/papers/Durst.pdf

Ermine, W. (2004). *The ethics of research involving Indigenous peoples*. Indigenous People's Health Research Centre. Retrieved from http://www.iphrc.ca/documents/ethics_review_iphrc.pdf on 07/20/2008.

Farris-Manning, C., & Zandstra, M. (2003). Children in care in Canada: Summary of current issues and trends and recommendations for future research. Unpublished paper prepared for the Child Welfare League of Canada for submission to the National Children's Alliance.

Findlay, J., Hardy, M., Morris, D., & Nagy, A. (2010). Mamow Ki-ken-da-ma-win: A partnership approach to child, youth, family and community well-being. *International Journal of Mental Health and Addiction, 8*, 245–257.

Foucault, M. (1977). Two lectures. In C. Gordon (Ed), *Power/knowledge: Selected interviews and other writings 1927–1977* (pp. 78–108). New York, NY: Pantheon Books.

Francis, D. (1992). *The imaginary Indian*. Vancouver, BC, Canada: Arsenal Pulp Press.

Fulcher, L. C. (2003). Rituals of encounter that guarantee cultural safety. *Relational Child & Youth Care Practice, 16*(3), 20–27.

Galley, V. J. (2010). *Summary of the review of Aboriginal over-representation in the child welfare system*. Regina, Saskatchewan, Canada: Saskatchewan Child Welfare Review Panel.

Garfat, T., & Fulcher, L. (2011). Characteristics of a child and youth care approach. *Relational Child and Youth Care Practice, 24*(1–2), 7–19.

Ghelani, A. (2010). Evaluating Canada's drug prevention strategy and creating a meaningful dialogue with urban Aboriginal youth. *Social Work with Groups, 34*(1), 2–40.

Haig-Brown, C. (1988). *Resistance and renewal: Surviving the Indian residential school*. Vancouver, BC, Canada: Arsenal Pulp Press.

Haig-Brown, C., & Nock, D. A. (Eds.). (2006). *With good intentions: Euro-Canadian and Aboriginal relations in colonial Canada*. Vancouver: University of British Columbia Press.

Hallett, D., Want, S. C., Chandler, M. J., Koopman, L. L., Flores, E., & Gehrke, E. C. (2008). Identity in flux: Ethnic self-identification and school attrition in Canadian Aboriginal youth. *Journal of Applied Developmental Psychology, 29*(1), 62–75.

Hand, C. A. (2006). An Ojibwe perspective on the welfare of children: Lessons of the past and visions for the future. *Children and Youth Services Review, 28*, 20–46.

Harding, R. (2010). The demonization of Aboriginal Child Welfare Authorities in the news. *Canadian Journal of Communication, 35*(1), 85–108.

Hare, J., & Pidgeon, M. (2011). The way of the warrior: Indigenous youth navigating the challenges of schooling. *Canadian Journal of Education, 34*(2), 93–111.

Henry, F., & Tator, C. (2005). *The colour of democracy: Racism in Canadian society*. Toronto, ON, Canada: Thompson Nelson.

Higgins, J. R., & Butler, N. (2007). Characteristics of promising Indigenous out-of-home care programs and services. *Promising practices in out-of-home care for Aboriginal and Torres Strait Islander carers, children and young people (Booklet 1)*. Melbourne, Australia: Australian Institute of Family Studies.

Hughes, J. (2012). Instructive past: Lessons for the royal commission on aboriginal Peoples for the canadian truth and reconciliation commission on indian residential schools. *Canadian Journal of Law and Society, 27*(1), 101–127.

Indian and Northern Affairs Canada. (1996). *Royal Commission on Aboriginal Peoples*. Ottawa, ON, Canada: Indian and Northern Affairs Canada. Retrieved from http://www.ainc-inac.gc.ca/ch/rcap/sg/cg_e.html.

Jones, M. (2010). Systemic/social issues Aboriginal child welfare. *Relational Child and Youth Care Practice, 23*(4), 17–30.

Lavergne, C., Dufour, S., Trocmé, N., & Larrivée, M. (2007). Visible minority, Aboriginal and caucasion children investigated by Canadian protective services. *Child Welfare, 87*(2), 59–76.

Leclair, M. (2007). Working with First Nations youth. *Relational Child and Youth Care Practice, 20*(3), 73–74.

McKenzie, B., Seidl, E., & Bone, N. (1995). Child and family service standards in First Nations: An action research project. *Child Welfare, 74*(3), 633–653.

Neegan, E. (2005). Excuse me: Who are the First Peoples of Canada? Aboriginal education in Canada then and now. *International Journal of Inclusive Education, 9*(1), 3–15.

Ortiz, L., & Jani, J. (2010). Critical race theory: A transformational model for teaching diversity. *Journal of Social Work Education, 46*(2), 175–193.

Pazaratz, D. (2005). Maintaining cultural integrity in residential treatment. *Residential Treatment for Children and Youth, 22*(1), 15–31.

Richards, K., Rosevear, L., & Gilbert, R. (2011). Promising interventions for reducing Indigenous juvenile offending. *Indigenous Justice Clearinghouse, Brief 10.* Canberra, ACT, Australia: Indigenous Justice Clearing House.

Ross, R. (1992). *Dancing with a ghost: Exploring Indian reality.* Markham, ON, Canada: Octopus Publishing Group.

Sinha, V., Trocmé, N., Fallon, B., MacLaurin, B., Fast, E., Propkop, S. T., ... Richard, K. (2011). *Kiskisik Awasisak: Remember the children. Understanding the overrepresentation of First Nations children in the child welfare system.* Ontario, Canada: Assembly of First Nations.

Skott-Myhre, K., & Skott-Myhre, H. A. (2011). Theorizing and applying child and youth care as politics of care. *Relational Child and Youth Care Practice, 24*(1–2), 42–52.

Smith, L. T. (2012). *Decolonizing methodologies: Research and Indigenous peoples* (2nd ed.). London, UK: Zed Books.

Solórzano, D. G., & Yosso, T. J. (2002). Critical race methodology: Counter-storytelling as an

St. Denis, V. (2011). Silencing Aboriginal curricular content and perspectives through multiculturalism: "There are other children here." *Review of Education, Pedagogy, and Cultural Studies, 33*(4), 306–317.

St. Denis, V., & Hampton, E. (2002). Literature review on racism and the effects on Aboriginal education. Prepared for Minister's Working Group on Education. Ottawa, Canada: Indian and Northern Affairs Canada.

Stacey, K., & Associates (2004). *Panyappi Indigenous Youth Mentoring Program: External evaluation report. Panyappi, Metropolitan Aboriginal Youth Team.* Adelaide, Southern Australia: SA Department of Human Services.

Styres, S. D. (2011). Land as first teacher: A philosophical journeying. *Reflective Practice, 12*(6), 717–731.

Tator, C., & Henry, F. (2000). The role and practice of racialized discourse in culture and cultural production. *Journal of Canadian Studies, 35*(3), 120–137.

Tiffany, G. (2010). Detached youth work in the United Kingdom. In W. Specht (Ed.), *Mobile youth work in the global context: Reaching the unreachable* (pp. 66–73). Stuttgard, Germany: Series of the International Society for Mobile Youth Work.

Valverde, M. (2012). The Crown in a multicultural age: The changing epistemology of (post)colonial sovereignty. *Social & Legal Studies, 21*(1), 3–21.

Wane, N. N. (2008). *Contested site, contested topic: Teaching anti-racism studies in a teacher education program.* In A. Wagner, S. Acker, & K. Mayuzumi (Eds.), *Whose university is it anyway?* (pp. 203–213). Toronto, Canada: Sumach Press.

Whattam, T. (2003). Reflections of residential schools and our future: "Daylight in our Minds." *Qualitative Studies in Education, 16*(3), 435–448.

Wilson, S. (2008). *Research is ceremony: Indigenous research methods.* Winnipeg, MB, Canada: Fernwood Publishing.

World Health Organization (2007). *Health of indigenous peoples.* Geneva, Switzerland: World Health Organization.

Zinga, D. & Davis, M. (2006). Canada's educational challenge: A Eurocentric curriculum in a multicultural country. In D. Zinga (Ed.), *Navigating multiculturalism: Negotiating change* (pp. 216–247). Newcastle, UK: Cambridge Scholar's Press.

Zinga, D., Styres, S., Bennett, S., & Bomberry, M. (2009). Student Success Research Consortium: Two worlds community-first research. *Canadian Journal of Native Education, 32*(1), 19–37.

Unsettling Representational Practices: Inhabiting Relational Becomings in Early Childhood Education

FIKILE NXUMALO
*School of Child and Youth Care, University of Victoria,
Victoria, British Columbia, Canada*

This article seeks to unsettle representational practices enacted through dominant multicultural pedagogical approaches in the early childhood classroom. Drawing from a research study in early childhood centers that investigated practitioners' and children's negotiations of racial difference, I explore how multicultural pedagogical approaches in early childhood spaces present a risk through the potential for static representations of difference and diversity. I argue that these approaches potentially reproduce inequalities and delimit ways of engaging with difference and diversity through prescribing identity and dampening capacities for certain bodies in certain spaces. I offer possibilities for movements away from pre-defined and prescriptive approaches toward complexified approaches that require close attunement to the emergence of material-discursive assemblages. Attention to relational becomings has the potential to open possibilities for socially just early childhood pedagogies that enact a micropolitical engagement with the material-discursive entanglements of everyday encounters.

Getting it Right...

On a small table in a preschool classroom in British Columbia sits a mirror, white paper, a package of eight markers ranging in colors from dark brown to light cream marked as "apricot," "peach," "tan," "sepia," *"burnt sienna," "mahogany," "Black," and "White." On the bright yellow and green package of markers there is a green and blue earth globe, inside of which are the drawn faces of four smiling children of different hues surrounded by the words "multicultural" "multiculterel." A four-year-old girl child-body sits on a chair facing the mirror. She moves to pick up a light cream "peach"-colored marker. She presses the marker down on a white piece of paper, and then looks intently at her face in the mirror. She repeats this several times, with different markers. She moves to put down yet another marker, and then pick up a darker-colored "tan" marker. She removes the lid, and presses the tip down on the paper. She looks in the mirror, and then picks up the lid, places the lid back on the marker, and looks around the table. She exclaims loudly, "I got the right color!" with a big smile at the two female-adult bodies that sit near her. She presses the marker on the paper and draws a dark brown oval face.*

Matching, Mixing and Matching...

A large and thick black book holds together pages of pedagogical narrations throughout the preschool year. One narration is named "Mixing the Colors of Us." The narration describes how the educators instruct all the children to take the paint and paintbrush and match their skin color with the paint. Images of the children are shown with paintbrush, paint, and paper, around a table. As several child-bodies gather and look at the colors, one child notices that one of the children is different. The child says, "Her skin is a lot yellower then ours." The educators point out to the children how all the skin colors are different from each other. The children are then instructed to take their "skin color" paint and mix all the colors together. One light cream color emerges. An image shows the children looking at the light cream color. The children are next instructed to take the light cream color and add colors to it to match it back to their own skin color.

OPENINGS

Everything depends on the dense entanglement of affect, attention, the senses, and matter. This is not exactly intended or unintended, not the kind of pure agency we imagine marching forward...but a balling up and unraveling of states of attending to what might be happening... (Stewart, 2010, p. 6)

Several authors have pointed to the need to unsettle the notion of a pre-defined and singular relationship between self and cultural identity and the underlying assumptions of a coherent and stable, homogenous identity in multicultural education (see, e.g., the work of Ghosh & Abdi, 2004; Hoffman, 1996; Kirova, 2008). In this article I seek to build on this work through an engagement with how the fixities and repetitions produced through dominant multicultural pedagogies might be transformed by attending to material-discursive assemblages and the affective becomings that emerge in intra-activities between human and more-than-human[1] bodies (Barad, 2007; Lenz Taguchi, 2010; Whatmore, 2002, 2006). As the preceding quote by Stewart (2010) indicates, I suggest a close attunement to the situated trajectories and multiplicities of subjectivities as they emerge in the affective material-discursive spaces of everyday encounters (Stewart, 2007, 2010, 2011). I use relational becomings as a productive concept for creating movement toward a pedagogy that blurs and complexifies the categories created by dominant multicultural pedagogical approaches while attending to emergent and embedded power relations (Braidotti, 2006a). I suggest attending to the material-discursive mobilities of subjectification as "an experimentation in contact with the real" (Deleuze & Guattari, 1987, p. 12). Experimental approaches to early childhood education practices that engage with the "qualities, rhythms, forces, relations, [and] movements" (Stewart, 2011, p. 445) through which embodied subjectivities emerge might hold promise for creating movement away from getting one's cultural identity "right"; a common underlying premise of dominant multicultural pedagogies (Kirova, 2008).

Importantly, my intent here is not to establish inhabiting material-discursive relational becomings as the right way of seeing and doing. My interest here is to explore how responsive attunement to material-discursive relational becomings can be put to work toward unsettling representational pedagogies (Bird, 2004). My hope is to affirm relational material-discursive becomings in early childhood spaces that complexify ways of seeing and engaging with multiculturalism and that center "our own implication in meaning-making materiality" (Haraway, 1995, p. 49). In this regard, the questions this article explores include:

- What becomings might attending to the material-discursive bring into view; becomings that might otherwise be obfuscated in dominant multicultural pedagogies?
- How might situated relational becomings work toward creating movements and openings in early childhood pedagogies to include the affective, the unforeseen and unexpected?
- How might close attunement to material-discursive "trajectories of difference and repetition" (Stewart, 2010, p. 14) as they emerge in everyday pedagogical encounters be seen as micropolitical acts?

To help engage with these questions, I draw on pedagogical encounters from an ongoing research project investigating practitioners' and children's negotiations of racial difference. The first section of the article situates the current work within critiques of multiculturalism in Canada and more specifically in early childhood education. I then turn to a discussion of key conceptual tools I experiment with toward unsettling the fixities of multicultural pedagogies, before illustrating this with examples from practice, including the vignettes which opened this article. I conclude the article with an opening toward a pedagogy of relational ethics that complexifies encounters with difference in the early childhood classroom.

MULTICULTURAL FIXITIES

In Canada, multiculturalism became national policy in 1971, and became national law through the Multiculturalism Act of 1988 (Abu-Laban, 1998). A large body of work has engaged critically with multiculturalism and the effects on those marked as multicultural subjects (see Pacini-Ketchabaw (2007) and Pacini-Ketchabaw and Nxumalo (2010) for examples within the context of early childhood education in Canada). While a comprehensive review and analysis of critiques of multiculturalism is beyond the scope of this article, I offer here a few insights from this work, with particular emphasis on the fixities created by practices predicated on tolerance, acceptance and recognition of cultural identity, as it is the fixities that are enacted through these seemingly benign representational practices that this article seeks to unsettle. For expanded discursive analyses and critiques of multiculturalism within the Canadian context see Bannerji (2000), de Finney (2010), Ghosh and Abdi (2004), Kirova (2008), Lee and Lutz (2005), and, Razack, Smith, and Thobani (2010).

The circulation of tolerance and recognition relies on the maintenance of power relations that fix the desired identity of "tolerated" "recognized" others as well as those deemed outside of the nation-state's liberal benevolence; including the underlying conditionality of fulfilling the demands of tolerance and acceptance (Ahmed, 2000, 2008; Ang, 1996; Brown, 2006). Tolerance can also be seen as a normalized taken-for-granted nation-state "value" that governs through seeming to accept the Other—while setting individual "limitations, controls, forms of coercion, and obligations" (Foucault, 2008, p. 63, as cited in Read 2009, p. 29) for tolerated Others. As Bannerji (2000) explains, multiculturalism, "relies...on reading the notion of difference in a socially abstract manner, which also wipes away its location in history, thus obscuring colonialism, capital and slavery" (p. 51). Pedagogies predicated on tolerance and recognition are thereby entangled with racialized neocolonial and neoliberal relations that reproduce hierarchies and exclusions without interrogating the underlying hegemonies (Dirlik, 2008; Giroux, 1992).

The rhetoric of acceptance and tolerance of diversity also masks technologies of assimilation. As Ang (2001) writes, "racially and ethnically marked people are no longer othered today through simple mechanisms of rejection and exclusion, but through an ambivalent and apparently contradictory process of *inclusion by virtue of othering*" (p. 139, emphasis in original). The circulation of tolerance and acceptance within normative predefined goals and deficit assumptions also extends to the context of early childhood education in Canada. Pacini-Ketchabaw (2007) has foregrounded the inequities created and amplified by multicultural pedagogies which place educators in the role of detached technician presenting children who "lack" knowledge with the tools for assimilation, and define children according to static categories of difference. As she explains, "liberal multicultural discourses present a homogenized view of migrant populations and at the same time constructs them as deviating from the norm" (p. 224).

Taken together, these perspectives highlight the potential effects of multicultural education practices to fix identity while masking inequitable power relations and the complex material and discursive relations within which subjectivities emerge. This very brief review illustrates how difference, as configured through dominant multicultural approaches, has been largely configured as a *lack*—a construction of fixed "identities on the basis that they lack access to dominant structures of privilege and domination" (Skott-Myhre, 2012, p. 305). While some of the work reviewed above has highlighted the effects of tolerance, acceptance and recognition in fixing relations between bodies and spaces, much of the focus of this work has been human-centric through a focus on the discursive. This article seeks to extend this important work, within the specific context of early childhood education, by exploring what relational engagements with and close attunement to the more-than-human might open up. What movements and possibilities might attention to human and more-than-human bodies, things and spaces and the material-discursive subjectivities produced in early childhood classroom encounters create and bring into view? I now turn to a consideration of the theoretical tools that I experiment with toward a productive relational attunement to everyday material-discursive becomings that unsettle multicultural representational practices.

ON MATERIAL-DISCURSIVE ENTANGLEMENTS

In this article I use material-discursive to signal the intrinsic relationality and mutual intertwining of matter and discourse; unsettling the binaries between language or discourse and the material world (Barad, 2003, 2007; Grosz, 1994; Haraway, 1997, 2008; Hultman & Lenz Taguchi, 2010). In these understandings, "the material and the discursive are mutually implicated" in knowing and becoming (Barad, 2007, p. 152). Subjectivity is conceptualized as emerging in continual material-discursive configurations, affinities and connections between human and more-than-human bodies in a multiplicity of encounters (Hultman & Lenz Taguchi, 2010; Springgay, 2008). These affinities and connections come together to form transient assemblages—a coming together of diverse material and discursive elements in the emergence of subjectivity. As Bennett (2010) explains,

> Assemblages are not governed by any central head: no one materiality or type of material has sufficient competence to determine consistently the trajectory or impact of the group. The effects generated by an assemblage are, rather, emergent properties, emergent in their ability to make something happen. (p. 24)

RELATIONAL BECOMINGS

I use becomings to refer to processes of subject formation that foreground relationality. In this view, becomings are "always in-the-making" (Whatmore, 2006, p. 603) through relational affinities between spatially and temporally located human and more-than-human bodies (Coleman, 2008; Deleuze & Guattari, 1987). This perspective provides an opening to attending to the ways in which bodies become through affirmative relations. Becomings enact productive possibilities for stepping outside of static identity; for embracing the "in-between" (Deleuze & Guattari, 1987, p. 277). New material feminisms and feminist technosciences (Barad, 2007; Braidotti, 1998, 2011; Grosz, 1994; Haraway, 2003) theorize subject formation through more-than-human relationalities—emerging as becomings through "co-constitutive relationships in which none of the partners preexist the relating, and the relating is never done once and for all" (Haraway, 2003, p. 12). This already-entangled relationality includes materialized and discursive more-than-human and human encounters situated within particular literary, cultural, political, economic, and social affective assemblages (Renold & Ringrose, 2011).

Material feminisms view subject formation as not only figured through discursive positionalities, but also as emergent in relation to dynamic material and affective processes of becoming. In this view the material and the discursive are in intertwined intra-activity and subjectivities emerge as effects of these intra-activities (Barad, 2007; Braidotti, 2011; Grosz, 1994; Lenz Taguchi, 2010). This view of subjectivity foregrounds relationality; envisioning the subject as multiple and hybrid assemblages of intrinsically creative, relational, rhizomatic, and intensive desiring forces that exceed humanistic conceptions and embrace the more-than-human (Braidotti, 1998, 2011; Deleuze & Guattari, 1987; Grosz, 1994). Bodies include human and more-than-human multiplicities which assemble in particular spatial and temporal encounters (Coleman, 2008; Deleuze & Guattari, 1987). The body is conceptualized as:

> processes, organs, flows, energies, corporeal substances and incorporeal events, speeds and durations...[and is understood]...in terms of what it can do, the things it can perform, the linkages it establishes, the transformations and becomings it undergoes, and the machinic connections it forms with other bodies. (Grosz, 1994, pp. 164–165)

Bodies, their actions and affects interact with things, spaces, and discursive elements in the emergence of subjectivity as an embodied and embedded processual assemblage of multiple belongings where "the subject is but a force among forces, capable of variations of intensities and inter-connections and hence of becomings"(Braidotti, 2006b, para. 5). This is an embodied subjectivity that brings attention to material-discursive relational becomings in each event rather than the pre-defined and fixed identity of multiculturalism.

Disrupting fixed categories, placing borders into "constructive and transformative tension" (Timeto, 2011, p. 161) and, transgressing borders are all important potentialities of a situated relational pedagogical orientation. Further to this, attending to the material-discursive affects, interactions, and tensions that might be transformed, created or re-enacted through relational becomings, also perhaps illustrates how things take "shape in specific ways and cannot take shape just in any way" (Haraway, 1997, p. 142). I now turn to a pedagogical encounter that illustrates how differences come to matter in the early childhood classrooms in ways that might not be "seen" through a multicultural lens. I explore how a relational entanglement with becomings might open new possibilities for grappling with difference; micropolitical possibilities that escape the coding striations of representational identity yet also make visible dampening effects of systemic inequities (Deleuze & Guattari, 1987).

INTERFERENCES AND INTERRUPTIONS—BROWN-CLAY WATER ENCOUNTER

A large block of brown clay and a small glass bowl of water have been set out on a drop-cloth on a table. Several child-bodies gather around the table and begin to mix water with clay...girl-child-arms and clay-water emerge in mutual engagement (Hultman & Lenz Taguchi, 2010) (Figure 1):

"I need a little more butter so it can melt."
[Rubbing brown clay-water into her arms]: "The butter is going up my sleeve."
"Look what I've got on my whole arm!"
"I'm rubbing it on my whole arm."
"Daba dab dab dab dab dab dab."
"Now I have brown skin instead of skin."
"Now you have brown skin?"
"Lindy, I have brown skin right now."
Rachel looks over at my adult-researcher-body and smiles as she rubs clay into her hands.
She looks back down at her arms smiling.
[Loudly]: "I have brown skin!!!" [smiling]

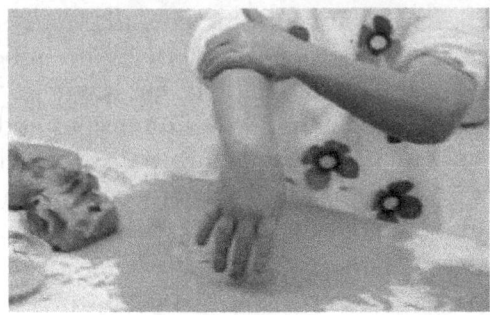

FIGURE 1 Brown clay-water encounter. (Color figure available online)

She looks over at my adult-researcher-body again while smoothing clay into her arms and hands and looks back down; studying her arms with a serious expression.
[Humming and singing, rubbing clay into her arms]: "a-a-a-a . . . eh-eh-eh-eh."
[In a sing-song voice]: "I ain't going to wash my hands, I ain't going wash my hands before my mom gets herrrre."
[Gasping]: "How come, how did that happen?"
[Educator laughing]: "That's what mom would say?"
"Yeah." [Later after washing and wiping off the clay];
[Loudly]: "No more brown skin!"

INHABITING RELATIONAL BECOMINGS

Following Haraway (1988, 1997), I view the interpretations that follow not as representations of objective, detached "truths" but as partial knowledges-in-the-making from my embodied material-discursive situatedness both in the event and after the event as I re-encountered the dialogue and images. I do not sit outside of and unimplicated in that which I narrate, but situate myself materially and discursively as a part of events (Bird, 2004; Haraway, 1997). Inhabiting relational becomings in located, accountable and implicated knowledge-making creates movement away from claims to detached and neutral objectivity (Haraway, 1988, 1997). Inhabiting relational becomings is an affective, embodied and embedded story-telling—an ethics that requires a "passionately connected form of presence . . . [which creates] . . . greater vulnerability as well as greater connectivity (Bird, 2004, p. 214). I intentionally seek to make the otherwise un-noticed visible, to engage with uncomfortable possible meanings, and to resist deflecting away from questions of racialization (Mac Naughton, 2005).

In my interpretations of this moment I draw from theoretical conceptions of difference as a productive material-discursive event that emerges and is enacted in encounters between discourse, things, affects, bodies and space (M'charek, 2010; Saldanha, 2006). Using this theoretical lens, I map the emergence of specific affective encounters with difference that connect to racialization and multiculturalism. Here mapping is understood not as a representation of what is, but rather as an opening to new knowledges and becomings (Haraway, 1992). In this encounter, meanings of "brown skin" emerge in the intense relationalities of encounters to form an assemblage of becomings that includes:

> the distribution of phenotypes around the room and the table—table—white drop cloth—brown clay/water—the children's and educator's bodies clustered around the table—the smell of the clay—clay's smooth, wet, slippery texture—sensation of wet clay against skin-the ease with which clay stains and slides across skin—the marks clay makes on skin—Rachel's singing, humming and other joyful exclamations: "I have brown skin!"—what other bodies do when she makes these proclamations (smiles, looks of surprise, a side glance)—the openness to experimentation with the clay in the room—memories of previous encounters and conversations about skin color—discursive constructions of difference—the affective processes activated through the smiles Rachel and I exchange—the effects of the camera....

All of these active participants, and more come together to "perform actions, produce effects and alter situations" (Bennett, 2004, p. 355). The relational assemblage of affects, things, and other human bodies seems to create an opening for new mutable becomings and new subjectifications where these material partners are always already entangled (Haraway, 2003). Clay-water and girl-child-body become-with as they are mutually transformed in the experimentations with brown clay-water on skin. Perhaps the brown clay-skin-girl-child-body assemblage embodies a relational becoming that is about lines of movement, "transitions and passages without pre-determined destinations" (Braidotti, 2011, p. 60; Deleuze & Guattari, 1987).

Envisioning becomings in this encounter in relation to desiring forces and contingent formations is an important move toward extending subjectivities beyond "the traditional image of thought and the pedagogical practices that assume a unitary vision of the self" (Braidotti, 2010, p. 408). Brown clay-skin-girl-child as a relational becoming is filled with "condensation, fusion and implosion" (Haraway 1997, p. 12) that disrupts the bounds of developmental temporality. Rather, the emphasis is on the ethical potentialities of this encounter, on the possibilities for deterritorializations of reified categories of difference—becoming clay-brown-skin-girl - without a reduction of difference to sameness but opening to the simultaneous processual proliferation of differences and multiple relational belongings including phenotypical affinities in this encounter (Saldanha, 2006). This encounter then, foregrounds becoming as always a *becoming-with* that is marked by messy, contingent and unpredictable affinities between a multitude of human and more-than-human actors (Deleuze & Guattari, 1987; Haraway, 2008). An important aspect of these material-discursive affinities is that they cannot be known beforehand; while solidarities that cut across difference and adhere to shared commonalities are both important, material-discursive relational becomings disrupt the notion that these commonalities determine what affinities and assemblages are possible. Relational becomings offer possibilities for exploring the complexities, contradictions and multiplicities inherent in everyday life; in particular encounters such as this, where taken for granted knowledges on conceptions of identity don't seem to fit or work as ways of seeing (Braidotti, 2010, 2011, Haraway, 1988). As Braidotti (2010) explains this conception of subjectivity:

> renders our image of thought in terms of a decentered and multilayered vision of the subject as a dynamic and changing entity; as such it can be taken as a dramatization of processes of becoming. This process assumes that identity takes place in between nature/technology; male/female; Black/White; local/global; present/past—in the spaces that flow and connect such seeming binaries. We live in permanent processes of transition, hybridization and nomadization. (p. 410)

Relational becomings then provide an affirmative perspective to conceptions of subjectivity (Braidotti, 2010). Attention to relational becomings creates possibilities to experiment with multiple transformative ways of envisioning subjectivities as contingent and embodied material-discursive becomings that are continually and materially configured and reconfigured in a dynamic, already-hybrid world (Springgay, 2008). This encounter suggests that subjectivities in early childhood classrooms, contrary to the reified differences highlighted in multicultural pedagogies, are always in movement, always already hybrid and emergent. This orientation offers possibilities to trouble the fixities of and representations of these knowledges; to reconfigure them and produce interferences (Haraway, 1992; Pacini-Ketchabaw, forthcoming)—to produce something different, with openings to the new, and with more ethical, relational, co-implicative and transgressive possibilities (Bastian, 2006; Braidotti, 2002; Haraway, 1992; Timeto, 2011).

Perhaps the loud and joyful expressions of *I have brown skin!* could also be seen as an enactment of power relations that circulate through the room and produce affective intensities (Foucault, 1980). Brown skin seems to be a desirable transformation in this momentary encounter that creates new flows of creative power. Brownclay-skin seems to produce a kind of pleasurable solidarity or affinity; an intense "relationality of difference" (M'charek, 2010, p. 310) particularly in the moment where she first looks over at my adult–researcher-brown body; the only brown-skinned body in the room, and smiles and then looks down at her arms. In this moment, it perhaps possible to see how phenotypic differences between bodies matter not only in relation to understanding how bodies may conform to representational boundaries, but also how they may create affects, affinities and possibilities that exceed the enclosures and repetitions of representation (Saldanha, 2006; Slocum, 2008). In this moment I see becomings that disrupt and complexify dampening flows of power and

> allow desire to flow in different directions, producing new possibilities and potentials. Revolutionary becomings. Becomings that can transform a single body... Brief lines of movement that move away from organisation and stratification... these connections or assemblages... allow desire to flow and... have the capacity to transform bodies and produce new social formations. (Malins, 2004, pp. 88-89)

Perhaps the moment when Rachel looked up at me, smiled and then looked back down at her arms can be seen as a transient blurring of the dichotomous boundaries between child/adult, Black/White, non-human clay/human skin (Pacini-Ketchabaw, forthcoming; Skott-Mhyre, 2008). Braidotti (2010) reminds us that becomings emerge through transitory, hybrid and fluid material-discursive relational processes. In this encounter, the girl-child-body as always *becoming-with* creates an opening toward a moment that is "unsure, heterogeneous, desiring, noninnocent, leaky, and situated" (Bastian, 2006, p. 1029) and filled with "visceral intensities," many of which escape my attempts at articulation (Swanton 2010, p. 459). Some of these visceral affective intensities might include:

> her joyful articulation of "I have brown skin"— my embodied, affective implicated presence as the only differently phenotyped presence in the room— the smile exchanged—the affects created by brown clay-arms and hands—

Perhaps this assemblage of things, affects and human and more-than-human bodies, and all that they "do" this moment can be seen as an "ethical engagement with otherness" (Saldanha, 2006, p. 14) that is filled with multiple potentials that escape representation. In my perception this assemblage enacts a transformative and ethical encounter with difference; an intense line of flight created through unpredictable material experimentation (Olsson, 2009). While Rachel seems to make a connection between my brown body and her "brown-skin" clay arms; I did not sense my presence in that moment as an "out-of-place-body," but instead a responsive relationality. In this encounter, brown skin seems to connect to joyful expressions, to shared smiles, to the specific material and discursive dynamics in the room at that moment—to produce an embodiment of brown skin as desirable—at least temporarily (M'charek, 2010). In other words, while the racial politics of skin are ever-present, how skin emerges as a racial object is highly contingent and intensely relational; in assemblages of becoming there are potentials for creating trajectories away from dampening relations (Fritsch, 2010). The relationality between my brown skin and the girl child-body's brown-clay skin is "the very materiality of the difference that is being enacted" in unsettling normativity (M'charek, 2010, p. 313). This perhaps illustrates how a focus on material-discursive becomings does not seek to erase difference but rather proliferates difference, and in doing, complexifies the formations that oppressions based on fixity and categorizations take (Grosz, 1994; Saldanha, 2006). This is a productive and creative view of difference where differences "are not given "entities" out there, awaiting dis-covery; rather they are effects that come about in relational practices" (M'charek, 2010, p. 307).

MOLAR VISCOSITIES

> Molar lines are those hard and sedimented structures which work to constrain and bind subjects in social space (e.g., gender, race, class identities) and the molecular are those micro process and tiny movements in everyday relations which make visible (if seen) the fragility and malleability of the molar...the molecular is about that moment or "becoming" when, however fleetingly, the normative molar segments are ruptured. (Renold and Ringrose, 2011, p. 394)

Molar viscosities[2] create "sticky" affects that fix bodies while becomings are molecular relational movements that "traverse, create a path, destabilize, energize instabilities, [and make visible] vulnerabilities of the molar unities" (Grosz, 1994, p. 172). The molar and the molecular "co-exist and cross over into each other" (Deleuze & Guattari, 1987, p. 213) and this is perhaps visible in this encounter which does not appear to be innocent and seems filled with contradictions and incoherences. As we exchanged glances a second time, I felt a shift in the mood as though it became very heavy compared to the moments before as she studied her arms and began to sing: "I ain't going to wash my hands, I ain't going wash my hands before my mom gets herrrre." An encounter with her mother's reaction is also felt by her gasp and the words, "How come, how did that happen?" And an educator laughing and saying— "that's what mom would say?" Rachel's words after she washes her arms "No more brown skin!" also present a stutter in attempts to fix meanings of this encounter. New meanings and questions emerge when these moments (the enactment of her mother's reaction, the song of not washing hands, the loud proclamation of "no more brown skin!") are placed side-by-side.

Perhaps these moments also illustrate how embracing hybrid, and more-than-human subjectivities does not silence materially and discursively produced power relations; rather it highlights the urgency of creating of new ways of thinking and practicing ethically and politically (Braidotti,

2006). For instance, these dampening encounters can be seen as momentary molar fixities where the relational assemblages of human and more-than-human bodies and discursive power relations together produce particular desires, affects, knowledges and accompanying acts that coagulate within "processes of stratification, over-coding and control" (Chesters & Walsh, 2005, p. 188). In this moment perhaps an engagement with the hierarchical categories of skin difference is one such molar viscosity. Perhaps there is a performative element in the song about washing hands and the shouting of "No more brown skin"?—perhaps there is a sensation that the experimentation with "brown skin" is risky and creates different affects amongst the adult-bodies in the room. I also wonder how brown skin is understood in relation to skin in this encounter? Perhaps it is in the words: "Now I have brown skin instead of skin." Perhaps this encounter also highlights what M'charek (2010) refers to as "fragile differences, the kind of differences that emerge and vanish in split seconds" (p. 318) where what seemed an affirmative and affective engagement with difference was also tightly connected to something else; something that is difficult to name but that seemed to have a discernible dampening effect on the affectivity felt at the beginning of the encounter with brown skin. Perhaps this encounter illustrates how molecular lines or becomings always occur within a field of molar segmentation where "the two lines are constantly interfering, reacting upon each other, introducing into each other either a current of suppleness or a point of rigidity" (Deleuze & Guattari, 1987, p. 196).

MULTICULTURAL FIXITIES

A typical multicultural response to the encounter with brown clay might center on the recognition and acceptance of difference, and on getting identity "right":

> Several days following the encounter with brown clay, an educator shows me a book she has bought to read to the children. As I flip from page to page I see images of children in boxes with labels underneath them. I look from the labels and to the children pictured. On one page two children are contrasted in boxes, one child is labeled "dark" and next is a child labeled "light." "Ordering of bodies" I think, as a familiar unease spreads over my skin. I flip to another page where a row of children are labeled: cinnamon, tan, and coffee. I stop on another page. The image shows a brown-bodied child leaning over a piece of paper. The child is holding a paintbrush, and is painting in a brown face with black curly hair.

In this encounter, it appears that the contingent, contextual, ambiguous, and hybrid emergence of difference, as seen in becoming clay-brown-skin-girl, remains obscured by dominant static and essentialized representations of difference in multicultural pedagogies (James, 2005; Pacini-Ketchabaw, 2007). The recognition of difference in dominant multicultural early childhood pedagogies is a form of orientation that "produces and positions subjects, orchestrates meanings and practices of identity, marks bodies, and conditions political subjectivities" as it mobilizes dampening affects toward "tolerated" others, regulates conditional belonging and shapes relations of power between certain bodies (Ahmed, 2004; Brown, 2006, p. 4). The seeming innocence and neutrality of recognizing and naming difference as "dark, light, cinnamon, tan, coffee," masks the ways this acts to fix certain subjectivities—particularly in relation to creating bounded hierarchies of belonging. This imposition of identity is in disjuncture with the complexities of racialized and immigrant subjectivities such as the diverse particularities and hybridities of people of color as positioned and negotiated within and across sociocultural, linguistic, national-citizenship boundaries and other contexts (Braidotti, 2008, 2009; de Finney, 2010). Such multicultural approaches can thereby be interrogated as potential contributions to the persistence of racism in which pluralism is emphasized but systemic injustices and exclusionary practices on the basis of race, class, language are depoliticized, minimized or silenced (de Finney, 2010; Pacini-Ketchabaw, White, & Armstrong de Almeida, 2006).

The vignettes that opened this article might also be seen as examples of multicultural fixities in the emphasis on getting identity "right" and teaching acceptance of diversity through representing skin color differences (Kirova, 2008; Lipton, 2010). In the first encounter a girl child-body works hard to match her skin with multicultural markers and in the second encounter, children are instructed to mix a color that matches skin using a light cream color as the base. How does "tolerance" or "acceptance" act on the body marked as "yellow" in this encounter? How does "tolerance" circulate to shape educators' responses and to discipline bodies and orient relations (Ahmed, 2008)? Perhaps the focus on matching skin color could also be seen as a re-ordering of child-bodies along developmental lines in multicultural approaches. This pedagogical approach closes down openings to the intensities, viscosities and potentialities for lines of movement created by the naming of "yellow" skin. The focus on naming and creating shades of skin—where light skin forms the base from which children are instructed to mix their skin color in this encounter could be seen as problematic in relation to concealing racializing structures and encounters while simultaneously normalizing Whiteness, invisibilizing its role in constructions of difference (Kirova, 2008). In these events molar viscosities appear to be sedimented through static representations of difference "with every outwardly progressive gesture, which works to normalize" (Roberts & Mahtani, 2010, p. 254). Contrary to an appearance of neutrality, these gestures of acceptance and recognition in early childhood pedagogies are intensely racialized (Nxumalo, Pacini-Ketchabaw, & Rowan, 2011).

In these encounters with materials such as books, paint and markers, perhaps we can also see their active participation in material-discursive assemblages that create normative limits on what a body can do (Deleuze & Guattari, 1987); a dampening of possibilities for relational becomings including the contingent, contextual, ambiguous, and hybrid emergence of difference (James, 2005; Pacini-Ketchabaw, 2007). Bodies are subject to stabilizing forces in these encounters. While "the body is subject to the social history it has inherited and is the site in which the social norms and structures of the society are performed and confirmed," even in these stratified encounters, there appear to be leakages, contestations, escapes, and complexities—becomings that seem to elude clear explanations (Skott-Mhyre, 2008, p. 59). For instance the child-body that works to match the skin to the marker in the first encounter is not a racialized body. I wonder then how or if it is even possible to make "sense" of her final choice of a dark brown marker and the exclamation of "I got the right color!" it seems to me though, that there is "something" happening here; human and more-than-human materialities entangle and come together to matter in this encounter but clear explanations appear elusive.

I think it's important to point out that multicultural tools, such as the markers in the opening vignette present a risk; such as when the pedagogical implication to children is that they need to represent and align themselves within particular fixed and prescribed categories of difference. At the same time my intent is not a simplistic dismissal of these tools; such a dismissal is also dangerous. One only needs to look at a recent suggestion by an American conservative talk show that multicultural crayons are politically correct "pandering" to liberals to see an example of these dangers (Fox News, April 10, 2011). Rather than a solely oppositional critique or dismissal of these tools, in this article I have attempted to map how paying close attention to their affects and effects in the classroom and continually seeking new ways to disturb their potentially striating effects might offer productive possibilities. I suggest moving toward relational attunements to the unexpected, to subtleties and incoherences and relational grapplings with all kinds of materials not just those designated as "multicultural."

ON MICROPOLITICAL ACTS

By embracing partial and multiple perspectives, situated relational becomings can be seen as "form of political resistance to hegemonic, fixed, unitary and exclusionary views of subjectivity" (Braidotti, 2011, p. 58; Haraway, 1991). These disruptions of fixed identity and dualistic categorizations are intensely ethical and political events that embrace partial, fluid and contradictory constructions of subjectivity (Haraway, 1991, p. 157) and "other ways of travelling and moving: proceeding from the middle, through the middle, coming and going, rather than starting and finishing" (Deleuze & Guattari, 1987, p. 25). An important question to consider is how might an emphasis on material-discursive becomings engage with ongoing inequitable power relations? As the encounter with clay illustrates, attending to embodied encounters includes situated entanglement within the at times subtle and contradictory interconnections with flows of power (Ahmed, 2004; Berlant, 2008; Stewart, 2007). Kathleen Stewart eloquently captures this attunement to the intricacies and socio-material textures of everyday encounters as an attempt to "wrest a 'something' out of an everyday life saturated with dragging, isolating intensities of all kinds" (Stewart, 2007, p. 119). For instance, engagement with the complexities, contradictions and capriciousness through which racialization is effected on and implicated through bodies and the ways in which bodies escape these limits, needs attunement to how systemic forces might be held in place in the intensities in everyday encounters, especially in ways that might otherwise remain obscured (Nxumalo et al., 2011).

Attention to material-discursive entanglements suggests understandings of not only dampening relations that reinscribe dominant understandings, but also the potentials for new unpredictable and transformative becomings where: "the body as the realm of affectivity, is the site or sites of multiple struggles, ambiguously positioned in the reproduction of social habits, requirements and regulations and in all sorts of production of unexpected and unpredictable linkages" (Grosz, 1994, p. 181).

Attention to material-discursive relational becomings then, might be seen as micropolitical acts through creating openings for different "ways of seeing" categorical stratifications and micro processes of becoming (Haraway, 1988). Importantly, while resisting the striations of representation and the fixities of categories of difference, this perspective does not suggest a dislocation or detachment from location nor does it seek to nullify the need for productive political action based on particular situated affinities (Haraway, 1988); on the contrary it accounts for one's embodied, geopolitical, historical and temporal locations while simultaneously emphasizing their limits and seeking multiple configurations of these locations that are "partial in all of [their] guises" (Haraway, 1988, p. 586). I see this as an important move toward engaging with the nuances of exclusionary positioning and conditional conceptions of belonging, including those implied by the bounds of multiculturalism (Braidotti, 2002; Haraway, 1988). Attention to the affective resonances of encounters with difference, including the "ability of inanimate things to animate, to act, to produce effects dramatic and subtle" (Bennett, 2004, p. 351) can thus be seen as a micropolitical act. A situated micropolitical activism is an "affective politics [which] seeks the degrees of openness of any situation" and in so doing confronts inequities on their slippery, contingent, and creative effects in everyday life (Massumi, 2009, p. 7).

CONCLUSIONS: TOWARD A PEDAGOGY OF RELATIONAL ETHICS

This article has sought to consider how close attunement to relational material-discursive becomings might create movement away from representational practices and engage with the affective and unforeseen in material-discursive worlds. I have experimented with relational becomings as a way to displace the fixities created by tolerance, acceptance and recognition of difference. Relational entanglements with situated becomings seem to hold potential for unsettling abstract notions of difference and diversity and the idea that materials have fixed properties that determine what knowledge they can transmit about identity. This relational perspective centres becoming-with children and more-than-human materialities in ways that actively animate and create worlds (Pacini-Ketchabaw, forthcoming). Mobilizing considerations of difference in ways that create movement from multicultural fixities creates openings for ethical relationalities that embrace new becomings, complexities, and multiplicities.

I see productive possibilities in early childhood pedagogies that centre ethics as the ability to build and enhance relations and connections to others (Braidotti, 2009). Such a pedagogy of relational ethics "proposes an enlarged sense of inter-connection between self and others, including the non-human or 'earth' others...It is a nomadic eco-philosophy of multiple belongings" (Braidotti, 2008, p. 34). In other words relational ethics can be seen as an entangled "presence-to-the-world" (Bird, 2004, p. 213) that is open to multiple possibilities as they emerge in relationship between people, things and place. This is an important move away from prescribing what practice should be, toward engaging with particular events and encounters.

For instance, rather than pre-defined pedagogical goals or looking for what is lacking in childrens' understandings of difference, interesting questions to consider could be: what materialities and discursivities have come together to produce a particular encounter with difference (Pacini-Ketchabaw & Nxumalo, 2010)? What particular arrangements and connections between bodies, discourse and material elements can be made visible as a part of both children's and educators' race and racialization negotiations? What does racialization do in this particular encounter? How does it connect to colonialisms? How do the pedagogical materials in the classroom act and how do they connect with the emergence of racialization? What possibilities emerge for pedagogical experimentation in ways that might increase other's capacities to act—what re-arrangements and new connections to things, spaces, bodies might create something new (Grosz, 2001)? This is an ethics of relational affirmation and becomings that grapples with the complexities of working with difference from inside the "thick of things" and foregrounds productive possibilities and ethical potentialities rather than a "hierarchical and dialectical vision of Otherness or difference" (Braidotti, 2010, p. 409). Situated entanglements with events or encounters, rather than pre-determined goals might provide productive possibilities toward "ethical engagement with otherness" (Saldanha, 2006, p. 14). As the encounters I have grappled with in this article suggest, "we can be thrown into becoming by anything at all, by the most unexpected, most insignificant of things" (Deleuze & Guattari, 1987, p. 322) and we need to remain open to all kinds of creative possibilities.

NOTES

1. I use more-than-human to refer broadly to all that exceeds the human, including non-human matter, relations, meanings and understandings. In this understanding both the human and non-human are active co-constitutive participants, and the human is "no less a subject of ongoing cofabrication than any other socio-material assemblage" (Whatmore, 2006, p. 603).

2. I borrow the term viscosity from Saldanha (2006) to refer to the "sticky" effects of the intermingling of molar fixities and molecular becomings or flows in particular spaces. Molar fixities act to constrain bodies causing "temporary thickenings of interacting bodies, which then collectively become sticky, capable of capturing more bodies like them.... Under certain circumstances, the collectivity dissolves, the constituent bodies flowing freely again" (p. 18).

REFERENCES

Abu-Laban, Y. (1998). Welcome/STAY OUT: The contradiction of Canadian integration and immigration policies at the millennium. *Canadian Ethnic Studies, 30*(3), 190–211.

Ahmed, S. (2000). *Strange encounters: Embodied others in post-coloniality*. New York, NY: Routledge.

Ahmed, S. (2004). *The cultural politics of emotion*. New York, NY: Routledge.

Ahmed, S. (2008). Multiculturalism and the promise of happiness. *New Formations, 63*, 121–137.

Ang, I. (1996). The curse of the smile: Ambivalence and the "Asian" woman in Australian multiculturalism. *Feminist Review, 52*(Spring), 36–49.

Ang, I. (2001). *On not speaking Chinese: Living between Asia and the West*. London, UK: Routledge.

Bannerji, H. (2000). *The dark side of the nation: Essays on multiculturalism, nationalism and gender*. Toronto, Canada: Canadian Scholar's Press.

Barad, K. (2003). Post-humanist performativity: Toward an understanding of how matter comes to matter. *Signs: Journal of Women in Culture and Society, 28*(3), 801–833.

Barad, K. (2007). *Meeting the universe halfway: Quantum physics and the entanglement of matter and meaning*. Durham, NC: Duke University Press.

Bastian, M. (2006). Haraway's lost cyborg and the possibilities of transversalism. *Signs: Journal of Women in Culture and Society, 31*(4), 1027–1049.

Bennett, J. (2004). The force of things: Steps towards an ecology of matter. *Political Theory, 32*(3), 347–372.

Bennett, J. (2010). *Vibrant matter: A political ecology of things.* Durham, NC: Duke University Press.

Berlant, L. (2008). Thinking about feeling historical. *Emotion, Space and Society, 1*(1), 4–9.

Bird, R. D. (2004). *Reports from a wild country: Ethics for decolonization.* Sydney, Australia: University of New South Wales Press.

Braidotti, R. (1998). *Difference, diversity and nomadic subjectivity.* Retrieved from http://www.ministeriodejusticia.cl/pmg/documentos/Differencem%20diversity%20 and%20nomadic%20subjectivity.pdf.

Braidotti, R. (2002). *Metamorphoses: Towards a materialist theory of becoming.* Malden, MA: Blackwell.

Braidotti, R. (2006a). *Transpositions.* Cambridge, UK: Polity.

Braidotti, R. (2006b). Affirming the affirmative: On nomadic affectivity. *Rhizomes, 11/12*. Retrieved from http://www.rhizomes.net/issue11/braidotti.html

Braidotti, R. (2008). Of poststructuralist ethics and nomadic subjects. In M. Düwell, C. Rehmann-Sutter & D. Mieth (Eds.), *The contingent nature of life* (pp. 25–36). Dordrecht, The Netherlands: Springer.

Braidotti, R. (2009). Animals, anomalies, and inorganic others. *PMLA, 124*(2), 526–532.

Braidotti, R. (2010). Nomadism: Against methodological nationalism. *Policy Futures in Education, 8*(3–4), 408–418.

Braidotti, R. (2011). *Nomadic subjects: Embodiment and sexual difference in contemporary feminist theory* (2nd ed.). New York, NY: Columbia University Press.

Brown, W. (2006). *Regulating aversion: Tolerance in the age of identity and empire.* Princeton: Princeton University Press.

Chesters, G., & Walsh, I. (2005). Complexity and social movement(s): Process and emergence in planetary action systems. *Theory, Culture and Society, 22*(5), 187–211.

Coleman, R. (2008). The becoming of bodies. *Feminist Media Studies, 8*(2), 163–179.

de Finney, S. (2010). "We just don't know each other": Racialized girls negotiate mediated multiculturalism in a less diverse Canadian city. *Journal of Intercultural Studies, 31*(5), 471–487.

Deleuze, G., & Guattari, F. (1987). *A thousand plateaus: Capitalism and schizophrenia.* (B. Massumi, Trans.). Minneapolis, MN: University of Minnesota Press.

Dirlik, A. (2008). Race talk, race, and contemporary racism. *PMLA, 123*(5), 1363–1379.

Foucault, M. (1980). *Power/knowledge: Selected interviews and other writings 1972–1977.* New York, NY: Pantheon.

Fox News. (2011, April 10). *PC gone too far? Crayola gets color sensitive* [Video file]. Retrieved from http://video.foxnews.com/v/4636817/pc-gone-too-far-crayola-gets-color-sensitive/

Fritsch, K. (2010). Intimate assemblages: Disability, intercorporeality, and the labour of attendant care. *Critical Disability Discourse, 2*, 1–14. Retrieved from http://pi.library.yorku.ca/ojs/index.php/cdd/article/view/23854

Ghosh, R., & Abdi, A. A. (2004). *Education and the politics of difference: Canadian perspectives.* Toronto, ON, Canada: Canadian Scholars' Press.

Giroux, H. (1992). *Border crossings: Cultural workers and the politics of education.* New York, NY: Routledge.

Grosz, E. A. (1994). *Volatile bodies: Toward a corporeal feminism*. Bloomington, IN: Indiana University Press.

Grosz, E. (2001). An interview with Elizabeth Grosz by R. Ausch, R. Doane, & L. Perez. *Found Object, 9*, 1–16. Retrieved from http://web.gc.cuny.edu/csctw/found_object/text/grosz.htm

Haraway, D. (1988). Situated knowledges: The science question in feminism and the privilege of partial perspective. *Feminist Studies, 14*(3), 575–599.

Haraway, D. (1991). A cyborg manifesto: Science, technology, and socialist-feminism in the late twentieth century. *Simians, cyborgs and women: The reinvention of nature* (pp. 149–181). New York, NY: Routledge.

Haraway, D. (1992). The promises of monsters: A regenerative politics for inappropriate/d others. In L. Grossberg, C. Nelson, & P. Treichler (Eds.), *Cultural studies* (pp. 295–337). New York, NY: Routledge.

Haraway, D. (1995). Interview by Gary A. Olson. "Writing, literacy, and technology: Toward a cyborg writing." In G. A. Olson & E. Hirsch (Eds.), *Women writing culture* (pp. 45–77). New York: SUNY Press.

Haraway, D. (1997). *Modest_witness@second_millenium. FemaleMan©_meets_OncoMouse TM: Feminism and technoscience*. London, UK: Routledge.

Haraway, D. (2003). *The companion species manifesto: Dogs, people, and significant otherness*. Chicago, IL: Prickly Paradigm.

Haraway, D. (2008). *When species meet*. Minneapolis, MN: University of Minnesota Press.

Hoffman, D. M. (1996). Culture and self in multicultural education: Reflections on discourse, text, and practice. *American Educational Research Journal, 33*(3), 545–569.

Hultman, K., & Lenz Taguchi, H. (2010). Challenging anthropocentric analysis of visual data: A relational materialist methodological approach to educational research. *International Journal of Qualitative Studies in Education, 23*(5), 525–542.

James, C. E. (2005). Introduction: Perspectives on multiculturalism in Canada. In C. E. James (Ed.), *Possibilities and limitations: Multicultural policies and programs in Canada* (pp. 12–20). Halifax, NS, Canada: Fernwood.

Kirova, A. (2008). Critical and emerging discourses in multicultural education literature: A review. *Canadian Ethnic Studies, 40*(1), 101–124.

Lee, J. A., & Lutz, J. S. (2005). Introduction: Toward a critical literacy of racisms, anti-racisms, and racialization. In J. A. Lee & J. S. Lutz (Eds.), *Situating "race" and racisms in space, time, and theory* (pp. 3–29). Montreal, Canada: McGill-Queen's University Press.

Lenz Taguchi, H. (2010). *Going beyond the theory/practice divide in early childhood education: Introducing an intra-active pedagogy*. New York, NY: Routledge.

Lipton, S. R. (2010). *Diversity matters—Canadian pedagogy and the problem with being different*. (Unpublished master's dissertation). Utrecht University, Utrecht, the Netherlands. Retrieved from http://igiturarchive.library.uu.nl/student-theses/2010-1029-200241/UUindex.html

M'charek, A. (2010). Fragile differences, relational effects: Stories about the materiality of race and sex. *European Journal of Women's Studies, 17*(4), 307–322.

Mac Naughton, G. (2005). *Doing Foucault in early childhood studies: Applying poststructural ideas*. New York, NY: Routledge.

Malins, P. (2004). Machinic assemblages: Deleuze, Guattari and an ethico-aesthetics of drug use. *Janus Head, 7*(1), 84–104.

Massumi, B. (2009). Of microperception and micropolitics. *Inflexions, 3*, 1–20.

Nxumalo, F., Pacini-Ketchabaw, V., & Rowan, C. (2011). Lunch time at the child care centre: Neoliberal assemblages in early childhood education. *Journal of Pedagogy, 2*(2), 195–223.

Olsson, L. M. (2009). *Movement and experimentation in young children's learning: Deleuze and Guattari in early childhood education*. New York, NY: Taylor & Francis.

Pacini-Ketchabaw, V. (2007). Child care and multiculturalism: A site of governance marked by flexibility and openness. *Contemporary Issues in Early Childhood, 8*(3), 222–232.

Pacini-Ketchbaw, V. (Forthcoming). Crafting new relationships in child and youth care: Human-nonhuman encounters. In K. Gharabaghi & H. Skott-Myhre (Eds.), *With children and youth: Emerging theories, practices, and discussions in child and youth care work*. Waterloo, ON, Canada: Wilfrid Laurier University Press.

Pacini-Ketchabaw, V., & Nxumalo, F. (2010). A curriculum for social change: Experimenting with politics of action or imperceptibility. In V. Pacini-Ketchabaw (Ed.), *Flows, rhythms & intensities of early childhood education curriculum* (pp. 133–154). New York, NY: Peter Lang.

Pacini-Ketchabaw, V., White, J., & Armstrong de Almeida, A. E. (2006). Racialization in early childhood: A critical analysis of discourses in policies. *International Journal of Educational Policy, Research, and Practice: Reconceptualizing Childhood Studies, 7*(1), 95–113.

Razack, S., Smith, M., & Thobani, S. (Eds.). (2010). *States of race: Critical race feminism for the 21st century*. Toronto, ON, Canada: Between the Lines.

Read, J. (2009). A genealogy of Homo-Economicus: Neoliberalism and the production of subjectivity. *Foucault Studies, 6*, 25–36.

Renold, E., & Ringrose, J. (2011). Schizoid subjectivities? Re-theorizing teen girls' sexual cultures in an era of "sexualization". *Journal of Sociology, 47*(4), 389–409.

Roberts, D. J., & Mahtani, M. (2010). Neoliberalizing race, racing neoliberalism: Placing "race" in neoliberal discourses. *Antipode, 42*(2), 248–257.

Saldanha, A. (2006). Reontologizing race: The machinic geography of phenotype. *Environment and Planning D, 24*(1), 9–24.

Skott-Myhre, H. (2008). *Youth and subculture as creative force: Creating new spaces for radical youth work*. Toronto, ON, Canada: University of Toronto Press.

Skott-Myhre, K. S. G. (2012). Nomadic youth care. *International Journal of Child, Youth and Family Studies, 3*(2–3), 300–315.

Slocum, R. (2008). Thinking race through corporeal feminist theory: Divisions and intimacies at the Minneapolis farmers' market. *Social & Cultural Geography, 9*(8), 849–869.

Springgay, S. (2008). An ethics of embodiment, civic engagement and a/r/tography: Ways of becoming nomadic in art, research and teaching. *Educational Insights, 12*(2), 1–11.

Stewart, K. (2007). *Ordinary affects*. Durham, NC: Duke University Press.

Stewart, K. (2010). Atmospheric attunements. *Rubric, 1*, 1–14.
Stewart, K. (2011). Atmospheric attunements. *Environment and Planning D, 29*(3), 445–453.
Swanton, D. (2010). Flesh, metal, road: Tracing the machinic geographies of race. *Environment and Planning D, 28*(3), 447–466.
Timeto, F. (2011). Diffracting the rays of technoscience: A situated critique of representation. *Poiesis and Praxis, 8*(2–3), 151–167.
Whatmore, S. (2002). *Hybrid geographies: Natures cultures spaces*. London, UK: Sage.
Whatmore, S. (2006). Materialist returns: Practicing cultural geography in and for a more-than-human world. *Cultural Geographies, 13*(4), 600–609.

Postcolonial Entanglements: Unruling Stories

VERONICA PACINI-KETCHABAW

*School of Child and Youth Care, University of Victoria,
Victoria, British Columbia, Canada*

In this article, I use Donna Haraway's philosophy to think about postcolonial encounters between different species. I follow entangled stories of the deer/settler-child figure to trouble colonialisms and untangle the histories and trajectories that we inhabit with other species through colonial histories. I shy away from generalizations and instead grapple with complexities that ordinary stories bring as I attempt to engage in nonhegemonic versions of childhood studies.

The child care center where I work on Vancouver Island, British Columbia, is located next to a forest that is home to many indigenous species, including mule deer. The children and educators at the center love this forest and we often take nature walks through it. The sounds, smells, and sights we encounter on these walks spark many conversations throughout the day. To our delight, the deer who live in these woods visit our center regularly, approaching the chain link fence that separates them from the children. The fence is a child care licensing requirement, ostensibly to restrain the children for their own safety. In reality, it restricts the deer more than it does the children, because the children, with adult supervision, can pass through a gate to the other side.

Mature deer visit the center in the fall and winter; in the spring we greet the new fawns with excitement. We adults remind the children not to startle

---

This article emerged from my readings of Donna Haraway and, importantly, from my many long conversations with graduate students Denise Hodgins, Fikile Nxumalo, Kathleen Kummen, Deborah Thompson, Scott Kouri, Vanessa Clark, and Carol Rowan.

the deer; when a deer approaches the fence, we ask those children who are in a different room to come quickly to the window; together, we watch as the deer walk the length of the fence; we pay attention to their every movement. We are all deeply interested in the deer.

I am curious, too, about the deer's interest in coming close to the fence to look at us, to look at the children. I wonder who is watching whom and what the risks are of the intersecting gaze. What is this relationship about? What happens when two species with different but entangled histories come together? What kinds of relations are being shaped, right at that moment, between indigenous and settler[1] species? As the deer and the children look at each other, histories are enacted, lives are changed, and new possibilities are generated for responding to each other. The responsibilities we have toward the deer we look in the eyes are real and actual; they shape us as beings and require a response. We cannot innocently ignore the ways in which the deer's lives—and our own—are shaped by our intra-actions. We are in the middle of who the deer are and the deer are in the midst of who we become. For example, in the moment of the gaze, the politics of wild animals might change. Food economies might shift as we encounter the deer face to face.[2] And, as these systems are altered, we and the deer are changed forever. Does this coshaping offer possibilities for learning how to live and to become together in less violent, more "equitable" ways? What can we learn from these encounters about life in a postcolonial state?[3] How has this encounter shaped, and been shaped by, colonial imaginaries? How might this encounter undo us as well as our practices with young children?

For some time now, cultural differences and diversity have been topics of interest in child and youth studies. Much has been written about difference and diversity, both in academic circles and discussions of practice. As an example of the latter, BC's *Early Learning Framework* (Government of British Columbia, 2008) includes the following statement to describe the importance of social responsibility and diversity when working with young children:

> Children benefit from opportunities to build relationships, to learn about their own heritage and culture and that of others, and to recognize the connection between their own actions and the wider world. These activities help build the ethical foundation for social and environmental health and well-being, now and in the future. (p. 33)

Academics, in recent years, have challenged colonialisms and neocolonialisms, including Canada's colonial history and contemporary neocolonial rationalities and mentalities within the context of Canadian childhood (de Finney, Dean, Loiselle, & Saraceno, 2011; Nxumalo, Pacini-Ketchabaw, & Rowan, 2011; Pacini-Ketchabaw, 2007, 2010; Pacini-Ketchabaw, White, & Armstrong de Almeida, 2006). The intention of much of this literature has been to situate contemporary childhoods within colonial enterprises and to engage in confronting, challenging, and undoing the dominative and assimilative forces of colonialism as a historical and contemporary process. Many questions have been addressed, including these: How do racial and economic hierarchies and categories from colonial pasts persist in today's social, political, and material landscapes within the context of childhood? How are neocolonialisms activated in Canadian childhoods? And, how do they shape their spatialities and temporalities? These questions remain extremely important. In the Canadian context, the effects of colonization bleed into the present in many ways, particularly in assimilation policies and ongoing material and cultural appropriations of Canada's Indigenous peoples.

One commonality of these texts is their focus on human relations—how humans come together, what happens when differently positioned humans come together, how differences among humans function in always already differential power dynamics, and so on. These discussions have been immensely helpful in a field that for too long has paid little attention to the intricacies and subtleties of colonialisms and neocolonialisms (de Finney, Gharabaghi, Little, & Skott-Myhre, 2012). However, when I sit with the children to watch the deer through the child care center's window, I am aware that this relationship involves much more than just an innocent look. What histories are we inhabiting here? What's going on through/within our act of looking?

In this article, I want to extend the important conversations that have shifted how we think about children and social justice by exploring the kinds of encounters I related in the opening paragraphs—encounters among humans and nonhumans in postcolonial states. What happens when human and nonhuman bodies come together? Through this inquiry, I follow a curiosity in child and youth studies around nonhuman others (see Pacini-Ketchabaw, 2012, forthcoming; Pacini-Ketchabaw, Kummen, & Thompson, in press; Skott-Myhre, 2012). By looking at human/nonhuman entanglements, I argue that the troubling of multiculturalism and colonialisms (the topic of this issue) is not limited to humans, and I engage with the following question: How can we conceive a politics for troubling colonialisms in which human individuals are not necessarily the central players, but players among nonhuman others?

To engage in this politics, I grapple with practices and stories that are both political and mundane, as is the story above. I hope that through these ordinary stories I can offer a challenge for responding to our colonial histories. I draw on biologist-philosopher Donna Haraway's (1995) "bag-lady story telling" in which she notes that "stories do not reveal secrets by heroes pursuing luminous objects across and through the plot matrix of the world" (p. 71); instead, they put "unexpected partners and irreducible details into a frayed, porous carrier bag" (p. 71). In the process, bag-lady stories "do not have beginnings or ends; they have continuations, interruptions, and reformulations" (p. 71). In other words, these stories build worlds. Affrica

Taylor (2011) explains this approach to storytelling as one that "grapple[s] head-on with knotty differences—not to minimize or discount them, not to try and assimilate them, not to reduce them to exclusively human concerns, but to let them be 'irreducible'" (p. 5). The key, she asserts, is "embarking upon the practice of 'loosening up' and 'untangling' the knots, so that [we] can 'pull out the threads' and trace their connections" (p. 5).

Through storytelling, Haraway (2008) has been exploring the figure[4] of a human/dog companion-species to think about what she calls natureculture entanglements:

> We are in a knot of species coshaping one another in layers of reciprocating complexity all the way down. Response and respect are possible only in the knots, with actual animals and people looking back at each other, sticky with all their muddled histories. Appreciation of the complexity is, of course, invited. *But more is required too.* (2008, p. 42, emphasis added)

Following Haraway's call, Taylor (2011), working in early childhood studies in Australia, traces the postcolonial figuration of wombat/settler-Australian by unraveling "some of the 'sticky knots' that they present and which are quite specific to postcolonial Australian commonworlds" (p. 3). Using a similar approach, Mindy Blaise, an early childhood scholar who works in Hong Kong, maps relations between dogs in prams in postcolonial Hong Kong. Blaise wrestles with the notions of context, difference, and complexity and emphasizes the practice of making the familiar unfamiliar by taking a contact-zone perspective. She invites us to attend to the coshaping that happens between species in ordinary events and to make room for the articulations and entanglements that exist across borders. Miriam Giugni (2011), in Australia, pays attention to the chicken/settler-child figure. Giugni grapples with activism, getting entangled in the proposition of doing activism by becoming relational and generative, by gathering and questioning. She says, let's engage in "an expansive and complex practice" of taking our relationships (with human and nonhuman others) seriously (p. 6). These three scholars collectively, following Haraway's work, question how to engage in an inclusive relational ethic that is less humancentric and more worldly (Taylor, Blaise, & Giugni, 2013), how to grapple with the dilemmas that differences bring, and how to "become with." I see these directions as the "more that is required" that Haraway (2008) asks for in the quote above. I find this approach helpful for my own mappings of natureculture entanglements specific to postcolonial Canada. In these mappings, I shy away from generalizations and instead grapple with some of the complexities that mundane stories bring.

In what follows, I map relations between indigenous deer and settler Canadians. I situate this mapping in the specific relations and entanglements of the lives of young children and of deer on Vancouver Island to argue that we need analyses of postcolonial entanglements that consider all partners and relational knots. As Haraway (1997) notes, "social relationships include nonhumans as well as humans as socially...active partners" (p. 8). She reminds us that "all that is unhuman is not un-kind, outside kinship, outside the orders of signification, excluded from trading in signs and wonders" (p. 8). Through the deer/settler-child figure, I hope to offer a renewed politics for child and youth care that engages with colonialisms by looking at the entanglements of human and nonhuman others in postcolonial spaces.

Thinking with the deer/settler-child figure allows me to engage in the politics of postcolonial relations—and in the kinds of lives that postcolonial relations organize—in the nodes and knots of living together in postcolonial spaces like Vancouver Island. I am curious about the ways in which these relationships, and the power-knowledge relations they embed, materialize certain worlds and not others. I wonder about the kinds of worldings, as Haraway (1997, 2008) calls them, that are generated. I am interested in the coshaping that takes place in encounters like the ones I related above and the ones below. Referring to dogs, Haraway (2008) says that nonhuman species "have not been unchangeable animals confined to the supposedly ahistorical order of nature. Nor have people emerged unaltered from the interactions. Relations are constitutive" (p. 62). This means that all encounters somehow matter because it is through these encounters that we emerge as "historical beings, as subjects and objects to each other, precisely through the verbs of their relating" (p. 62).

DEER/SETTLER-CHILD ENTANGLEMENTS

Black- and whitetail deer and their hybrid descendants, including mule deer, have been living in North America for more than two million years. Mule deer are plentiful in many parts of Vancouver Island. Although much of their value today is aesthetic and recreational, deer meat was an important part of the First Nations diet for thousands of years and, in many cases, still is. Deer were also an important link between First Nations and White Europeans. Not only did the European colonizers depend on deer meat to survive, they also "killed many in order to provision trading posts and also exported deer hides with other furs. In the late 1800s, market hunters supplied mining camps with deer meat" (British Columbia Ministry of Environment, Lands, and Parks, n.d., p. 5). Deer have taught us visitors in the territory we call North America something about this land. They have also participated in our capital accumulation and empire building. Since World War II, recreational hunting and tourism have boosted the value of deer in the North American economy to millions of dollars. Today, we have a profitable hunting industry built around killing deer, and we also showcase them to tourists who are delighted to see frightened deer in our beautiful forest parks.

Our relationship with the deer becomes a bit more "testy" when we encounter them in our gardens. Simply put, we don't like deer to eat the flowers and vegetables we have worked so hard to grow after long, bare winters. Living beside a ravine, I encounter these creatures all the time in my little garden. They love the roses and, even more, my neighbors' figs. There is always someone in the neighborhood who comes to the rescue and ensures that the deer go back to the ravine where they belong: in nature. Some of the neighbors have enclosed their gardens, or parts of them, with fences to deter unwanted visitors.

Fences, children, and deer form interesting assemblages. For example, the fence that separates the child care center from the deer becomes a material/semiotic marker of hyperseparation between the "civilized" domesticated world of the child and educator on one hand and the "uncivilized" indigenous world of the deer on the other. On one side of the fence, we find the manicured child care center playground, which has been recently renovated to meet "natural playground" stipulations. On the other side, the grass grows wild and huge pine trees provide shade. As Lesley Instone (2010) notes, "the fence is an arresting delineation of native/non-native, introduced/indigenous, colonial/postcolonial" reflecting material and discursive practices of "neat/messy, familiar/unfamiliar, accessible/inaccessible" for the children, educators, and deer (p. 93). The fence does the work of boundary maintenance—although these boundaries become blurry, as I explain later on.

These stories might imply that our relationship with deer is sometimes violent. Foucault (1977) would tell us, however, to look at points of resistance. Better yet, we could look at our coshaping (Haraway, 2008) with the deer. In my research for this article, I came across the following quote on an American hunting website that explains how we and deer emerged together:

> The early and ongoing colonization of America did little to diminish the whitetail's presence. To the contrary, it helped increase and broaden deer populations. Before colonization, our forests were large, dense and contiguous. As humans cleared the land, deer moved into diverse new habitats and flourished. Deer fed and mated in open fields and cutovers. Nearby woodlands provided cover and warmth. Today, as the suburbanization of America continues, whitetail herds continue to grow and thrive in small, broken habitats. (Outdoor Adventures Network, 2012, para. 2)

These stories make me wonder about living with difference. How are different species entangled together? How do we shape each other? Can this shaping be done in a respectful way? The deer who look at us (and we who look at the deer) are part of colonial conquest, trade, economies, ecologies, resistances, tourism, and entertainment (Haraway, 2008). How do we learn to live together in this "knotty" relation in less violent ways? Following Haraway (2008), I suggest that we take these questions and complexities seriously as we think about our own demands on the Other, on those whose lands and lives we have come to impose ourselves. Let's ask how we got here together and how we have shaped each other's lives and histories.

Many stories speak specifically about the entanglement of children's and deer's lives. Walt Disney's *Bambi* (1942) provides a productive space to think about the place deer occupy in the North American settler imaginary, and it is through this film that many North American children have established an affectionate relationship with deer. Hastings (1996), in "Bambi and the Hunting Ethos," describes the film's affectionate tone:

> [The film] presents an idyllic forest without active carnivores. One could argue that the movie's real theme is love in all its varieties, as the opening song, "Love Is a Song" suggests. Bambi opens with an evocation of maternal love, as the newborn fawn nestles against his mother's side while the smaller animals gather to greet the "young prince." The early part of the film shows Bambi's first year of life and primarily develops the relationship between mother and fawn, along with childhood (same-sex) friendships. The second part of the film, following the death of Bambi's mother, develops a more mature love theme, as Bambi and his friends each pair off with an appropriate female, and his developing relationship with the doe Faline takes center stage. At the end, the cycle of love relationships is completed as Bambi and Faline become parents themselves. The peaceable kingdom of the opening is recapitulated as Bambi's twin fawns become the focus of adoration by the smaller animals, and the film ends with Bambi's father ceding the rule of the forest to his son. (para. 3)

This film is far from innocent, however, and we know that how children relate to troubling messages in films like *Bambi* is not straightforward (Tobin, 2000). In *Bambi*, as in many other Disney stories, we find a gestating space of corporate interests, colonization of desires, idealized versions of North America, racialized and gendered discourses, and much, much more (Kasturi, 2002). Since *Bambi*, hunting will never be seen the same way. And this, of course, brings material consequences for those who depend on deer as an important part of their diets. Whose meals are more important? These are the kinds of "knotty" spaces that Haraway (2008) suggests we take head-on instead of just analyzing them from a distance. Further, these knotty spaces "require action and respect," but without a final "resolution" (p. 300).

In addition to stories like *Bambi*, direct encounters with deer further complexify the deer/settler relationship. Deer occupy an ambivalent place in the lives of many Vancouver Island children. As this article's opening alludes, children do have regular "friendly" encounters with deer through the window or the fence. The fence separates the children and educators from the deer, but it also allows for boundary blurrings and crossings that help to undo the categorical divisions it creates between colonized/colonizer and human/nonhuman. Children and educators alike enjoy their special excursions into the forest. These are now even easier through the gate that was installed during the playground renovations. Crossing the fence gives the children pleasure and a sense of novelty as they excitedly hope for encounters with the animals and trees they know live there, including deer. These fence crossings and encounters, as I argue later, have much potential for learning to live in postcolonial spaces.

But children's encounters with deer are not always as pleasant as the ones that take place at the child care center. My doctoral student, Denise Hodgins, tells of her son being terrified of deer, specifically of an eventual deer attack. Wild animals are often feared in places like Vancouver Island. It's mostly cougars and bears that are feared, but reports of deer attacks have recently gained some momentum. It is common to hear in the news about the need to push deer out of urban areas as they become more and more accustomed to humans. Deer, the story goes, have become aggressive, not only toward humans but also toward pets.

Unlike *Bambi* or stories of deer attack, other encounters and stories compel me to look at the deer that pass the child care center—and the deer that eat my roses, and the deer that are written about on hunting websites—from another vantage point. These stories raise different kinds of questions. A few months ago, I heard an interview on CBC radio with wildlife photographer Isobel Springett (2012), who lives on Vancouver Island and has seen a bond develop between two species. Springett's Great Dane, Kate, and a fawn called Pippin have become companion species. As Haraway (2008) would say, they have become political companions, messmates at the table who are engaged in a "dance linking kin and kind" (p. 17) and simultaneously making a mess out of categories. What made this story a sensation in Canadian news is that Springett's actions of "domesticating" a wild animal are deemed unethical and illegal. A manager for the British Columbia Society for the Prevention of Cruelty to Animals (BC SPCA) contends: "The susceptibility of a young fawn being imprinted like that has been well-documented, and it's really inappropriate because it sets the deer up for a hard life.... That deer is not going to have a wild life and it has no idea what predators are" (Clarke, 2011, para. 10). Springett has clarified that Pippin is not really a domesticated wild animal. She has learned to do what all wild animals do, but she has also learned to be in a close, loving relationship with Kate.

The story I want to tell about Kate and Pippin, though, is the one that many children on Vancouver Island are likely to encounter—*Kate & Pippin: An Unlikely Love Story* (Springett, 2012), a picture book written by Springett's brother and illustrated by Springett herself (see http://kateandpippin.com). This tale begins with a fawn who lies on the ground for three days awaiting her mother, who never comes back. After listening to the fawn crying, Isobel carried her home, where Pippin and Kate encountered each other. After gazing at each other, "Kate gave the young deer a nuzzle and a lick" (p. 6) and a new and unlikely relationship began—a relationship in which both parties had to figure out what role to play and how to play it. The relationship changed both Kate and Pippin forever. At the end, Pippin returns to the forest and becomes an independent deer, but she never abandons her friend Kate, whom she visits regularly.

There are other stories like this one, as my colleague Shanne McCaffrey knows well. Her cat Orono and Nora, a deer, are getting to know each other in the old cedar grove in Shanne's back yard.

Haraway (2008) suggests that these stories can act as "microcosms" for thinking about both "how to inherit the history" of gaze with the deer and "how to shape becoming with them" in a potentially productive way (p. 105). Taylor (2011) warns us that these are not merely innocent stories of a cute deer with a caring dog. Instead, these stories bring species face to face to encounter their relationships head-on. They do not anthropomorphize deer and dogs "as infantilized humans in furry suits" like many children's stories do. Nor is this "a domestication story that celebrates human mastery of nature" (p. 8). These stories, Taylor says, are "queer kin stor[ies] of knotty [deer/settler] co-existence of an unexpected and opportunistic kind" (p. 8) that allow us to think about "cross-species relational grapplings that are the direct consequence of settler practices that disturb and endanger" lives (p. 8). Taylor suggests that, "by offering children the paradoxically mundane-yet-unusual details of such daily [multispecies] grapplings," these kinds of stories incite children to ask "What else is going on here?" and to be curious about the specific circumstances that bring species "together as queer kin in the first place" (p. 8). Simultaneously, these stories create spaces "for children to think about how they live with the differences of more-than-human others in their own commonworlds" (p. 8).

In the case of the children at the child care center, the fence becomes, as Instone (2010) says, "a line of communication, not just a division": "Far from being stationary and fixed the fence is a dynamic space of contestation and interaction that activates all manner of work" (p. 97). The fence, as contested space, might "enact shifting relations between native/non-native, nature/culture" that are unknown (Instone, 2010, p. 98). The fence was constructed to prevent children's encounters with the "wild," the "outside." But as it stands there, it also presents a way to relate differently to the "wild" and the "native," and to the deer that inhabit the forest. Instone (2010), referring to fences that "protect" grasslands in Royal Park in Australia, writes:

> Back at the fence we can understand a different relation than that of division and dualism, instead considering the fence as enacting an encounter, a space of conjunction and the possibility of a sideways

movement across and along. From this perspective, other forms of connectivity more attuned to uncertainty, context, situation and multiplicity, more open to earthly others and lively encounters, may serve us better. (p. 110)

The fence is not just one thing; it has become entangled in human/nonhuman histories and networks without clear boundaries. Surprising possibilities might emerge from these entanglements from which we might learn new ways to live together in postcolonial spaces. As Instone says, these entanglements might "nudge us towards an ethics of co-transformation" that is full of uncertainties (p. 111).

HUMAN/NONHUMAN POSTCOLONIAL ENCOUNTERS

In this article I have endeavored to tell stimulating and challenging stories of postcolonial entanglements between human and nonhuman species. These stories, I believe, are worth telling as we attempt to engage in nonhegemonic child and youth studies (de Finney et al., 2012). Threading Haraway's texts and learning from her entanglements with nonhuman species, I have outlined some ideas about what more might be required (Haraway, 2008, p. 42) when we think about how we might live our lives with children in postcolonial spaces in "responsible" ways. Haraway reminds us that every encounter makes us worldly and connects us with layers and layers of local and global histories and webs. Once we have come face to face with the species we live with, "obligations and possibilities for response change" (p. 97). Haraway puts it beautifully:

> Like it or not, flesh-to-flesh and face-to-face, I have inherited these histories through touch [or vision] with my dogs, and my obligations in the world are different because of that fact. That's why I have to tell these stories—to tease out the personal and collective response required now, not centuries ago. Companion species cannot afford evolutionary, personal, or historical amnesia. (p. 98)

Here, I believe, are lessons for those of us working with children. Perhaps we can begin to pay attention to children's encounters with nonhuman species so that we can find ways to respond to histories of colonization. "How are we going to respond to these mundane encounters?" might be the question we need to ask and grapple with.

If we tell these mundane stories, Haraway writes, we might begin to remember other stories—"stories about immigration, indigenous worlds, work, hope, love, play; and the possibility of cohabitation through reconsidering sovereignty and ecological developmental naturecultures" (p. 98). Deborah Bird Rose (2004) refers to an "ethics for decolonization" as one that "work[s] with harm, twisting violence back into flourishing and life-affirming relationships" (p. 8). This is an ethics about connections that is "situated in bodies and in time and in place" (p. 8). Rose writes:

> The ethical challenge of decolonization illuminates a ground of powerful presence. Against domination it asserts relationality, against control it asserts mutuality, against hyperseparation it asserts connectivity, and against claims that rely on an imagined future it asserts engaged responsiveness in the present. (p. 213)

If we tell these situated stories and pay attention to how we are entangled in a web of histories, we may begin to see our relationships with children differently. If we ourselves or children themselves are not seen as the center of our troubles, but instead we become more worldly, then we might find possibilities for new worlds and new relations to emerge. Looking at the deer who visit our playgrounds and following the stories that connect and entangle us with them cannot but make us "more worldly, more enmeshed in webs of history that demand response today" (p. 100). These encounters generate meanings and generate us and the deer and multiple species. More importantly, these encounters coshape us all and our histories. There is nothing simple about these entanglements. No generalizations can be made as to how we practice, what we do, or how we respond. Each encounter requires a different kind of attention. There are no shortcuts for any of us. Haraway (2008) writes: "There is no happy ending to offer, no conclusion to this ongoing entanglement, only a sharp reminder that anywhere one really looks actual living [nonhumans] are waiting to guide humans into contested worldings" (p. 39).

We need to figure out, together, how we want to live as heterogeneous species that are now entangled in colonized common worlds.

NOTES

1. The term "settler" refers to, as Deborah Bird Rose (2004) notes, "the conquerors and their descendants" (p. 2). It implies invasion or occupation of lands where people were already residing; in particular, it refers to settler colonialism and European colonial expansion.

2. Levinas's (1969) ethics of face-to-face relations makes us answerable to the call of the other: "In the face-to-face relationship the individual experiences being obligated before the Other, and is called to response and responsibility in relating to the person who is other than himself or herself" (Cook & Young, 2004, p. 343). I argue that this ethics can be extended to human-nonhuman relations (see Rose, 2004).

3. My use of the term "postcolonial state," both here and throughout, does not denote the end of colonization. I use the term to be attentive to colonized, racialized, and gendered histories entwined with state formation (see Jiwani, 2006; Razack, Smith, & Thobani, 2010).

4. Haraway (1997) uses figures as reclamations that have "real" meanings, a kind of personification and, simultaneously, *a making of knowledge*. Figures are not about representations or significations, but they can be inhabited "to map universes of knowledge, practice and power" (p. 11). Figures, Haraway (1997) says, "involve at least some kind of displacement that can trouble identifications and certainties"; they "can be condensed maps of contestable worlds" (p. 11). Claudia Casteneda (2002) writes:

This concept of figuration makes it possible to describe in detail the process by which a concept or entity is given a particular form—how it is figured—in ways that speak to the making of worlds. To use figuration as a descriptive tool [not as representation] is to unpack the domains of practice and significance that are built into each figure. A figure, from this point of view, is the simultaneously material and semiotic effect of specific practices. Understood as figures, furthermore, particular categories of existence can also be considered terms of their uses—what they "body forth" in turn. Figuration is thus understood here to incorporate a double force: constitutive effect and generative circulation. (p. 3)

REFERENCES

Blaise, M. (2011, October). *Grappling with contact zones of species assemblages: Dogs/humans, children/adults.* Paper presented at 19th Reconceptualizing Early Childhood Education Conference "Politics of Care: Sharing Knowledges, Love and Solidarity," University of East London, UK.

British Columbia Ministry of Environment, Lands, & Parks. (n.d.). *Mule and black-tailed deer in British Columbia.* Retrieved from: http://www.env.gov.bc.ca/wld/documents/muledeer.pdf

Castaneda, C. (2002). *Figurations: Child, bodies, worlds.* London, UK: Duke University Press.

Clarke, B. (2011, September 20). A dog and the deer who's dear to her become Internet sensations. *The Globe and Mail.* Retrieved from http://www.theglobeandmail.com/news/national/british-columbia/a-dog-and-the-deer-whos-dear-to-her-become-internet-sensations/article2173831/

Cook, P., & Young, J. (2004). Face-to-face with children. *Journal of Curriculum Studies, 36*(3), 341–360.

de Finney, S., Dean, M., Loiselle, E., & Saraceno, J. (2011). All children are equal, but some are more equal than others: Minoritization, structural inequities, and social justice praxis in residential care. *International Journal of Child, Youth and Family Studies, 2*(3–4), 361–384.

de Finney, S., Gharabaghi, K., Little, J. N., & Skott-Myhre, H. (2012). Conversations on "Conversing in Child and Youth Care." *International Journal of Child, Youth and Family Studies, 3*(2–3), 128–145.

Foucault, M. (1977). *Discipline and punish: The birth of the prison.* New York, NY: Vintage.

Giugni, M. (2011, October). Breakfast "with" the chicken: Worldliness as another kind of activism in early childhood. Paper presented at 19th Reconceptualizing Early Childhood Education Conference "Politics of Care: Sharing Knowledges, Love and Solidarity," University of East London, UK, October 25–29.

Government of British Columbia. (2008). *British Columbia early learning framework.* Victoria, BC, Canada: Ministry of Education.

Haraway, D. (1995). Otherwordly conversations, terran topics, local terms. In V. Shiva & N. Moser (Eds.), *Biopolitics: A feminist and ecological reader on biotechnology* (pp. 69–92). London, UK: Palgrave Macmillan.

Haraway, D. (1997). *Modest_witness@Second_Millennium.FemaleMan©_Meets_Onco Mouse^{TM}: Feminism and technoscience.* New York, NY: Routledge.

Haraway, D. (2008). *When species meet*. Minneapolis, MN: University of Minnesota Press.

Hastings, A. W. (1996). 'Bambi and the hunting ethos. *Journal of Popular Film and Television, 24*, 53–59. Retrieved from http://www.questia.com/PM.qst?a=o&d=94295827

Instone, L. (2010). Encountering native grasslands: Matters of concern in an urban park. *Australian Humanities Review, 49*, 91–117.

Jiwani, J. (2006). *Discourses of denial: mediations of race, gender and violence*. Vancouver, BC, Canada: University of British Columbia Press.

Kasturi, S. (2002). Constructing childhood in a corporate world: Cultural studies, childhood, and Disney. In G. Cannella & J. Kincheloe (Eds.), *Kidworld: Childhood studies, global perspectives and education* (pp. 39–58). New York, NY: Peter Lang.

Levinas, E. (1969). *Totality and infinity: An essay on exteriority*. Pittsburgh, PA: Duquesne University Press.

Nxumalo, F., Pacini-Ketchabaw, V., & Rowan, C. (2011). Lunch time at the child care center: Neoliberal assemblages in early childhood education. *Journal of Pedagogy, 2*(2), 195–223.

Outdoor Adventures Network. (2012). *Deer habitat*. Retrieved from http://www.myoan.net/huntingart/deer_habit.html

Pacini-Ketchabaw, V. (2007). Child care and multiculturalism: A site of governance marked by flexibility and openness. *Contemporary Issues in Early Childhood, 8*(3), 222–232.

Pacini-Ketchabaw, V. (2012). Acting with the clock: Clocking practices in early childhood. *Contemporary Issues in Early Childhood, 13*(2), 154–160.

Pacini-Ketchabaw, V. (Forthcoming). Crafting new relationships in child and youth care: Human-nonhuman encounters. In K. Gharabaghi & H. Skott-Myhre (Eds.), *With children and youth: Emerging theories, practices, and discussions in child and youth care work*. Waterloo, ON, Canada: Wilfrid Laurier University Press.

Pacini-Ketchabaw, V., Kummen, K., & Thompson, D. (In press). Making developmental knowledge stutter and stumble: Continuing pedagogical explorations with collective biography. In V. Pacini-Ketchabaw & L. Prochner (Eds.), *Resituating Canadian early childhood education*. New York, NY: Peter Lang.

Pacini-Ketchabaw, V., with Nxumalo, F. (2010). A curriculum for social change: experimenting with politics of action or imperceptibility. In V. Pacini-Ketchabaw (Ed.), *Flows, rhythms, and intensities of early childhood education curriculum* (pp. 133–154). New York, NY: Peter Lang.

Pacini-Ketchabaw, V., White, J., & Armstrong de Almeida, A. E. (2006). Racialization in early childhood: A critical analysis of discourses in policies. *International Journal of Educational Policy, Research, and Practice: Reconceptualizing Childhood Studies, 7*(1), 95–113.

Razack, S., Smith, M., & Thobani, S. (2010). *States of race: Critical race feminism for the 21st century*. Toronto, ON, Canada: Between the Lines.

Rose, D. B. (2004). *Reports from a wild country: Ethics for decolonization*. Sydney, Australia: University of New South Wales Press.

Skott-Myhre, K. (2012). Nomadic youth care. *International Journal of Child, Youth, and Family Studies, 3*(2–3), 300–315.

Springett, M. (2011). *Kate & Pippin: An unlikely love story*. Toronto, ON, Canada: Penguin.

Taylor, A. (2011, October). *Haraway's method: Earthy grapplings and worldly visions*. Paper presented at 19th Reconceptualising Early Childhood Education Conference "Politics of Care: Sharing Knowledges, Love and Solidarity," University of East London, UK, October 25–29.

Taylor, A., Blaise, M., & Giugni, M. (2013). Haraway's "bag lady story-telling": Relocating childhood and learning within a "post-human landscape." *Discourse: Studies in the Cultural Politics of Education, 34*(1).

Tobin, J. (2000). *"Good guys don't wear hats": Children's talk about the media*. New York, NY: Teachers College Press.

Reconceptualizing Multicultural Discourse as Shifting Geographies

J.N. LITTLE and M. WALKER
Department of Child and Youth Studies, University of Victoria, Victoria, British Columbia, Canada

The authors come together as student and instructor to explore the limitations of learning and teaching multicultural practice in Child and Youth Care. Specifically, they posit that models available to undergraduate students are limited in their foci on norm-centric orientation and static singularity. In response, they conceptualize a post-multicultural pedagogy as geography, whose maps and territories are to be contested.

My partner requests one simple gift for her birthday: a world map. Large enough to fill the wall behind the stereo that pumps out CBC every morning. "I don't want to buy you a map," I say, "because it will be outdated in one breath, one war, one peace agreement." She replies: "maps show the sentiments of a political reality and the boundaries of resentment." (D. Loubardeas, personal communication, May 13, 2012)

Maps are problematic—they demarcate the boundaries of what can be known, what is unknown; what has been taken, what can be taken. What we see, as organized "truth," is marred by colonizing practices, violence, and displacement. In response to constrained mapping, geographies morph, resist and evolve. This can result in cultural "enclaves" debated recently on the CBC (*On the Coast*, 2012), or it may result in resisting what is considered fixed or permeable boundaries.

Csikszentmihalyi (1993) reflected "we bring up children to take their places in a culture that in reality, no longer exists" (p. 276). We were inspired to write this piece based on what we witness in post-secondary education—proposing maps of cultural competence that do not match what students encounter. As Korzybski (1958) famously declared "the map is not the territory" (p. 750). Multicultural educational initiatives are similar to maps—they demarcate the territory but do not deterritoralize it. We see Korzybski's idea as a helpful parallel in critiquing how diversity as multiculturalism is taught, discussed and not taught and discussed in our subjective Child and Youth Care (CYC) educational contexts. In this article, we will explore the problematic assumptions embedded within the use of "multicultural" as it pertains to curriculum delivery, the tension of privileging social location as reflexive praxis, and propose decolonizing pedagogy through the lens of geography.

WHO'S MULTICULTURALISM?

For those of us who live in Canada, multicultural policy and practices are often lived experiences of violence that have continuous, problematic articulations of social location, inclusion, and conceptions of "the other" (Ellsworth, 1992; Garcia, 2002; Thompson & Tyagi, 1993). As Bell (1993) not so-tongue-in-cheek reflects:

> A thousand years from now, anthropologists of their thirty-first-century successors will wonder. Pouring over the recorded remains of what was the United States, they will search for reasons. "How," they will ask, "could so great a nation with so many advantages over its outside adversaries allow itself to be destroyed from within?" In search of answers, social scientists will undoubtedly discover that ours was a society that preached inclusiveness and equality while vigorously practicing an ever more pernicious and ultimately destructive discrimination that disadvantaged all those not affiliated with mainstream, upper-class Whiteness. (p. ix)

While we are referencing the Multiculturalism Act (Canadian Multiculturalism Act (R.S.C. 1985, c.24 (4th Supp)) in Canada, and Bell (1993) is referencing the educational trajectory of the United States, the result is one of the same: assimilation and tokenism. Under this banner of multiculturalism, set on the ambiguous stones of federal and educational policies, come forth ideas of niceness and tolerance actualized as politically correctness. Of course, in time the term diversity has surpassed multiculturalism as linguistic currency, but in our experience this does not radically change how such differences are approached and the enduring challenges they present. We remain vexed, like Shapiro (1995) who states:

> Justifying pedagogical strategies purported to have revolutionary intent with such terms as liberation, equality, and democracy is in essence constructing new variation of the same theme of 'enlightened' development, and no radical shift of liberatory social practice ever seems to come of them. (p. 7)

The dialogues we experience around diversity in the classroom as student and instructor are ones that reflect a necessity to be nice and a near paralysis to not be offensive (Bemak & Chung, 2008), which is perhaps a hangover of ambiguous policy statements including the idea to "advance multiculturalism throughout Canada in harmony to the national commitment to the official languages of Canada" (Canadian Multiculturalism Act). In other words: let's talk about inclusion in our own official paradigms. Diversity is loudly celebrated to distract from the echoes of its shadow. Linell, Bansel, Ellwood, and Gannon (2008) reflect:

> More than a call to say nice things it is also a call to remain silent, to not say the unsayable, the messy, the difficult, the unpleasant. It is an aesthetics of speech that prefers harmonious melody over discord. It is an aesthetics of speech that contains within it an ethic, an ethic of harm minimization, of preservation of goodwill and approval, of self-preservation of the Other. It also implies an ethic of censorship and silence: Do not speak the unspeakable! But might we still think the unthinkable? (p. 301)

As student and instructor, we are painfully aware of how the ethic embedded in multicultural discourses creates disconnections, anxieties and artificial borders. The language of inclusion in itself creates an environment of isolation and exclusion. By creating inclusive pedagogical and practice environments, we are overtly creating a norm to which the other can be included. By virtue of the gracious dominate norm, the other is afforded concessions so that they may be included. In our interpretation of what is implicit in multicultural policy we see a norm that, under the guise of graciousness, dominates the non-dominant with its own ambitions and aspirations to appear heterogeneous.

GROOMING MULTICULTURAL SUBJECTS

Part of this hospitality afforded and/or affronted includes the ways in which we groom citizens, CYC practitioners included. For example, Zipin (2003) asserts that:

> More or less unconsciously, each person actively embodies subjective dispositions for sensing (1) "self" as distinct from "others" within a complex

identity nexus; (2) one's centrality or marginality in relation to rules of ethics and perception that define a "normal" self-norms that are partial historical constructions of "truth," passed off as timeless universal verities; and (3) styles of behavior that is one's distinctive "nature" as raced, sexed, classed, or otherwise identified subject, to perform in relation to dominant norms. (p. 316)

The discursive processes of self and other as they relate to processes of sexualization, gender, racialization and class are clearly evident in the educational process, despite our attempts under the multicultural agenda to unseat them. How we come to understand our subject/subjugated positions in our CYC training, then, becomes the map taken forward into practice. As Zipin (2003) reflects above, these maps of experience demarcate what become the stories you tell of yourself and of others. As humans we are deeply impressionable and vulnerable in the face of a story, even in the face of the stories we tell about ourselves (Adichie, 2009).

As with Corson (1998), we recognize that:

Dominant people are trying to work out in advance, from their own interests as dominant individuals, what arrangements would be chosen by other people whose interests may not be readily understood by anyone who is not from the relevant class, gender, race or culture. Of course, this point is very relevant to present-day schools, which are filled with students from diverse backgrounds, but where teachers and administrators are rarely in a position to understand the real interests of the diverse communities they serve. (p. 11)

Likewise, in CYC, the development and delivery of curriculum is informed by dominant cultural orientations that mimic both the privilege of the curriculum writer(s) and also the prevailing theoretical preferences of the field. Specifically, the latter frames how identity, location and self-reflection on diversity are taken up-or assumed to be fixed tactics of practice. In some regards, the "internationalization" or "diversifying" of curriculum is merely palimpsest.[1] We argue that these a priori approaches to multicultural initiatives not only rarely represent diverse interests (i.e., what is offered in curriculum) but also silence actual experiences in relation to dominance. For example, Schick and St. Denis (2005) state that, "when racism is recast as a problem of 'cultural difference' instead of an everyday experience, the solutions take on particular forms that serve to obscure the systemic and structural relations of racial domination" (p. 306). Racialised difference is replaced by the term of cultural difference and the discussion around racism is erased. As Zerbe Enns and Forrest (2005) claim "promoting [s] a tourist or an add and stir approach to diversity" (p. 17, emphasis in original), pedagogy becomes a process of understanding difference and compensating for cultural divergence by comparing to a White norm (Schick and St. Denis, 2005).

MULTICULTURALISM AS AN ISSUE OF "RACE"

In our experience as a student and teacher on unceeded territory, "race" as a cultural construct, paradoxically the most avoided and referenced aspect of diversity in the classroom. Whiteness is not often talked about in our experience of education and schools and consequently is centered as the invisible norm to which all visible differences are compared (Schick & St. Denis, 2005). As illustrated by the recently debated one hundred dollar bill in Canada[2]

A discourse of cultural difference denies the power relations on which racial privilege and inequality depend. When racism is denied the conversation about it is easily replaced by a celebration of diversity, heroes and roles models. "The celebration of heritage and heroism not only maintains difference but also allows a multicultural Canada to congratulate itself on achieving tolerance" (Schick & St. Denis, 2005, p. 307). This tolerance, of course, is not limited to racial identity but any one of the multiple identity markers we bring into the classroom. Tsolidis (2001) suggests that:

> Teachers have an obligation to assist in the construction of schools as spaces which allow students to contest, negotiate and recreate cultural identifications. We should not expect these cultural identifications to be familiar to us. Indeed if they were familiar, they would not be new. (p. 126)

While we anticipate most CYC practitioners would agree with Tsolidis's championing of multiplicity, Roy (2003) reflects that "[t]here is only increasing pressure on institutions to find ways of managing difference that keeps things evermore the same, resulting in deep frustration for those on the margins" (p. 33, emphasis in original). This difference is managed through disciplining subjects through multicultural policy and habits of speech that leak into practice. Training programs may be considered essential to creating competent CYC practitioners, "but from the very moment the practitioners use the academic system to build the field its already structured organizations and venues act to format their activities" (Messer-Davidow, 2002, p. 129).

SELF LOCATION OR SELFISH LOCATION?

Difference, in our experience, is managed through the pedagogical imperative of self-location. How do you criticize conventional declarations of social location and concurrently enact them? In many respects, we are both products of our training, advocacy alliances, and education in that acknowledgment of such is expected and respected. We also anticipate that readers may be curious to know who has invited themselves into your course pack or into your electronic device(s). We may be invited or not. We may at best, be welcomed roommates; at worse, guests who overstay their welcome. But we cannot anticipate which.

We offer what we both consider as critical to our self locating narratives. In our first drafting of this article, we offered this first as a means to establish from whence we were writing. Upon reflection, however, we have opted to use these narratives as a means to address what we find so limiting in creating "transcendent" conversations regarding multiculturalism, social location and praxis.

Dr. Little

There is a lot of power in how you name yourself. There is a lot of power in what others name you. I am both and more. For example, by virtue of including Dr. in my introduction, I state my privilege. By virtue of initials, I make you guess, if you do not know me, to name me female, male, both or neither. If I introduce my nickname, you are privy to a certain chronological chapter of my life, and may continue to question my gender based on connotation of common names. Yet the point of naming one's social location is not to make a mystery, but rather certainty. There is an implicit shortcut that occurs when we acknowledge, through language, who we are. On the one hand, I ask my students to do this so as to recognize what unacknowledged privilege they come with or what unacknowledged knowledge(s) they are bringing forth (you might notice both are binaries). At the same time, there is a palpable tension in the classroom, the conference room, the practice space where acknowledgment of social location allows the "other" to put you on the map of multiculturalism. If you are such a geographer, then it might also be of benefit to acknowledge that I am a White, queer femme settler who lives on Coast Salish and Strait Salish territories which is also known as Victoria, British Columbia. I make my living as a contract worker who collages instructional, writing, and practice pieces together.

Mattie Walker

In writing, the privilege within my name is not as salient as it might be. I do not have letters before or after my name denoting my status within the inner circle of academia; however, these letters are on their way. I neither have an overtly masculine name nor a strikingly feminine one. I wonder if explicitly stating who I am puts more value on my statements or less. Does announcing who I am and where I come from do my story and opinion justice? Does admitting who I am plant myself in a place of humility or a place of superiority? How can one line about myself tell you enough to know me? As I lay this before you, you will see that I am an undergraduate student, that I am a White Canadian and that I am living and studying in Victoria, British Columbia, on the unceded land of the Coast Salish people. By locating myself on our metaphorical map of social and cultural location has the value in my opinion been justified or guaranteed to impact you in profound and moving ways? No. By locating myself as a White undergrad that is choosing to voice my opinions on issues of "multiculturalism" in CYC have I excused myself from the responsibility that comes with my words? No. As an undergraduate, I am privy to the teachings of the more experienced and the voices of the students. The conversation(s) of White privilege, difference, diversity and multiculturalism in practice is woven in and around the various pieces of course work and the comments of my peers—I have listened, I have critiqued and I have questioned. With my White privilege, my higher educated status, and other aspects of my social location, I arguably have the power to stay out of the conversation but as a new voice in the field I feel as though I am already a part of it and must continue the dialogue.

Recognition of Self

Pillow (2003) reflects that there are four components to reflexive strategies: "reflectivity as recognition of self; reflexivity as recognition of other; reflexivity as truth; reflexivity as transcendence" (p. 181). While her thesis is particularly targeting qualitative research, it can be aptly applied to pedagogical initiatives. For example, our narrations above speak to the first category of her reflexive strategies, recognition of self. In our experiences as student and instructor, this is, unfortunately, where reflexivity begins and ends. In no way do we place blame on those who enact this localizing but rather suggest that the multicultural policies and pedagogical imperatives discussed previously demand it. It is our challenge to expand it.

Ball (n.d.) states that people are "culturally complicated" and that when educating practitioners working in multicultural contexts there is a united goal toward equity and dignity for all; however, there continues to be an us versus them problem to learning about cultural differences. We believe, along with others in this volume, the focus needs to move away from becoming "competent" in another culture outside of one's own and move toward a more self-reflexive and fluid practice, where practitioners are keenly aware of their own shifting and inscribed identities, locations and cultures that they bring into a relational moment and the history that comes with them (Ball, n.d.). This is not to suggest the promotion of cultural naval gazing. Lather (1991) describes reflexivity as "those stories which bring the teller of the tale back into the narrative, embodied, desiring, investing in a variety of often contradictory privileges and struggles" (p. 129).

Unfortunately, in our experience, it is the contradictory piece that, due to its complexity, gets left out of the conversation. Instead, students and practitioners polarize their social locations despite asserting their wish to bridge entrenched identity binaries. "When we make people 'other' we group them together as the objects of our experience instead of regarding them as fellow subjects of experience with whom we might identify" (Wendell, as cited in Schick & St. Denis, 2005, p. 305, emphasis in original). Fellow subjects, however, must not be confused with cultural relativism. Yet how do we teach this self-reflexivity without basing it on a context of other versus norm? Pillow (2003) suggests:

> A reflexivity that pushes toward an unfamiliar, towards the uncomfortable, cannot be a simply story of subjects, subjectivity, and transcendence or self-indulgent tellings. A tracing of the problematics of reflexivity calls for a positioning of reflexivity not as clarity, honesty, or humility, but as practices of confounding disruptions-at times even a failure of our language and practices. (p. 192)

What we are struck by in her comments is a moving away from static, individual states of reference to more curious and uncertain questions. Individuals and their communities are more than a single aspect of themselves (Adichie, 2009). Adichie (2009) states that is impossible to engage fully with a person without engaging in all of the stories of that person, to focus on one aspect, especially a negative aspect, is to "flatten" the person and his/her experience. If we only allow ourselves to see one story of a person and base our methods of practice upon this preconceived "single story" (Adichie, 2009) of an individual, we have we robbed him/her of his/her dignity (Adichie, 2009). The stories we tell about ourselves and the stories others tell about us matter. If we move away from our "single stories" of those whom with we work we can move toward an ontology of multiple truths and possibilities. But to do so requires a different approach to how we locate ourselves as practitioners, students and instructors on the map of multiculturalism.

A DIFFERENT GEOGRAPHY

At this point, we have introduced the reader to considerations of the problematic multicultural discourse and the role of reflexivity within that. In wrestling with how to trouble the concept of multiculturalism in a manner that had meaning for practitioners and educators, we conceptualized multicultural pedagogy initiatives as a particular geography. Popkewitz and Brennan (1998) reflect:

> We can think of educational studies, then, as a social mapping of the region and its inscribed boundaries. The notion of region embodies a

varied notion of time to account for different patterns of ideas and social practices that come together to produce the subject. (p. 13)

A geographical lens views particular ecological spaces as territories that require borders, boundaries and languaging of space that becomes fixed in socio-historical contexts. Once a geography is "recognized" through law, a subject may orient I to it through proximal familiarity—hometowns, neighborhood, or through geographical resonance—I am not from here but I belong here. Geography invites belonging or alienation and works in tandem with discursive practices of power to determine which of the aforementioned categories you might find yourself subjugated to. If we view CYC as a human geography, we can tangibly trace these practices. Barnett (1991) reflects:

> The importance of context in human geography is both substantive and theoretical (Sunley, 1996). Substantively, there is a strong sense that geography is actually all about contexts. "Place" is once again a favoured reference point for research, a theme that can be traced back to debates in the 1980s over localities, regions and structure and agency (Massey 1984; Thrift, 1983). These debates laid the groundwork for what is now a much broader appreciation of the place-specific constitution of social processes, registered not least in the turn to "culture" in various subdisciplines. "Context" is shorthand for a sensitivity towards the ways in which general processes are embedded, modified and reproduced in particular, local places. Theoretically, this concern is related to a critique of universalist epistemologies. Ideas, representations and theories are understood to be intrinsically connected to the particular contexts in which they are produced. (p. 279)

What Barnett suggests, then, is recognition of space and context but simultaneously raises the challenge of how those weave into contentious issues of geographical resonance as it pertains to multiculturalism. However troubling this idea may be, the subject of multiculturalism and what it means to work within multicultural contexts is not a stranger to the CYC curriculum. Nevertheless, it seems as though teaching and learning multiculturalism is approached as a way of giving practitioners travel tools so that they may go out exploring and discovering different areas in the metaphorical geography that is our society. These tools allow practitioners to approach so-called strange and foreign areas with confidence and competence necessary to scale the unfamiliar terrain, standing atop new points on the map and admiring their progress. We congratulate ourselves on our inclusive environments and our politically correct terminology yet cease to evolve beyond it. The question remains: How can we teach students how to be in relation with others when we still cannot fully articulate what this means?

Instead of supplying maps, we reply by "suggesting that the way we treat the most mundane or apparently inconsequential experiences may have the most to offer in suggesting a larger vision of social transformation" (McNiff, 2008, p. 37). What this means is the geography of diversity is created through addressing local climates in the context of global intersectionality; if a racist, classist or homo/trans phobic comment is not confronted and worked through in the classroom, it inevitably leaks into practice and reifies the maps of multiculturalism. If, on the other hand, we assume no maps, but emergent geographies, we can have these conversations with a decolonizing perspective that does not predetermine how we might encounter the other—in the children, youth, families and communities who with we work and in ourselves.

In the spirit of Roy (2003):

> Instead of being passively affected by conditions...look for ways in which teachers [and students] can affect the situation in which they find themselves by breaching or rupturing the old boundaries that can lead to a release of new intensities. This is the notion of "deterritialization" in Deleuze—a movement by which we leave the territory, or move away from spaces regulated by dominant systems of significance that keep us confined within old patterns, in order to make new connections. (p. 21, emphasis in original)

It is time to leave the territory of multiculturalism and the aforementioned "systems of significance" and create new means of connection.

CONCLUSION

Lather (1991) once asked "how have I policed the boundaries of what can be imagined?" (p. 84). Likewise, we have asked how multicultural discourses have limited our understanding of what it means to be decolonizing practitioners. We have also explored the role of self location and reflexivity in this. We acknowledge that there may be no fixed map and no static model with which to embark on new conversations surrounding these lived, breathed and sometimes agonizing experiences. To trace is to erase. If we accept that the available maps are palimpsest, we can be better prepared to create maps of practice that center difference, that avail permeable boundaries and flexible and multiple locations. In our shared experience, Child and Youth Care practitioners and educators continue to search for an appropriate, singular formula to apply to the work that we do in the name of multicultural competence. It is not available; it never has been. However, many other voices (as seen in this issue) in the field have recognized these limitations and are beginning to challenge them. We are confident a new geography is emerging. It may not look familiar but that is the point.

NOTES

1. For those unfamiliar, Wooldridge (1996) defines palimpsest as "a text written over an earlier text that was erased, with a few traces showing" (p. 154).

2. For more information see: http://www.cbc.ca/news/canada/story/2012/08/17/pol-cp-100-dollar-bills-asian-scientist-image.html.

REFERENCES

Adichie, C. (2009). *Chimamanda Adichie: The danger of a single story* [video file]. Retrieved from http://www.ted.com/talks/lang/en/chimamanda_adichie_the_danger_of_a_single_story.html

Ball, J. (n.d.). *Cultural competence in health care for Aboriginal peoples*. Retrieved from http://www.ecdip.org/docs/pdf/Cultural%20safety%20in%20health%20care%20compr.pdf.

Barnett, C. (1999). Deconstructing context: Exposing Derrida. *Transactions of the Institute of British Geographers, New Series, 24*(3), 277–293.

Bell, D. (1993). The power of prophets. In B. W. Thompson & S. Tyagi (Eds.), *Beyond a dream deferred* (pp. ix–x). Minneapolis, MN: University of Minnesota Press.

Bemak, F., & Chung, R. C.-Y. (2008). New professional roles and advocacy strategies for school counselors: A multicultural social justice perspective to move beyond the nice counselor syndrome. *Journal of Counseling and Development, Multicultural and Diversity Issues in Counseling, Special Issue, 38*, 372–381.

Canadian Multiculturalism Act (R.S.C. 1985, c.24 (4th Supp)). Retrieved from http://laws-lois.justice.gc.ca/eng/acts/c-18.7/page-1.html#h-3.

Corson, D. (1998). *Changing education for diversity*. Bristol, PA: Open University Press.

Csikszentmihalyi, M. (1993). *The evolving sense: A psychology for the third millennium*. New York, NY: Harper Collins.

Ellsworth, E. (1992). Why doesn't this feel empowering? Working through the repressive myths of critical pedagogy. In C. Luke & J. Gore (Eds.), *Feminism and critical pedagogy* (pp. 90–119). New York, NY: Routledge.

Garcia, K. (2002). Swimming against the mainstream: Examining cultural assumptions in the classroom. In L. Darling-Hammond, J. French, & S. P. Garcia-Lopez, *Learning to teach for social justice* (pp. 22–29). New York, NY: Teachers College Press.

Korzybski, A. (1958). *Science and sanity*. Lakeville, CT: The International Non-Aristotelian Library Publishing Group.

Lather, P. (1991). *Getting smart: Feminist research and pedagogy with/in the postmodern*. New York, NY: Routledge.

McNiff, S. (2008). Arts-based research. In J. G. Knowles & A. L. Cole (Eds.), *Handbook of arts in qualitative research: Perspectives, methodologies, examples, and issues* (pp. 29–40). Thousand Oaks, CA: Sage.

Messer-Davidow, E. (2002). *Disciplining feminism: From social activism to academic discourse*. Durham, NC: Duke University Press.

On the Coast. (2012, May 28). Ethnic enclaves in high school [Radio broadcast]. Retrieved from http://www.cbc.ca/onthecoast/episodes/2012/05/28/ethnic-enclaves-in-high-school/

Pillow, W. (2003). Confession, catharsis or cure? Rethinking the uses of reflexivity as methodological power in qualitative research. *International Journal of Qualitative Studies in Education, 16*(2), 175–196.

Popkewitz, T. S., & Brennan, M. (1998). Restructuring of social and political theory in education: Foucault and a social epistemology of school practices. In T. S. Popkewitz & M. Brennan (Eds.), *Foucault's challenge: Discourse, knowledge, and power in education* (pp. 3–35). New York, NY: Teachers College Press.

Roy, K. (2003). *Teachers in nomadic spaces: Deleuze and curriculum.* New York, NY: Peter Lang Publishing.

Schick, C., & St. Denis, V. S. (2005). Troubling national discourses in anti-racism curricular planning. *Canadian Journal of Education, 28*(3), 295–317.

Shapiro, S. (1990). *Between capitalism and democracy: Educational policy and the crisis of the welfare state.* New York, NY: Bergin & Garvey.

Thompson, B. W., & Tyagi, S. (1993). The politics of inclusion: Reskilling the academy. In B. W. Thompson & S. Tyagi (Eds.), *Beyond a dream deferred* (pp. 83–99). Minneapolis, MN: University of Minnesota Press.

Tsolidis, G. (2001). *Schooling, diaspora, and gender: Being feminist and being different.* Philadelphia, PA: Open University Press.

Wooldridge, A. G. (1996). *Poemcrazy.* New York, NY: Clarkson Potter Publishers.

Zerbe Enns, C., & Forrest, L. M. (2005). Toward defining and integrating multicultural and feminist pedagogies. In C. Zerbe Enns & A. L. Sinacore (Eds.), *Teaching social justice: Integrating multicultural and feminist theories in the classroom* (pp. 3–24). Washington, DC: APA.

Zipin, L. (1998). Looking for sentient life in discursive practices: The question of human agency in critical theories and school research. In T. S. Popkewitz & M Brennan (Eds.), *Foucault's challenge: Discourse, knowledge, and power in education* (pp. 316–347). New York, NY: Teachers College Press.

Fleeing Identity: Toward a Revolutionary Politics of Relationship

HANS SKOTT-MYHRE

*Department of Child and Youth Studies, Brock University,
St. Catherines, Ontario, Canada*

This article explores relationship as foundational to multicultural praxis and theory. The question of who arrives in the encounter will be examined through the concept of identity politics. In their text Commonwealth Hardt and Negri state that "It is inevitable that identity should become the primary vehicle for struggle within and against the republic of property since identity itself is based on property and sovereignty." This article will trace the ways in which the violence of identity might become more visible and propose the abolition of identity as a fixed aspect of an existing subject.

Many years ago, when I was directing a runaway shelter program in Santa Fe New Mexico, the elders of the Eight Northern Pueblos approached our organization to establish a runaway shelter on the Nambe Pueblo. We approached the project with some degree of trepidation understanding the highly contested history of the Tewa people with both the U.S. federal government, who would fund the project, and the predominantly Anglo social service system that we represented. We felt honored to be invited and worked quite hard to establish a collaborative and respectful working relationship. To this end, we had a number of meetings with tribal elders that were largely relational and focused on getting to know each other as people. Unlike many other collaborations in which personal relationships followed formal agreements of collaboration, the Tewa elders wanted to know us as the elders of our organization and as people before formally agreeing to work together.

In one of our first meetings together, one of elders opened by talking about the Tewa people and their history on the Pueblo. He explained some of their values and traditions as well as some prohibitions and exclusions for those of us outside the tribe. Unlike many indigenous people subjected to the colonial genocidal rule of the United States government, the Tewa people had not been moved from their traditional land, but had been on the same land for hundreds, if not thousands, of years. This is not to say they were unaffected by colonialism. Indeed, they had suffered other depredations at the hands of the Spanish in the fifteenth and sixteenth centuries and then U.S. government programs that attempted to disrupt traditional practices of living. In the face of these incursions, however, they sustained much of their traditional way of life.

At one point, an elder turned to me and asked, so who are your people? I was taken aback. I had never really been asked this question so seriously and personally. I stammered that I was adopted and didn't really know my heritage outside the one I had been adopted into. He looked at me with pity and sorrow and told me how sorry he was that I had no people. I found myself ashamed, confused and embarrassed. I had never missed having a people, but now I wondered if I should have.

This interchange echoed an earlier experience, where I found myself living and working in a largely African American context in Richmond Virginia. In the context of the American south, I discovered that in both Black and White communities the first question that anyone asked was, who are your people? Indeed, there could be a rather long preamble to any further conversation that included a listing of genealogy and a contextualization of one's identity within a matrix of a certain lineage and familial history. Once again, I had found myself culturally adrift. I could certainly trace my adopted family lineage; after all, on my mother's side we were Mormons with an intense interest in genealogy. I certainly remembered that at my family gatherings there had always been long evenings of storytelling and the sharing of traditions from cooking, to songs, to quilting and so on. So I had a people and a history, even if adopted. What difference blood?

I found, however, that in the American south my Yankee heritage had little currency. In the White community, I was an interloper with no established pedigree and in the Black community, I was simply White. This is not to say that people were not generous, warm, and helpful. But there was little place for a person of no significant lineage. My culture was not culture in that vernacular. It did not signify the possibility of belonging.

Certainly, these stories could lead us into a discussion of what is culture and what is its relationship to belonging. We could explore the various signifiers of cultural identity and perhaps trouble the boundaries of culture, as Bhabha (1994) does when he proposes that culture is fluid and premised in collisions between peoples that always result in hybrid constellations of shifting traditions and practices. Such traditions and practices are an amalgam of intersecting historical trajectories forged by trade, nomadic contingent encounters along game routes, war, diasporas, and famine. This might lead us to a discussion of whether culture has any stable form. If so, who controls and defines the purity of that form? We could argue that culture is a continually contested space in which, what Deleuze and Guattari (1987) call the molar lines of the state, are in perpetual constitutive relation with the war machine composed of lines of flight that undo and dissemble the order and structure of definition and structure.

My intention here, however, is somewhat different than that. I have no interest in defining culture. To paraphrase Baudrillard (1995), I am not interested in arguing over the validity of a particular system of signification. Instead, I am interested in challenging the sign system per se. In another vernacular, as Deleuze and Guattari (1987) state, we might, "experiment, don't signify and interpret! Find your own places, territories, deterritorializations, regime...Semiotize yourself instead of rooting around in your prefab childhood and Western semiology" (p. 587).

To experiment, however, is not to simply try out new ideas or practices thoughtlessly. To experiment requires a certain degree of rigor both personal and conceptual. Certainly, one of the most contentious and powerful constructions in Western semiology is that of Whiteness. In my experience, this centrally defining identification is largely absent from our thinking about CYC practice and ethics. To focus on what it means to identify as White is an extremely challenging exercise. How many of us, who identify as White, have taken the time personally or collectively as staff to unpack the complex history and powerful effects of this identity. In one agency where I worked we attempted to do this in a year-long series of meetings and trainings we called decolonizing our conversations. We attempted to work collectively in focusing on the ways in which our cultural and racial identification in relation to Whiteness influenced our practice with the young people we encountered. It was incredibly challenging and in the end only marginally successful. However, the process was incredibly informative about our own personal investments in the actual practices of power, control and privilege.

In his writings on the development of Whiteness as an identity in North America, Roediger (1991) addresses the question of black face in the minstrel show. He suggests that the appropriation of black face by the White working class was a complicated expression of the hidden costs of becoming White for previously subaltern groups such as the Irish. In particular, he argues that European immigrants arriving as indentured servants and later as, what was termed at the time wage slaves, entered into an extremely problematic class and identity configuration. They were initially identified with African slaves in their indentured servitude. In fact, sold on the same slave blocks, traveling together in chains and living and at times inter-marrying within slave communities. With the founding of the new republic, however, the indentured

Europeans were freed from chattel slavery while the Africans remained enslaved.

This freedom for the previously indentured immigrants came with a cost. In order to be fully assimilated as White they were forced to give up their cultural identities rooted in Europe and become American. The freedom promised at the expense of their indigenous heritage, however, was quickly betrayed through the industrialization of the United States and the development of a new form of slavery; the capitalist wage.

Roedigger (1991) argues that the use of black face and the assumption of the faux-black musical form in the minstrel show was a complex expression of profound confusion, rage, guilt, and despair over the costs of becoming White. The racism of the early working class Whites against the Africans who previously shared their enslaved status was a reflection of abject fear of being identified with any group that could be enslaved and a resentment of the enduring rich indigenous culture of Black Americans.

How much of this framework might apply to the relationship we have with young people in terms of our own fears about being identified with any group that is marginalized or penalized for their identity by the dominant social? How much of our burn out is premised in our confusion, guilt and despair over the conflict between our best intentions regarding young people and the necessity to carry out the disciplinary mission of the agency? How deep does our resentment lie in regards to those young people who make us uncomfortable in our role as technicians of social control?

It is Nietzsche (1967) who warns us of the dangers of resentment. Resentment he tells us is premised in reaction and indulgence in the negative. He discusses what he calls the slave revolt in morality that begins with resentment. Slave morality as a form of revolt is premised in the identity associated with being in a subaltern or subjugated position. Such a revolt is doomed to failure because slave morality operates as a negation of all that is different. It only has the capacity to say "no" to the forces that oppose it or that challenge its hegemonic resentment. It can only react to the forces of oppression within the logic of that very oppression. It is a failure of constitutive affirmation; a tacit acceptance of the forces of domination masked (literally in the case of black face) as deviant creativity or resistance. Resentment always focuses backward to that which has been lost. It lives in a realm of abstraction where mythically homogenous people lived idyllic lives before the catastrophe that severed the past from the horrors of the present.

According to Deleuze and Guattari (1994) this was the great philosopher Heidegger's mistake in allying himself with the Nazi regime in Germany. He sought the idyllic world of the Greeks in the world of perfect order the fascists promised. "He got the wrong people, earth, and blood" (p. 109). The Germany that Heidegger was responding to was in midst of a great economic catastrophe. The great depression was a world-wide phenomenon, but in Germany the effects were particularly devastating.

Certainly, we could argue that we live in a time of catastrophe and transition. The services we deliver cannot be exempted from the social upheaval that surrounds them. We operate in a time of uncertainty in which it is almost impossible to find a center or social certainty. In the advent of catastrophes such as an economic crisis, war, famine, slavery, pestilence, diaspora and plague, everything is thrown into chaos. The war machine of contingency and disruption deterritorializes all. There is a rupture in the order of things that throws the dice and when it lands, a new territory is formed, a new earth and a new people to come. Such a becoming earth, a becoming people cannot be sought in any outside purity, ideal form or call to a romantic vision of days gone by. It is to be found instead in "an oppressed, bastard, lower, anarchical, nomadic and irremediably minor race" (Deleuze & Guattari, 1994, p. 109). If the future is not be found in any ideal form of the existing system, then as workers who engage the coming generations, how are we to inform our practices so as to bring forth the world to come? We might answer that this is not our job or our mission. I would argue that it *is* what we do, whether we intend to or not.

In their text *What is Philosophy* Deleuze and Guattari (1994) propose that our most difficult task is believing in this world, this life. This is to say two things:

1. To believe in this world, this life is to eschew resentment because there is only this world, this life. There is no world outside. There is no life other than this. This is what Spinoza (2000) asserts when he says that what should be, is precisely what is.
2. Of course, what emerges is in constant becoming. This life is not a point. It is an infinitude of intersecting lines of force in constant movement, driven by the idiosyncratic capacity of each line to extend itself in space and to intensify its effects in any given point in time. To believe in this world requires an understanding that life is beyond description or category.

Or, we might propose that life is perhaps not beyond description, but requiring a different form of description. Deleuze and Guattari (1987) explore what they call a minoritarian literature. This is writing that is informed by an ontological constitutive creative force that does not set out to challenge the dominant descriptions of the world. Instead by its very nature, it cannot help but do so. They characterize such writing as a language that a minority constructs within a majority that is always political and collective (pp. 16–17). One such style of writing is what has been termed magical realism. Faris (2004) informs us that magical realism "has provided literary ground for significant cultural work; within its texts, marginal voices, submerged traditions and emergent literatures have developed and created masterpieces" (p.1). She goes on to say that this genre challenges the primary modes of representation in western literature and destabilizes it as a "decolonizing agent."

In Faris's (2004) description there is a minoritarian collective of marginal voices and submerged traditions. There is also the politics of colonial and postcolonial relations and the linguistic challenge of Latin America to the traditional linguistic structures of Europe and the United States. In this context, it has been argued that the magical realist genre owes a great deal to the traditions of European surrealism (Oberhelm, 1991), but Faris argues that the two genres are radically distinct. She asserts that the culture of realism in industrialized Europe that the surrealist's responded to with their interpellations of dreams and the absurd never really existed in Latin America. For the surrealists to delve into the "primitive" unconscious was an excursion. Latin American culture was the site of such excursions. Faris notes that the

> Distinctly American phenomenon where church sculptures depicted the intercultural phenomenon of angels playing the maracas, where outrageous otherworldly plants grew in profusion... was in no need of the artificial juxtaposition, such as sewing machines and umbrellas on dissecting tables, to which the European surrealists had recourse in their desperate search for the extraordinary. (p. 33)

The European surrealists sought to construct representations of the unconscious through depictions of the perverse and extraordinary. That is to say, they sought to portray a landscape of an outside they found in the interior world of dreams. For the magical realist, there is no outside any more than dreaming is separable from waking. This world encompasses within itself all experience, from the mundane to the extraordinary.

From this view there are no metaphors. Nothing stands for anything else. The black face of the minstrel show does not represent the cost of becoming White. It is the expression of that experience in all its complexity and contradiction. In this sense, one's people are not to be found in any outside lineage somewhere in the past. One's *people* is not a representation. It is a contemporary web of interconnected lines of force and capacity that cannot be described or adequately accounted for in any linguistic form. It is not a lineage to which one belongs. This is why Hardt and Negri (2004) warn us against the concept of a people.

They argue that a people, as an outside regime to which one belongs, constitutes a form of rule and domination. It subjects one to the definitions of a certain geography, history and practice. While this may seem a comfort in times of confusion, alliance to a people always puts one at odds with those who are not your people.

Of course, under colonial rule, a dominant people seek the assimilation or genocidal elimination of those people's outside the center. Under such circumstances, there may be a moment in which the preservation of subaltern knowledges and practices engages the protective enclosure of a nominalized people. This moment is an affirmation of the lines of the creative capacities blocked by colonial domination. Its purpose is not to freeze in time any set of beliefs, affiliations or practices. To produce a people from such a moment, is to subject the dynamic living force of a diverse and idiosyncratic assemblage of bodies to an abstract or transcendent set of non-living definitions. Such an effort holds great danger of falling into fascism, resentment or both.

The alternative movement is to recognize the creation of tradition and affiliation as a momentary tactic. I would propose that any given tactic should be deployed only as long as it is both necessary and effective. It is an error to become attached to any tactic. One must understand the ground and necessity of the tactic and always look to see if it has been successful or is no longer effective or relevant to current historical conditions.

In the case of sustaining the practices, beliefs and languages of a group under assault by a dominating force, it is important to recognize that this tactic is designed to keep the creative capacities of these practices as living force. It can become dangerous if tactics become romanticized or historicized. If this should happen tactical options stand the risk of becoming calcified and the effort to preserve their living force will be for naught.

Revolt against domination cannot be found in the dead repetition of practices performed because they should be or always have been. Revolt is to be found in the ways that these practices open fissures and ruptures in the field of domination that allow such practices to create new worlds and new peoples. Of course, we cannot step outside our historical moment. As Deleuze and Guattari (1994) remind us, we are not outside our time but "continue to undergo shameful compromises with it" (p. 108). The question is what comprises our time and what are the shameful compromises we make? I would argue, along with Hardt and Negri (2000) that our time is the time of global capitalist empire. That is, the epoch wherein the logic of capitalism, with the money sign as its abstract signifier, colonizes every aspect of our lives including our very definitions of our values, identities and practices. There is no one exempt from this form of colonization.

Capitalism is a global system of rule that operates parasitically like Acquired Immune Deficiency Syndrome (AIDS), entering our very subjectivities and social forms, altering our social codes and cultural DNA. It leaves the structural similarities intact, but empties our identities and civil structures, replacing them with the money sign. Such a system, would like us to believe that the disease is the cure. That the advent of global capitalism is both the terminal event for all historical and economic forms that preceded it. Perhaps most cogently it would have us believe that capitalism is the only available future.

Capitalism as an abstract parasitic system seeks to collapse all human creative forms of society, culture, gender, sexuality, art, music and technology into capital; to the reductive machinery of profit and loss. In this implosion of creative force into the empty abstraction of abstract signification, living force is blocked and constricted like a sclerotic artery. The realm of living force begins to weaken and finds itself ill. A sociocultural malaise infects our lives. Our thinking becomes weak and confused. We develop a cultural and social Alzheimer's disease in which we act as though the past is present and the present is forgotten. We become frightened and engage in a process of bargaining with the disease itself as though we were terminal and our only hope was to beg for just a little more time, a little pain; a few more memories. In short, we make shameful compromises and forget that the disease is founded in illusion and fantasy.

In fact no system of abstraction can produce terminal conditions for life. The only way such an effect can be sustained is if living beings can be convinced to destroy themselves in service to the parasite that infects them. In this respect, the cure cannot be found in producing more of the disease; more signs and significations. The cure is in recognizing the profoundly ephemeral and unstable nature of signs and signifiers. The realm of representation is always dependent upon life as the originator of what it represents. Life, however, does not need signs or signification to continue, although it might co-evolve such systems to extend its field of thought and imagination.

Central to the contested field of life and signification is the question of who we are. In the field of Child and Youth Care, we place significant value on the self and the development of identity (Fewster, 1990, 1999; Krueger, 2007; Phelan, 2008). Such value makes sense in the respect that much of original theoretical formulations have come about in the sphere of relational encounter (Garfat, 2008). We have theorized the encounter that occurs in a Child and Youth Care institutional setting as having a unique constitutive force. Framed in phenomenological terms, this encounter between selves has a certain capacity for reflection and self-discovery. Indeed, as Krueger (2007) has pointed out, even in the most mundane of encounters significant life shifting revelations and connections can be forged. New and life affirming identities can be discovered and acted upon through ongoing authentic interactions and relationships.

I would, in large part agree that relationships are key ingredients in the work that we do as Child and Youth Care workers. However, I would expand the field of inquiry about relations, beyond the binary configuration of the Western semiology of the self. I would suggest along with Pacini-Ketchabaw (2012 [this issue]) that there are more than the human self and the human other in any given encounter. There are cross-species elements and non-animate elements in any encounter between two perceived humans. I say perceived, because along with Luhmann (1995) I find the linguistic nomenclature of human both incomplete and inadequate.

As Foucault (1980) has pointed out, every encounter is comprised of multiple lines of force, each line comprised of idiosyncratic elements of virtual capacity. In any given atomic fragment of time there are constitutive collisions of viruses, bacteria, technological possibilities, linguistic variabilities and differences, electrical and chemical variations, and exchanges within and between bodies both animate and inanimate. Each of these myriad and distinctive lines hinges on what Bergson (1990) described as the horizon of the world or that ontological condition of possibility that is always receding as we approach it.

For Deleuze and Guattari (2003), all encounter is premised in a "desiring-production" that,

> is at work everywhere, functioning smoothly at times, at other times in fits and starts. It breathes, it heats, it eats. It shits, it fucks...Everywhere Everywhere it is machines—real ones, not figurative ones: machines driving other machines; machines being driven by other machines, with all necessary couplings and connections. An organ machine is plugged into an energy-source-machine: the one that produces a flow that the other interrupts...Hence we are all handymen: each with his [sic] little machines. (p. 1)

The encounter in CYC is never a simple arithmetic of one plus one, or a directed flow of senders and receivers. Relationships are always composed of infinite and multiple flows connecting and blocking the little machines that we designate as our identity. Which is itself, of course, a little machine comprised of flows that continually exceed and overflow our epistemological designations. We are indeed handy folk continually adjusting the levels of force streaming through, opening new and unanticipated channels and blocking and blowing old and established systems of calibration and homeostasis.

In our time, we have come to name some of these flows in temporal and spatial terms based on flows across geography that have thrown bodies together in configurations we call society and culture, as though they have always been know this way. Out of this rich and fecund field we have derived a semiological strata we have designated as who we are; our identity. Of course, this word identity is both historically and geographically contingent, although like all naming, identity is a habit not a description. Deleuze and Guattari (1987) address this when they say,

> The two of us wrote Anti-Oedipus together. Since each of us was several, there was already quite a crowd. Here we have made use of everything that came within range, what was closest as well as farthest away. We have assigned clever pseudonyms to prevent recognition. Why have we kept our own names? Out of habit, purely out of habit. (p. 3)

The pseudonyms we have assigned ourselves in our encounters in the field of CYC include affiliation by categories such as profession and race; gender and class; sexual identity and nationality; family and people; political party and subculture; age and sports team etc. We weave stories of affiliation and misunderstand them as solid edifices rather than trail markers. We try to live in them rather than through them. We forget that we are always several and look for a core unity of one. Perhaps most importantly, as Foucault (1971) points out, we mistake the habits and beliefs of our own age for the truth about who we are.

Our habitual naming, however, fails to come anywhere close to adequately describing our identity. As Deleuze and Guattari (1987) point out, we are comprised of what is closest and what is farthest away. In this sense, we are maximal intensity temporally, affectively and spatially as well as radical extension in all the same registers. We are an indeterminate point on an infinite line. Our identity becomes the contested space for the immanent encounter between semiotic abstract systems of domination and ontological lines of immanent revolutionary force. The politics of identity, then, are central to any version of Child and Youth Care interested in liberatory practices.

A number of years ago I was the clinical director of a large multiservice runway and homeless youth program. The program served an extremely diverse population ranging from suburban upper middle class runaways to inner city homeless youth, LGBTTIQQA[1] young people, and gang affiliated youth. The mix was at times volatile as culture, class, race and sexuality collided in the intensity of a crisis based shelter. The staff, when I arrived, was largely White and upper middle class. I was told that there simply weren't sufficient qualified CYC workers of color in the available job pool. Over the next few years we magically discovered that this was no longer the case in our community and we managed to balance the staff with reasonable representations of race, class, sexuality, gender, professional degrees and lived experience. Indeed, we had a staff that was quite proportional to the categories of young people we were seeing in the shelter. We assumed that, over time, this mix along with an array of trainings in anti-racism, anti-homophobia and sensitivity to class issues would result in far more equitable and welcoming environment for the young people and families we served.

In fact, what we found was that as differing backgrounds, histories, personal lineages and struggles collided on the floor, in staff meetings and attempts to develop and agency culture, fixed identities emerged that reinforced divisions and resentments between staff. These identities also emerged in assumptions about proper modes of discipline, codes of morality and behavioral expectations of young people. As we attempted to make sense of this complex and troubling reification of identity politics in our program, it occurred to us that a different level of conversation might be necessary. Perhaps, we needed to explore as a staff the ways in which our personal lineages and practices of identity were forged in the history of colonial rule. Of course, we had learned about this is in our training and most of the staff could discuss this comfortably when addressing the issues a family or young person might be experiencing. But, we had never made it personal for ourselves.

In their text *Commonwealth* Hardt and Negri (2009) state "it is inevitable that identity should become the primary vehicle for struggle within and against the republic of property since identity itself is based on property and sovereignty" (p. 326). They remind us that capitalism is founded on ownership. Indeed, without the capacity for private property capitalism would have no ability to demand of us that we work for others in order to survive. If the means of production were owned by all of us in common, we would be working for all of us in common and we would receive the benefit of our work directly rather than in the form of an abstract wage. If we are to take Deleuze and Guattari (1994) seriously and acknowledge the fact we cannot live outside our time, then the relationship between identity and property has to be taken seriously, particularly in a field of endeavor premised in relationship.

Hardt and Negri (2009) propose that property is central to the production of identity through its association with hierarchy and forms of dominant rule. They cite the deep association of capitalism and property in the construction of the slave trade:

> Property is so profoundly entangled with race...not only because in many parts of the world the history of property rights is deeply embedded in the sagas of slave property but also because the rights to own and dispose of property are racialized. (p. 326)

Similarly, they note how the construction of gender is founded on notions of ownership and property, from the idea that a female child is owned by her father and can be sold into marriage so as to be owned by her husband, to the trafficking of women in the sex trades, inheritance laws and battles over reproductive rights. Of course, it might be argued that struggles for LGBTTIQQA rights are deeply founded in the constructions of patriarchal ownership of the body and the resulting hierarchies of control and discipline (Foucault, 1980). In some sense, these struggles over who owns the body are somewhat familiar. However, Hardt and Negri (2009) go on to state that "On...a more profound level...identity *is* property" (p. 326, emphasis in original).

They reference the philosophy of the Enlightenment in its production of concepts of individual self-rule and possession that lie at the heart of the bourgeois/ capitalist political and philosophical project. They cite the political philosopher John Locke, who maintains that all men have the property of their own person. This, they argue, extends to levels of privilege premised on the ownership of certain identities such as Whiteness and masculinity. It is in this register that we can read Roediger's example above about black face, class and the "purchase" of White status.

To turn identity from its appropriation as property, Hardt and Negri (2009) propose three tasks. The first, as we have noted above, in our comments on the tactics of subaltern people under colonial rule, is to "reveal the violence of identity as property and thereby in some sense re-appropriate that identity" (p. 327). This is, of course, the terrain of traditional identity politics. The civil rights, gay rights, feminist, indigenous and workers movements are all founded on this notion of re-appropriation of an identity forged by dominant colonial incursions. This is a fundamental step toward revolutionary politics and if we were to ever doubt its force, we should note how intent the current regime of rule is on dismantling it. We, as CYC workers, live in an age of compassion fatigue and post-racial, post-feminist ideologies. We are surrounded by media that insists we have put racism, sexism, and class behind us and no longer need to concern ourselves with these troubling ghosts from the past.

This is a great comfort to many of us who identify as White. As Hoskins points out in this journal issue, it is uncomfortable dealing with our complicity and shame over the violence done to others. However, as Deleuze and Guattari (1994) tell us "we are not responsible for the victims but responsible before them" (p. 108). We may not be directly responsible for what happened, but we are responsible for the results. Both in the sense that we continue to benefit from the economic and social privilege we inherit in our status as White, but also in our responsibility to care for those with whom we are in relationship. As anyone who has worked with survivors of sexual assault knows, caring cannot occur without the acknowledgement of suffering. It is necessary to reveal the violence of property in all its painful aspects by bearing witness to it without flinching.

Deleuze and Guattari (1994) state that under certain circumstances there is catastrophe such that "friends can no longer look at each other or each at himself without a weariness or perhaps a mistrust which does not suppress friendship but gives it its modern color" (p. 208). In a field such as CYC, premised in relationship, the first task is to find a way to look at each other and ourselves without weariness or mistrust. This cannot happen if the catastrophe is denied or elided. As we know from working with young people, you cannot build trust by pretending that adults are not dangerous or hurtful, or by denying that you, as an adult, are beyond suspicion.

Hardt and Negri (2009) tell us that re-appropriation as a first step, however, is not sufficient in and of itself. They suggest that forging an identity as an exercise in self-affirmation and pride is a weak and watered down version of what could be a powerful mode of liberation. The foundational function of a forceful identity politics is not to be found in the configuration of the identity. It is instead, the drive to freedom as a "resistance to enslavement." (329) They cite Linda Zerilli who proposes that "freedom centered feminism...is concerned not so much with knowing (and revealing for example, the ways in which women are socially subordinated) but rather with doing—'with transforming, world building, beginning anew' " (pp. 229–230). Such doing includes the formation of what Deleuze and Guattari (1994) call a "new earth, a new people" (p. 101). This new world Hardt and Negri tell us cannot be found in any existing subject. Indeed, as we mentioned above it cannot be found in any of our existing habits. We are not aiming to free an existing configuration of identities and habits so that they can be sustained. This only leads to the kind of regressive politics and new forms of domination exemplified by self proclaimed radical feminist Sheila Jeffreys who, according to Roz Kaveny (2012), has been at the forefront of refusing trans people admittance to the radical feminist conference RadFem 2012 and has identified:

> post-modernism and queer theory [as] the enemy, and [maintains that] piercing, tattooing, BDSM and role play are all pollutions of a feminism that is nothing to do with choice or preference, everything to do with commitment. Indeed, the Radical Feminist Hub, to which she contributes regularly, links to resources arguing that what it calls "penis-in-vagina" sex is a bad idea, from which women should choose to refrain.[2]

Of course, this same dynamic can be found in other social formulations such as the log cabin Republicans in the United States who promote their economic agendas at the cost of siding with the very agents of their own oppression, or Black nationalists essentialists who replicate colonialism and obfuscate Indigenous voices by only naming Black issues, and so on.[3] This form of identity politics seeks to enforce and discipline on the basis of identity through rigid formations of community dependent on exclusion from others. We must be wary of any form of politics remised on notions of authenticity. As we have noted above this was Heidegger's error. It is a politics based in resentment and slave morality that leads to an affirmation of existing conditions rather than creating new peoples that can challenge the existing order. Hardt and Negri (2009) remind us that identity is a means not an end.

In our work in CYC we might well be cautious of true or authentic identity constructions. Those who would claim new privilege or hierarchy on the basis of their more perfect understanding of identity simply supplant one order of hierarchy with another. Any claim of a pure or unsullied lineage that needs to be sustained against the incursions of our time might also be suspect. Any such notion is undoubtedly founded in certain forms of resentment and slave morality.

That is not to say that re-appropriating lineage or marginalized identity are not important steps in the process of rebellion. They are simply not the end points. Any time we find ourselves producing identity as truth, we are verging on a regressive line. While rediscovery of our marginalized lineages, particularly for those identified as White is important work, it is just the beginning of a process. "To become revolutionary, the politics of identity has to find a means to keep moving forward." (Hardt & Negri, 2009, p. 331)

In this regard, Hardt and Negri (2009) make a distinction between emancipation and liberation. Emancipation they tell us allows for an affirmation of who we really are. Liberation allows for "the freedom to determine *what you can become."* (p. 332, emphasis in original). Liberation therefore, engages what we have noted above as the horizon of the world, that indeterminate space of infinite capacity always receding as we proceed toward it. The freedom to become is premised in a revolutionary identity politics that "strives for its own abolition" (p. 332). Hardt and Negri state in this regard that,

> The primary object of class struggle, in other words, is not to kill capitalists but to demolish the social structures and institutions that maintain their privilege and authority, abolishing too, thereby, the conditions of proletariat subordination...Revolutionary feminism is distinguished from other feminist perspectives by its aim of the abolition of gender...Queer is less an identity than a *critique of identity*... Only a project of liberation that destroys not just blackness as an identity of subordination but blackness as such along with whiteness and all other racial identities makes possible the creation of a new humanity. (pp. 332–336)

This creation of a new humanity begins in relationship; a relationship to all both animate and inanimate. It is a dynamic relationship that forms and reforms identity as a living art composed of all elements of any given moment. This compositional relation does not seek to reject or ignore pain or suffering, histories of injustice or existing systems of hierarchy or dominance. It acknowledges their continuous force by mounting alternatives that say yes to the future rather than no. The creation of new worlds and new peoples involves affirmation and extension, not exclusion and negation. Identity is always political and any disparagement of identity politics misunderstands the fundamental and revolutionary importance of who we are becoming.

Many years ago I went to see a guru by the name of Sunyatta. He was reputed to be very holy and to be able to see into the truth of all matters. Many disciples, dissatisfied with their lives would come to him to find out what was wrong with them. They would ask him to look deep within them and tell them what was wrong. They would frame their question premised in their assumption that they were flawed and ask "Look at me and tell me what do you see?" Sunyatta would answer "I see God." They would respond, "Yes, yes—but what do you really see." And he would respond, "I see God." This could go on for some time, until the disciples, frustrated and feeling misunderstood, would give up. Or, occasionally and rarely they would understand what he was saying to them and a revolution would occur in who they imagined themselves to be.

Imagine if we were to form our relationships in CYC in this way. What if we saw the infinite possibilities of becoming in each and every encounter with all elements of our work? With the staff, the buildings, the streets, the gardens, the empty lots, the cars, the youth, the families. Not any ideal outside that would tie them to some preconceived notion of who they could be according to our fantasy. Instead, a co-becoming assemblage of all the material reality inclusive of our common and divergent histories and the struggles of our peoples, the harm we have done each other, the catastrophes of our encounters, the structures of domination and running through and across it all the line of flight that is living liberation.

WHO ARE YOUR PEOPLE: REDUX

If I could return to the question that I discussed at the beginning of this piece about "who are your people." If I could approach it with new eyes, I might well respond, "you are my people." Of course, given the contested and painful history of our joint lineages, such a statement might be misunderstood as an avoidance or even an insult. As a result, at times it is perhaps best to approach such an understanding through the slow accumulation of trust earned through struggle together. The first step in such struggle is to be responsible before the victims of our privilege. The details diverge according to history and lineage but each of us has someone before whom we need to be responsible. Such acts of careful and meticulous response-ability unlock proliferating fractal extensions of relationship that have the capacity for revolutionary force; the force that can create a new world, a new people.

NOTES

1. Lesbian, gay, bisexual, two-spirited, transgendered, intersex(ed), queer, questioning, and ally.
2. See http://www.guardian.co.uk/commentisfree/2012/may/25/radical-feminism-trans-radfem2012?fb=native&CMP=FBCNETTXT9038).
3. Thanks to one of my reviewers who pointed out the necessity of broadening the scope beyond feminists alone and who provided these two excellent examples.

REFERENCES

Baudrillard, J. (1995). *Simulacra and simulation (The body, In theory: Histories of cultural materialism)* (S. F. Glaser, Trans.). Ann Arbor, MI: University of Michigan Press.
Bergson, H. (1990). *Matter and memory* (N. M. Paul & W. S. Palmer, Trans.). New York, NY: Zone Books.
Bhabha, H. K. (1994). *The location of culture*. New York, NY: Routledge.
Deleuze, G., & Guattari, F. (1987). *A thousand plateaus: Capitalism and schizophrenia* (B. Massumi, Trans.). London, UK: Athlone Press.
Deleuze, G., & Guattari, F. (1994). *What is philosophy?* London, UK: Verso.
Deleuze, G., & Guattari, F. (2003). *Anti-Oedipus: Capitalism and schizophrenia*. Minneapolis, MN: University of Minnesota Press.

Faris, W. B. (2004). *Ordinary enchantments: Magical realism and the remystification of narrative*. Nashville, TN: Vanderbilt University Press.

Fewster, G. (1990). *Being in child care: A journey into self*. New York, NY: Haworth.

Fewster, G. (1999). Turning myself inside out: My theory of me. *Journal of Child and Youth Care, 13*, 35–54.

Foucault, M. (1971). Human nature: Justice vs. power. Retrieved from http://www.chomsky.info/debates/1971xxxx.htm.

Foucault, M. (1980). *The history of sexuality*. New York, NY: Vintage Books.

Garfat, T. (2008). The inter-personal in-between: An exploration of relational child and youth care practice. In G. Bellefeuille & F. Ricks (Eds.), *Standing on the precipice: Inquiry into the creative potential of child and youth care practice* (pp. 7–34). Edmonton, Canada: McEwan Press.

Hardt, M., & Negri, A. (2000). *Empire*. Cambridge, MA: Harvard University Press.

Hardt, M., & Negri, A. (2004). *Multitude: War and democracy in the age of empire*. New York, NY: Penguin Press.

Hardt, M., & Negri, N. (2009). *Commonwealth*. Cambridge, MA: Harvard University Press.

Kaveney, R. (2012). Radical feminists are acting like a cult. Retrieved from http://www.guardian.co.uk/commentisfree/2012/may/25/radical-feminism-trans-radfem2012?fb=native&CMP=FBCNETTXT9038.

Krueger, M. (2007). *Sketching youth, self, and youth work*. Rotterdam, the Netherlands: Sense Publishing.

Luhmann, N. (1995). *Social systems. Writing science*. Stanford, CA: Stanford University Press.

Nietszche, F. (1967). *On the genealogy of morals and ecce homo* (W. Kaufmann & R. J. Hollingdale, Trans.). New York, NY: Vintage.

Oberhelman, H. D. (1991). *Gabriel Garcia Marquez: A study of the short fiction*. Boston, MA: Twayne Publishers.

Phelan, J. (2008). A developmentally responsive approach to child and youth care intervention. In G. Bellefuelle & F. Ricks (Ed.), *Standing on the precipice: Exploring the creative potential of child and youth care practice* (pp. 73–106). Edmonton, Alberta, Canada: Grant MacEwan University Press.

Roediger, D. R. (1991). *The wages of whiteness: Race and the making of the American working class*. New York, NY: Verso.

Spinoza, B. (2000). *Ethics* (G. H. R. Parkinson, trans.). Oxford, UK: Oxford University Press.

Conclusion

Sketching the Outlines: CYC Multiculturalism(?)

HANS SKOTT-MYHRE

*Department of Child and Youth Studies, Brock University,
St. Catharines, Ontario, Canada*

J.N. LITTLE

*School of Child and Youth Care, University of Victoria,
Victoria, British Columbia, Canada*

In this issue of *Child and Youth Services* we have gathered a diverse array of scholars and practitioners to explore the parameters, definitions, and praxis of multiculturalism as it impacts and is shaped by the field of Child and Youth Care (CYC). In the preceding pages we have engaged multiculturalism as a generative term rather than seeking to foreclose or reduce it to any single definition. Indeed, one might well wonder, here at the end, whether we can say anything definitive about the term multiculturalism that might assist us in forming a praxis of CYC that would promote better relations between diverse cultures in our programs and interactions with young people and families.

The short answer is that the writings here seem to indicate that in the immediate future a seamless multiculturalism built on tolerance and best intentions will not and probably should not occur. It will not occur because the social architecture of racism, imperialism, and colonialism continue to permeate our daily habits and beliefs. It should not occur yet, because such an occurrence at this historical moment would have to be premised in what already exists as a massive repression and denial of the actualities of our current age. Our relations remain troubled and for CYC, as a field premised in relational practice, these tensions and traumas cannot simply be glossed over by well-intentioned policies, procedures, and endless cultural-awareness seminars. Instead, as we already know from our daily encounters, the work begins with ourselves. It is, after all, the only part of any given relationship in which we have any fully generative role to play.

We use the term generative here with a strong degree of intentionality. In the preceding pages, our colleagues have consistently suggested that central to any multicultural praxis is not an understanding of what multiculturalism is, but what the term generates. Multiculturalism from this perspective does not hold an intrinsic value or worth in and of itself. Its worth is not to be found in the modes of its successful implementation as a symbolic ideal of global and national harmony or even in the cry for us all to just get along. Instead, what has been proposed here, is that the power and force of multiculturalism lies in its capacity to promote new ideas, new identities, new sets of social relations, rebellion, and flight, as well as the endless return of disrupted and interrupted minoritarian practices ostensibly left behind by the colonial project.

It was in this sense that the title of this issue "Troubling Multiculturalism" came to fruition in two registers. First, troubling as an action. The articles in this issue have challenged, deconstructed, critiqued, and remonstrated with the term and its effects, troubling it so as to open it to alternative readings and inquiry. Second, troubling as an adjective. Our colleagues have engaged multiculturalism as a troubling term. They have suggested that despite the best intentions of policy makers and theorists, the conceptual and political edifice that constitutes multiculturalism in common parlance and practice operates perversely to reinforce all that it intends to redress.

Put in another term, and to paraphrase Foucault, because multiculturalism is designed to evade a serious interrogation of the cultural, geographical, and historical conditions of its inception, it brings much of the colonial project in through the back door. What does this mean for those of us who wish to work across, between, and within cultural contexts with integrity? Our colleagues in this issue seem to suggest that it means we cannot simply rely on the common parlance and understanding of multiculturalism to frame our work as CYC practitioners and theorists. Instead we must interrogate our own thoughts and practices preferably before, but of necessity in process, throughout our work.

Our colleagues, in this special journal issue, have argued for just such an interrogation. As Loiselle, de Finney, Khanna, and Corcoran have stated, "we need to talk about it." However, not discuss it as a set of social expectations or ideals added onto the field of theory and practice that is CYC. Instead, we need to place the discussion of "colonialism, normativity, social power, and social change" (p. 179) at the center of our self-interrogation and, by extension, at the center of our theories and practices. This would, of course, reorient the center of our field away from a psychologically developmental focus on the child, youth, family, or worker. This would move the question of political praxis from the edge of our field into the center. Loiselle et al. argue that such a shift would make room for those voices currently marginalized by dominant theories and practices in CYC. They suggest that this is a necessity, because a practically functioning multiculturalism must challenge our current social values and practices. Such a challenge must be mounted because our current practices are based in long standing beliefs and actions that have, over the past 500 years or so, "positioned Indigenous cultural and social norms as inferior" (p. 181).

Our colleagues here propose that in order for CYC to engage multiple cultures within its work and theoretical frameworks in any serious way, self-identifications that center or privilege Whiteness, patriarchy, individuality, rational choice or self realization must be re-thought in terms of their powerful negative effects on other ways of thinking and acting. To do this, they argue, we need new analytical tools that engage transtheoretical frameworks "drawn from Indigenous, postcolonial, queer, feminist, and poststructural perspectives" (p. 178).

Kouri, in his contribution, echoes the necessity for a new analytic if we are to open our field as a site of what he terms hospitality. He suggests that the drive within our field toward internal theoretical and practical coherence is problematic, and that instead we should apply pressure to the very possibility of such coherence. Framing his argument for a "CYC to come," Kouri proposes that we must deconstruct our hegemonic constructions of race and culture by "working-within and troubling-from-within" (p. 207). By this he means that all of our traditional ways of viewing our work and our world hold within themselves tensions created by the very possibility that our knowledge is neither stable nor uncontested. When we work within, we recognize that our own linguistic conventions require that we must find ways to repeat our worldview in ways that makes sense. Simultaneously, however, the concept of troubling-from-within challenges our traditional view as foreclosing and marginalizing alternative ways of knowing. This, he suggests, underlies what he calls "a doubling practice" (p. 207). Such a practice sustains and enriches traditional conceptual frameworks by opening them to fresh perspectives and productive reconceptualizations. Indeed, he argues that without this reinvigoration of the conceptual frameworks of CYC the field risks becoming both moribund and obsolete.

This special issue of *Child and Youth Services*, as we have noted, is comprised of just such a doubling practice. We might well read the contributions here as what Kouri calls a self-deconstruction of CYC. He argues that just such a deconstruction has always been active in our field and is precisely what has driven the field forward as innovative and somewhat outside of the traditional formats for working with young people and their families. In this sense, the current modes of deconstruction explicated here in the context of multiculturalism simply extend the traditional practice of the field of CYC to consistently and persistently reinvent itself. As Kouri notes, "Deconstruction, in this sense, is specifically not a method or critique applied from outside [our field]," (p. 207) but rather the rumblings of immanent instability of our field to determine knowledge and identity production.

It is this ongoing deconstruction that reconfigures the traditional parameters of CYC in such a way as to open it to the margins of both the dominant social and the field of academic discipline. Kouri argues that it is fixed and static systems of dominant ways of knowing that foreclose the possibility of true hospitality. In a field premised on relational work, the question of welcoming the other into both our personal and professional realms is central. This becomes amplified in contexts where multiple cultures come into contact with another. To close ourselves off to new concepts and vernaculars that allow us to rethink ourselves in relation to others whose practices and modes of thought vary from our own sense of what is and should be centered in our lives, is to necessarily exclude the other-as-other from our sense of what constitutes our own community. A process of ongoing deconstruction, Kouri argues, opens CYC contexts, communities, and relationships to the other and extends a certain hospitality to otherness through a self-interrogation that radically produces, even ourselves, in alterity to our own sense of certainty as to who we are. Indeed, Kouri characterizes the potential of such praxis as creating an openness to the "unexpected coming of the unanticipated other" (p. 211). And we might add, even when the unanticipated other is an unanticipated version of our self.

As might be surmised, this process of producing ourselves as alien to our self holds the potential for considerable anxiety. The elision of certainty and reliance on tried-and-true knowledge, whether those inherited from our upbringing or learned through various exposures to pedagogical truth factories, opens us to the unknown and the unknowable. To confront this anxiety in the encounter with the other is the challenge that Hoskins poses for us in her writing in this issue. She proposes that we "consider the complexities" (p. 239) of such encounter and that we avoid trying to find escape routes from the discomfort the encounter with the other entails.

Like many of the authors here, Hoskins reminds us that our encounters with the other entails a degree of painful accountability to the joint history of our peoples under the genocidal history of colonialism and its contemporary extensions under global capitalism. It is, as we have inferred earlier here, precisely this messy complexity of guilt, pain, suffering, and joint oppression that multiculturalism is designed to cover over. Hoskins encourages us instead to stay with our discomfort, to wrestle with it, without seeking a resolution that would bring an end to the existential encounter with the terror of our genocidal history. As with Kouri and Loiselle et al., Hoskins argues that it is important to engage in an indeterminate, open-ended engagement that stays with the painful complexities at a profoundly personal level in order to open "generative conversations." Hoskins outlines this as an emotional as well as an intellectual struggle that is profoundly challenging. As a person identified with the White, dominant culture, she asks, what are the prerequisites for productive engagement? Should one apologize? Can one even begin to grasp what role one has played and continues to play in the subjugation of aboriginal and other peoples who have suffered and are suffering the effects of colonial rule?

These are key questions for CYC as it confronts the trouble of multiculturalism. Such questions get even messier, Hoskins reminds us, when the deconstructive and poststructural theories that have proven so useful to activists and scholars in the European tradition are taken up by indigenous peoples whose own communities have entirely different historical trajectories and contemporary problematics. Lest we forget, of course both the colonizer and the colonized were and are changed and brutalized by the encounter with the emerging system of colonial rule that produces contemporary capitalism. However, the effects and problems for colonizer and colonized emerge and extend themselves through markedly different trajectories and across significantly different social and physical geographies. The oppressive force of class relations and subjugations of alternative knowledge for European subjects leads to philosophical and political responses that may or may not line up with or find resonance among indigenous peoples. This question of different projects premised in idiosyncratic positioning for different peoples is highlighted in work that calls for hybridity or forms of disaggregation of fixed identities. For communities dispersed and disrupted by subjugation under colonial rule, the task of recollecting identity and a renewed sense of the common may be the central task, while those whose identities have been forged into the homogenizing force of Whiteness have a different set of problems to solve. Conflating these projects or assuming that there are common theoretical lenses that can be used in the same ways for all peoples is a dangerous and dubious approach.

We can see this in the writings here. While there may a certain degree of commonality in the deployment of theories that deconstruct and critique dominant modes of knowing and practices of colonization, the application and appropriation of these ideas varies significantly. Dawn Zinga struggles with this complexity in writing about what she terms re-centering indigeneity. Implicit in her writing is the complex relations of her own role as a White researcher who must engage the task of decolonizing her own assumptions and positionality in relation to her indigenous colleagues, whose struggle to reverse their own internalized oppression functions in a similar register but on an entirely different field. Like the other authors in this volume, Zinga sees this work as deeply personal. For herself, decolonization requires deconstruction of language and meaning, but also a willingness to be accepting of new ways of knowing and practicing encountered in her work in an indigenous context. She suggests positioning oneself as a novice learner. She offers a strong caution that those of us from the dominant culture must be careful about our "limitations and ... abilities to challenge our mainstream privilege" (p. 274). She reminds us that in our encounters with other cultures, we run the risk of compounding the damage already done by replicating the betrayals, exploitation, and appropriation that have characterized multicultural relations so far.

For her indigenous colleagues, she suggests the task is somewhat different. The work of re-centering indigeneity is a process of struggling against internalized oppression, as a "brown face pushing White policy" (p. 274). The legacy of colonization places indigenous ways of knowing and acting in an ongoing relation of struggle with dominant practices and beliefs. While it is possible for those in the dominant culture to live their lives in complete ignorance of the ways western thought and social organization have been influenced by indigenous culture, the obverse is impossible for indigenous peoples who find themselves continually struggling to find a way clear of the western view of who they are and what they must do.

Nxumalo engages this struggle in the context of the pedagogical practices that promote multiculturalism and suggests that, as currently practiced, they reassert the colonial formations of race and identity they are ostensibly designed to subvert and challenge. Indeed, she suggests that the way in which children are inducted into forms of self-representation constitutes a risk to equitable practice and social justice. This risk lies in the "static representations of difference and diversity" (p. 281). She proposes that it is essential that we move away from these rigid ways of defining, for children, who they are. Instead, our work with young people might better be founded on an engagement with the world as surprising, unpredictable, and creative. In exploring multiculturalism through what she terms a "complexified" approach, children move away from "pre-defined and prescriptive" (p. 281) definitions of who they are toward an encounter with the world that opens possibilities of identity that fragment and disrupt colonial binaries such as race.

Nxumalo suggest that such work is not engaged in workshops or classes that teach children or young people about multiculturalism. Writing in the CYC tradition of relational practice, she tells us that the encounters that challenge the hegemony of dominant multiculturalism are to be found in the mundane activities of daily life. Such encounters constitute a rich and vibrant field of micro-political activity that holds the possibility of new forms of identity far more complex and creative than the binary residues of the colonial project. In her view, a simple encounter with the colors in a box of crayons can either result in a rigid definition of what is the right color for a self-portrait or an exploration of the multiple possibilities of self-perception and difference.

The subtleties of our induction into reifying the colonial patterns of identity through their repetition in our daily practices and relationships are both powerful and opaque. As Nxumalo points out, the social danger of distinguishing the other by race or ethnicity is no longer predominately one of exclusion. In contemporary society, the most dangerous practices that undermine equitable and just relations operate through the far more complicated process of assimilating the other as perpetually "other"—other defined and enforced through terms of difference controlled and distributed through the vernacular of multiculturalism; policies and practices that subtly invalidate any possibility of self-definition outside the prescribed characterizations provided by well-intentioned professionals who work with children at all levels of society. Such pedagogy functions through the vernacular of tolerance and acceptance, while predicating both terms on the right of the dominant social to define how you are to define yourself if you are to be tolerated or accepted. Clearly, if you must be tolerated or accepted by us then you must not be us.

The encounter of the child with the material world, however, is not inherently structured through the perverse logic of a predetermined and rigid set of identity parameters. The material world is complex and multiple in its array of forms and relationships. There are an infinite array of shadings and variations in all living form. It is this realm of potentiality that Nxumalo proposes as the praxis of daily encounter that can be shared between adults and children. Attention to difference in all things as a common field of becoming idiosyncratic and unique subjects exceeds, violates, subverts, and disrupts the lingering effects of bigotry.

The material world as an important alternative field of encounter that can provide challenges and new possibilities is also central to Pacini-Ketchabaw's contribution to this issue. The non-human encounter, she argues, allows us to step aside from our traditional stories about relationship, domination, and power. The encounter with non-human species replicates in important ways the power relations and colonial histories of human relations. In exploring the ways that children engage with other species in mundane encounters, such as those with deer or rabbits, we might be able to find new ways to engage new responses to human colonial histories. Pacini-Ketchabaw highlights the importance of paying attention to such mundane stories of interspecies encounter because of the force such stories may have in helping us to evoke other stories about our own histories.

Certainly, it could be cogently argued that it is precisely in the scission between non-human and human species that the logic of the colonial project is founded; that the primary othering is that of the non-human world. The loss of the stories of entanglement and connection in which non-human and human species are intertwined as mutually constitutive of the world, such as the coyote stories in indigenous culture, signals a particular and brutal form of alienation. Alienation, we would propose, is essential to any project that must use exclusion and genocide to extend its effects. In the aftermath of such calamity, the question becomes how we might re-engage with each other and ourselves. Indeed, as Hoskins has inquired, how might we face each other without shame? Or in another term, how might we overcome the alienation that has brought us to this place?

Pacini-Ketchabaw and Nxumalo both seem to propose the mediative value of the non-human encounter as a way of opening trajectories of both memory and contemporary practice. In engaging in a ecosystemic relation with both the worlds of other species and the nonorganic world, we might find new sets of relations and modes of engagement that both inform and exceed limited and dominant forms of multiculturalism. In expanding our realm of relations ecosystemically we might find ways to reconsider practices of domination and hierarchy. Possibly, in the revitalization of our relation to the non-human world, we might find new definitions of relationship that might inform our relations to our fellow humans.

However, Pacini-Ketchabaw, like the other authors here, warns us against utopic or simplistic impulses. She tells us that no relational entanglement is simple. There are no set and predictable practices or beliefs that will lead to a way out of the struggle or the accountability to our history.

This is the lesson of the coyote stories in indigenous cultures. Coyote is always looking for a shortcut out of his troubles, but each shortcut leads to deeper and more complicated troubles. Our colonial entanglements require attentiveness to all levels of the world in which we live. Each encounter holds an infinitude of information and possibility if we are willing to engage it seriously and reflectively. Any binary separation of ourselves from our environment ruptures our connection to our self. The practices of alienation are found in all everyday encounters, whether between adults and young people, children and deer, or a child and a box of crayons. Similarly, however, the infinite entanglement and co-evolutionary force of life itself can be found in each encounter as well.

Little and Walker invite us to consider the entanglements of the multicultural encounter as a kind of geography or mapping. The question becomes how and where one is positioned on any given map. They propose that the dominant map of multiculturalism is premised on teaching each subject where it fits in terms of belonging or exclusion. Indeed, in CYC, they argue we are trained to know how to read the map of entangled cultures like travelers moving across an alien landscape. The question implicit in such travel is one of belonging. Does one traverse the geography with the intimate sensate resonance of the native, the curious distance of the tourist, or the acquisitive eye of colonizer? How are we to determine our relation to the geography of multicultural entanglements in our teaching, work with young people, or in our relations with each other?

Placing ourselves on the map is a complex and troubling process. Indeed, the very construction of the map is inherently problematic. Any map includes certain aspects of a given terrain and excludes others. In a mapping of multiculturalism within a classroom or a program there will inevitably be exclusions and alienations of both adults and young people. And yet, Little and Walker point out that not only do we persist in creating maps of diversity and multicultural program environments, we take great pride in the maps we have created and encourage both staff and young people to use them to negotiate their relations. Of course, as the authors point out, this is to make the fundamental error that the map is the territory mapped.

Little and Walker offer an alternative approach to the constantly shifting geography of multiculturalism. Rather than creating fixed maps that generalize and offer ostensibly complete global mappings of the terrain, we might consider small, local, provisional mappings. Such maps would be experimental and premised in our actual experience of each other in day-to-day interactions. In this we might consider what Walker and Little term "emergent geographies" (p. 326) that may in fact not look like maps at all. Instead, such provisional sketches of the geography would open territories to constant revision and reconceptualizations. Living maps such as these constantly generate new possibilities for who we might become through the rich entanglement of the lived experience of the encounter. In such a geography we all belong because the map is comprised not of who we are defined to be but of who we are becoming together.

This question of who we are is engaged by Skott-Myhre as he interrogates the role of identity itself in multiculturalism. He challenges any form of essentialist identity such as the notion of a people and even reductive readings of culture. The notion of a true or authentic identity is dangerous in that it lays the groundwork for new practices of exclusion and hierarchy. He argues that placing oneself in the context of a "pure or unsullied lineage" (p. 341) that holds its force against the current historical moment runs the risk of a politics of resentment. The premise that identity can be fixed or located on an axis of truth, Skott-Myhre claims, can only lead to a reactionary social force. That is not to say that the recovery of marginalized or subjugated identities is not important or useful. However, such recovery is the beginning of a process, not the end point. Following Hardt and Negri, Skott-Myhre proposes that revolutionary multiculturalism isn't founded in a politics that affirms who you are. Instead, a truly radical multicuturalism is premised in "the freedom to determine *what you can become*" (pp. 341–342). In fact, he argued that for multiculturalism to operate as a fully functioning political project it must, in the end, seek its own abolition.

The work, in both theory and practice, that produces the field of Child and Youth Care is premised in a set of relations. In this special issue of *Child and Youth Services*, the authors have argued that this set of relations should not be engaged naively or without a profound sense of its complexity. None of us comes to our work-as-relationship untouched or immune to the complex and painful history of colonialism. That history is deeply influential in both conscious and unconscious levels of thought and action. It troubles us individually and collectively in our most personal encounters as well as at the level of community and global politics. It permeates our agencies in both our informal and procedural daily practices. In fact, there is no realm of encounter that is not constituted by the collision of cultures and our emergent globalized life space.

Multiculturalism is a term that has been designated to signify this infinitely complex and dynamic set of relations. The authors here have undertaken to trouble this term so as to open it to creative and productive interrogation. In this we hope they have troubled you, the readers, to interrogate your own practices and thoughts—to engage the relationships you have with young people and their families not simply as a site for solving problems or producing compliant subjects—instead, to work in ways that undo the old patterns of hatred and exclusion and open pathways toward new sets of relations, new identities, new forms of sociability; new worlds, and new peoples to come.

Index

acceptance 110–11, 120
activism 132
Adichie, C. 71, 150
adoption 156
affirmative politics 77–8
Alexander, J. 17
Alfred, T. 101–2
alienation 177, 178
American south 156
Ang, I. 110
Anna 23–5
anti-theory perspective 26–7
apologies 67–8
art 14–17
Artz, S. 43, 54, 67
assemblages, transient 111–12, 115–18
assimilation 88, 144–5
'at-risk' girls 21–5
authentic identity 166–7, 179

bag-lady storytelling 131–2
Ball, J. 149
Bambi 135
Bannerji, H. 110
Bansel, P. 145
Barnett, C. 40, 43, 51, 54, 56, 58–9, 59–60, 151
becomings 9–25; complex 13–17; freedom to become 167–9, 179; radical 21–5; relational *see* relational becomings; resurgence 9–13; untimely 17–21
being 47–8
believing in this world, this life 159
Bell, J. 144
Bennett, J. 111–12
Bhabha, H. 20–1, 156
Bird, R.D. 114
black face 157–8
Blackstock, C. 89
Blaise, M. 132
body 18, 24–5, 112–13, 121
boundaries: boundary crossings 136; professional 97
Braidotti, R. 77–8, 113, 116, 117, 123

Brennan, M. 150–1
brown clay-water encounter 113–19
Butler, J. 42, 60

Cameron, C.A. 44–5
capitalism 51–2, 161–2, 165
Caputo, J.D. 33, 35, 37, 43, 52–3, 54–5, 57, 58
Castaneda, C. 139–40
child/deer encounters 129–30, 132–8
child welfare services, history of 87–91
Chinook 73, 80
circularity 99
class traitors 100
clay, brown 113–19
closings, contexts as 43–6
collaborative research 13–17
collaborative working 26
collective identity 73–4
collective knowledge generation 23–4
colonial time 18–21
colonialism 160–1; contexts of CYC practice 7–8; history of child welfare services 87–91; resurgence and 9–13
colonization 65, 130–1, 175; *see also* decolonization
communication 54
community 52–60; communicative 54; deconstruction is hospitality 57–60; direction of 56–7; identity and tradition 52–4; tradition in transgression 54–6
community development approaches 89
Competency Document 46, 48
complex, becoming 13–17
complexified approaches 123–4, 176–7
conditional hospitality 58–9
conservative multiculturalism 84–5
context 36, 37–48, 51, 151; contexts as openings and closings in CYC 43–6; CYC professionalization as 46–7; CYC as transient context 33–5; deconstruction of 37–9; 'nothing outside text/context' 39–41; praxis as 47–8
contextual/essentialism binary 46
contextualization 41–3; practice of 43–6

INDEX

Corcoran, R. 12, 13–17
core values 92–3
Corntassel, J. 101–2
Corson, D. 146
coshaping 132, 134–8, 139
coyote stories 178
critical reflection 99–100
Csikszentmihalyi, M. 144
cultural competence training 77
culture, nature of 156–7
curriculum delivery 146–7
CYC Competency Document 46, 48

dampening encounters 118–19
De Cosson, A. 16
De Finney, S. 5, 9–13, 35–6, 47, 51–2
decolonization 100, 152, 175; decolonizing CYC practice 17–21; ethics for 138–9
deconstruction 32–62, 173–4; of context 37–9; is hospitality 57–60; hospitality, the impossible and 35–7; impossible approach 50–2; Marxism, praxis and 49–50
deer: attack by 136; child/deer encounters 129–30, 132–8; hunting 133, 135
degrees of suffering 70
Deleuze, G. 24, 157, 158, 159, 163, 164, 166
democratic discourses 85–6
denial 11–12
Department of Indian Affairs 75
Derrida, J. 36, 37, 38, 39, 40, 41, 43, 46, 47, 56–7, 59, 60
desire-based framework 8–9, 16, 27, 71
desiring-production 163
différance 42
difference 53–4, 64; conflating differences 70; relational becomings 114–15, 117–18, 119–20
direction of a community 56–7
diversity 2, 144–5
doing 47–8
dominant culture 64, 69, 79
domination 160–1, 167
Donald, L. 22
doors/entrances 57–8
doubling practices 33, 173
Downe, P.J. 11
Downey, L. 101
Du Bois, W.E.B. 66
Durst, D. 88

early childhood: interspecies encounters 2, 129–42, 177–8; unsettling representational practices 2, 107–28, 176–7
Early Learning Framework 130
Elders 20
Ellwood, C. 145
emancipation 167–8
emergent geographies 152, 179

Emily 16, 17
emotional response, Whiteness and 65–9
encounters 162–4; dampening 118–19; interspecies 2, 129–42, 177–8
engagement, praxis of 50
enhanced pedagogical spaces 76–9
Enlightenment 165
essentialism 41–2
essentialism/contextual binary 46
ethics: for decolonization 138–9; of Ojibwe parenting 94; relational ethics 57–60, 123–4
European immigrants 157–8
European surrealism 160

family-based mentorship 95
Fanon, F. 70
Faris, W.B. 159–60
Farris-Manning, C. 89
fawn-Great Dane relationship 136–7
fences 134, 136, 137–8
figuration 2, 132, 139–40
First Nations *see* Indigenous peoples
Forrest, L.M. 146
foster care 13–17; becoming a foster child 14–16
Foucault, M. 85, 162, 164
founders 9–11
Francis, D. 86
Fraser, S. 75
freedom to become 167–9, 179
freedom-centered feminism 166
French Canadians 68
Front de Libération du Québec (FLQ) 68

Galley, V.J. 89
Gannon, S. 145
gardens 134
gender 165; intersection with race and sexuality 18–21
generative conversations 2, 63–83, 174–5; working toward generative dialogues 69–74
geographical lens 2, 143–54, 178–9
Gergen, K.J. 78–9
Germany 158
Gharabaghi, K. 5, 56
Gibson, B. 101
Giugni, M. 132
Glavin, T. 73
global capitalism 51–2, 161–2, 165
'good child' 46
Gordon, A. 20, 71
Great Dane-fawn relationship 136–7
Griffin, S. 72
grooming multicultural subjects 145–7
Grosz, E.A. 112, 122
Guattari, F. 24, 157, 158, 159, 163, 164, 166
guilt 67, 68–9

INDEX

Hannah 11–12
Haraway, D. 112, 114, 115, 131, 132, 133, 135, 136, 137, 138, 139
Hardt, M. 160, 164–8
Hastings, A.W. 135
hauntings 20–1
hegemonic structures 85
Heidegger, M. 158, 167
helping relationships 11–13
Henry, F. 85–6
history of child welfare services 87–91
Hodgins, D. 136
hooks, b. 27
hospitality 2, 52, 173–4; deconstruction is 57–60; deconstruction, the impossible and 35–7
Hultman, K. 113–14
human/nonhuman encounters 2, 129–42, 177–8
hunting deer 133, 135

identity: collective 73–4; community 52–4; relational becomings 112–13, 116; relational identity formation 56; role of in multiculturalism 2, 155–70, 179; self-differentiating 55–6
'Imaginary Indian' 86
imagistic gaze 79
impossibility: deconstruction, hospitality and the impossible 35–7; deconstruction as impossible approach 50–2
inclusion 145
indeterminacy 42–3
Indian Act 7, 86
Indian time 18–21
Indigeneity, re-centering 2, 84–106, 175–6
Indigenous peoples: becoming resurgence 9–13; colonial policies regarding 7; health issues 80; relevant contributions 71–3; sovereignty 90
individual-based mentorship 95
Instone, L. 134, 137–8
integration 88
intensive mentoring 95, 96, 97–8, 99
International Child and Youth Care Network listserv debate 5–6
International Journal of Child, Youth and Family Studies (IJCYFS) Conference Issue 5, 33–4, 50, 55
intersectionality 18–21, 69
interspecies encounters 2, 129–42, 177–8
intertextuality 37–8, 49
Irwin, R. 16

Jayden 12–13
Jeffreys, D. 167
journeying with youth 94–9

Kate and Pippin: An Unlikely Love Story (Springett) 136–7

Kaveny, R. 167
Khanna, N. 17–21
knotty spaces 135
knowing 47–8; ways of 89–90
knowledge generation, collective 23–4
Korzybski, A. 144
Krueger, M. 162

labels 18–19, 23
language 87, 101
Laporte, P. 68
Lather, P. 33, 49–50, 149, 152
Latin America 160
leaning in 75, 76
Lee, D. 13
Lenz Taguchi, H. 113–14
Leonardo, Z. 67, 70, 75, 77
liberation 166–9
Linnell, S. 145
Little, J.N. 5, 47, 55–6, 148
Lizz 22
local control period 88–9
Locke, J. 165
'logic of genocide' 20
Loiselle, E. 21–5
Lugones, M. 7, 8

magical realism 159–60
Malins, P. 117
Mandy 14–15
maps 143–4, 178
Marxism 48, 49–50
Mary 23–4
Mason, M. 42
matching and mixing 107–8, 120–1
material-discursive entanglements 111–12; *see also* relational becomings
material feminisms 112
material world 177
McCaffrey, S. 137
M'charek, A. 118
McNiff, S. 152
medication 23–5
mental illness 23–5
mentoring 87, 91–9, 100, 101; journeying with youth 94–9; mentees 95–6; mentors 96–9
Messer-Davidow, E. 147
micropolitical acts 121–2
Mikel-Brown, L. 24
minoritarian literature 159–60
minstrel show 157–8
mixing and matching 107–8, 120–1
Mohanty, C.T. 17
molar viscosities 118–19, 120, 124
mule deer 129–30, 133
multicultural fixities 110–11, 119–21
Multiculturalism Act 110, 144–5

INDEX

multiple flows 162–3
multiplicity 73–4

Nambe Pueblo runaway shelter 155
names 163–4; self-location 148–9
nationalism 72
Nazi Germany 158
Negri, A. 160, 164–8
Nelson, B. 14
neocolonialism 7–8, 20–1, 130–1
neoliberalism 7–8
New Relationship Document, The 74
news coverage 90
niceness 144–5
Nietzsche, F. 158
non-hegemonic approaches 101
nonhuman/human encounters 2, 129–42, 177–8
'nothing outside of text/context' 39–41

objects 74
Ojibwe communities 94
openings, contexts as 43–6
openness, radical 51
other, hospitality toward the 37, 57–60
othering 110–11, 176–7
Outdoor Adventures Network 134
ownership 165

Pacini-Ketchabaw, V. 111
Panyappi Indigenous Youth Mentoring Program 92, 93
parasitism 161–2
participatory action research 17–25
pedagogical spaces, enhanced 76–9
pedagogy of relational ethics 123–4
people, alliance to a 2, 156, 160–1
Phillips, L. 44–5
Photovoice 9
Pillow, W. 149, 150
place 151
politicized praxis 1–2, 4–31, 172–3
politics: affirmative 77–8; micropolitical acts 121–2; of relationships 74–6, 78–9; revolutionary politics of relationship 2, 155–70, 179
Popkewitz, T.S. 150–1
Porter, R.K. 77
positionality 87
postcolonial entanglements 2, 129–42, 177–8
poststructuralism 39
poverty 22, 89
practice/theory divide 55–6
praxis: as context 47–8; deconstruction, Marxism and 49–50; politicized 1–2, 4–31, 172–3
presencing 13
privilege: acknowledging and discomfort 65–9; questioning 100–1

professional boundaries 97
professionalization 46–7
Project Artemis 21–5
property 165–6

questioning privilege 100–1

race: intersection with gender and sexuality 18–21; multiculturalism as an issue of 'race' 147
radical feminism 167
radical multiculturalism 167–9, 179
radical openness 51
radicalization 21–5
Razack, S.H. 10
'real' CYC 5–6
re-appropriation of identity 165–6
re-centering Indigeneity 2, 84–106, 175–6
recognition 73–4, 110, 120; of self 149–50
reflexivity 149–50
relational becomings 109, 112–24, 176–7; inhabiting 114–18; micropolitical acts 121–2; and multicultural tools 119–21
relational ethics: of hospitality 57–60; pedagogy of 123–4
relational identity formation 56
relational practice (Relational CYC) 27, 93
relationships: mentoring 93, 96, 97–8; politics of 74–6, 78–9; revolutionary politics of 2, 155–70, 179
relevance of Indigenous scholarship 71–3
Renold, E. 118
representational practices 2, 107–28, 176–7
resentment 158, 167
resurgence 9–13
rhizomatic inquiry 14
Richardson, C. 14
Ridley, C.R. 67
Ringrose, J. 118
risky behavioral patterns 90–1, 91–2
Roediger, D.R. 157–8
Rose, D.B. 138–9
Ross, R. 94
Roundtable Conversation 34–5, 55–6
Roy, K. 147, 152
runaway and homeless youth program 164

safe space discourse 77
Sameroff's unified theory 44–5
Saraceno, J. 34, 36, 46–7
Schick, C. 146, 147
Scott, D. 34, 37, 52
self, recognition of 149–50
self-actualization 93–4
self-differentiating identity 55–6
self-location 147–50
settler-child/deer entanglements 132–8
sexuality 17–21

INDEX

Shapiro, S. 144–5
shifting geographies 2–3, 143–54, 178–9
Shohat, E. 73–4, 76
Sienna 10
signs 39; looping effect 42
Simpson, L.B. 13
single stories, danger of 71, 72
skin color matching and mixing 107–8, 120–1
Skott-Myhre, H. 5, 16, 27, 38, 48, 50, 51–2, 53–4, 56, 57–8, 59, 85, 99–100
Skott-Myhre, K. 27, 47, 48, 85, 99–100, 111
slave morality 158, 167
slave trade 165
Smith, A. 20
Smith, L.T. 100
social diagrams 38, 59
social location 147–50
social realities 87–91
social responsibility 130
Sparks, J.A. 22, 25
spirituality 16–17
Springett, I. 136–7
St. Denis, V.S. 146, 147
St. Pierre, E.A. 39
stereotypes wall 23–4
Stewart, K. 108, 109, 122
storytelling 131–2
structural inequities 7–8, 25–8; *see also* transtheoretical frameworks
Styres, S.D. 94
suffering, degrees of 70
Sunyatta 168
superficiality 11–12
supportive mentoring 95, 96, 97, 99
surface changes 85–6, 99
surrealism 160
survivance 71, 72, 80

tactics 161
Tator, C. 85–6
Taylor, A. 131–2, 137
Taylor, R. 22
Tewa people 155–6
text 39–41
theory: importance of 26–7; theory/practice divide 55–6; *see also* transtheoretical frameworks
Thompson, A. 74
Tiffany, G. 85
time: becoming untimely 17–21; colonial and Indian 18–21

tokenism 144–5
tolerance 110–11, 120, 144–5, 147
trace elements 38
tradition 52–6, 72; community identity and 52–4; in transgression 54–6
transgression 54–6
transtheoretical frameworks 1–2, 4–31, 172–3; moments of entanglement 8–25
Trocmé, N. 89
troubling-from-within 33, 173
trust 166
Tsolidis, G. 147
Tuck, E. 8–9, 14, 16, 27, 66, 69, 71

uncertainty 159
unconditional hospitality 58–9
undergraduate education 2–3, 143–54, 178–9
unified theory model 44–5
untimely, becoming 17–21

Vancouver Island 129–30, 132–8
Victoria, BC 9–10
visceral intensities 117
Vizenor, G. 27, 71–2, 76, 79

Walker, M. 148–9
Wane, N.N. 102
water-brown clay encounter 113–19
ways of knowing 89–90
Westmoreland, M.W. 58, 59
White, J. 47–8
Whiteness 2, 36, 147, 157–8, 166; decolonizing CYC practice 17–21; difficulties of and generative conversations 2, 63–83, 174–5
whitetail deer 133, 134
working in context 44
working within 33, 173
World Health Organization (WHO) 94

Yoon, J.-S. 34
youth mentorship program (YMP) 87, 91–9, 100, 101

Zandstra, M. 89
Zerbe Enns, C. 146
Zerilli, L. 166
Zipin, L. 145–6

www.routledge.com/9780415834377

Related titles from Routledge

Diverse Spaces of Childhood and Youth: Gender and socio-cultural differences
Edited by Ruth Evans and Louise Holt

Diverse Spaces of Childhood and Youth focuses on the diverse spaces and discourses of children and youth globally. The chapters explore the influence of gender, age and other socio-cultural differences, such as race, ethnicity and migration trajectories, on the everyday lives of children and youth in a range of international contexts. These include the diverse urban environments of Istanbul, Copenhagen, Helsinki, Toronto, London, and Bratislava and the contrasting rural settings of Ghana and England. The analyses of children's, young people's, parents' and professionals' experiences and discourses provide critical insights into how gender and other socio-cultural differences intersect. Overall, the book provides an original contribution to geographies of children, youth and families and research on diversity and difference in global contexts.

This book was published as a special issue of *Children's Geographies*.

August 2013: 246 x 174: 240pp
Hb: 978-0-415-83437-7
£85/$145

For more information and to order a copy visit
www.routledge.com/9780415843377

Available from all good bookshops

www.routledge.com/9780415643993

Related titles from Routledge

Child Protection in Development
Edited by Michael Bourdillon and William Byers

Every day millions of children in developing countries face adversities of many kinds, yet there is a shortage of sound evidence concerning their plight and an urgent need to identify the most appropriate and effective policy responses from among the multiple approaches that exist. This collection of journal papers aims to engage with researchers and debates in the field so as to understand better some of the numerous risks confronted by children in developing countries.

The contributors are all experienced researchers and practitioners who have worked for many years with children in developing countries. The book offers suggestions for reform of current child protection policies, based on empirical findings around a range of child protection concerns, including children's work, independent migration, family separation, early marriage, and military occupation. Together, the contributions provide a body of knowledge important to humanitarian and development policy and practice.

This book was published as a special issue of *Development in Practice*.

October 2012: 246 x 174: 208pp
Hb: 978-0-415-64399-3
£85 / $145

For more information and to order a copy visit
www.routledge.com/9780415643993

Available from all good bookshops